THE BUSH DOCTRINE AND LATIN AMERICA

DATE DUE

JAN 1 3 2009	FEB 1 0 2010

The Bush Doctrine and Latin America

Edited by
Gary Prevost
and
Carlos Oliva Campos

10304670

THE BUSH DOCTRINE AND LATIN AMERICA
© Gary Prevost and Carlos Oliva Campos, 2007.

First published in 2007 by
PALGRAVE MACMILLAN™
175 Fifth Avenue, New York, N.Y. 10010 and
Houndmills, Basingstoke, Hampshire, England RG21 6XS
Companies and representatives throughout the world.

PALGRAVE MACMILLAN is the global academic imprint of the Palgrave Macmillan division of St. Martin's Press, LLC and of Palgrave Macmillan Ltd. Macmillan® is a registered trademark in the United States, United Kingdom and other countries. Palgrave is a registered trademark in the European Union and other countries.

ISBN-13: 978–1–4039–7387–0
ISBN-10: 1–4039–7387–3

Library of Congress Cataloging-in-Publication Data is available from the Library of Congress.

A catalogue record for this book is available from the British Library.

Design by Newgen Imaging Systems (P) Ltd., Chennai, India.

First edition: February 2007

10 9 8 7 6 5 4 3 2 1

Printed in the United States of America.

Contents

List of Illustrations

Figures

Tables

Maps

Editors

Carlos Oliva Campos is the executive director of the Association for Our America (AUNA) in Havana, Cuba, and former associate researcher of the Center for the Study of the United States at the University of Havana. He is an adjunct professor of history and philosophy at the University of Havana and has held visiting appointments at the University of Texas and Johns Hopkins. His publications include *La situación actual en Cuba: desafíos y alternativas*, and *Relaciones internacionales en America Central y el Caribe durante los anos 80*.

Gary Prevost is a professor of Political Science at Saint John's University and the College of Saint Benedict in Collegeville, Minnesota. He has published widely on Latin America and Spain. He has received numerous fellowships and awards including a Fulbright Central American Republics research grant. His books include *Politics in Latin America-The Power Game, Neoliberalism and Neo panamericanism-The View from Latin America, Democracy and Socialism in Sandinista Nicaragua, The Undermining of the Sandinista Revolution*, and *Politics and Change in Spain*. Professor Prevost also teaches courses on social movements and political change.

Contributors

Lourdes Regueiro Bello is a senior researcher at the Center for the Study of the Americas (CEA) in Havana, Cuba. She is author of numerous articles on inter-American trade issues.

Elsa M. Bruzzone is an adjunct professor of History at various universities in Buenos Aires. She serves as an advisor to the Argentine Congress on matters of natural resources. She is the secretary of the Interamerican Institute of Geopolitical Studies (ILADEG).

German Rodas Chavez is a professor of Latin American Studies at Simon Bolivar Andean University in Quito. He is head of international relations for the Broad Socialist Front of Ecuador and secretary of the Latin American Socialist Coordination.

David Alejandro Alvarez Dieppa is a researcher on inter-American issues at the Association for Our America (AUNA) in Havana, Cuba. He holds a degree in geography from the University of Havana.

Jorge Mario Sánchez-Egozcue is Assistant Professor in the Department of Economics and Research at Centro de Estudios de los Estados Unidos (CESEU) at the University of Havana. He holds a Ph.D. in International Economics at the University of Havana. His most recent publication is *Latin America and the Challenges of Globalization: The Limits of Integration*. His main areas of research are international integration, trade, dollarization, exchange rate policy, and macroeconomics.

Antonio Elizalde Hevia is a professor of sociology and rector of the Bolivarian University in Santiago, Chile. He was Chile coordinator of the Program for Sustainable Development in MERCOSUR. He has consulted with various international organizations on the environment and development, including the United Nations Development Program (UNDP) and the United Nations Children's Fund (UNICEF). He is the author of numerous books including *Human Development and Ethics for Sustainability*.

Raúl Moreno is an economist on the faculty of the University of El Salvador and a member of the Action Network Against Commerce and Investment. He received his doctorate from the University of Madrid.

Harry E. Vanden is a Professor of Political Science and International Studies at the University of South Florida, Tampa. He received his Ph.D. in political science from the New School for Social Research and also holds a graduate Certificate in Latin American Studies from the Maxwell School of Syracuse University. He has lived in several Latin American countries, including Peru, where he was a Fulbright Scholar and later worked in the Peruvian government's National Institute of Public Administration. His scholarly publications include numerous articles, book chapters, and the following books: *Mariátegui, influencias; National Marxism in Latin America; A Bibliography of Latin American Marxism; Democracy and the Socialism in Sandinista Nicaragua,* coauthored with Gary Prevost; and *The Undermining of the Sandinista Revolution,* coedited with Gary Prevost.

Enrique Amayo is a Peruvian-born professor working in Brazil, in the Economics Department of the University of the State of Sao Paulo (UNESP), in the Graduate Program of Sociology, and the International Relations program "Santiago Dantas". PhD in History from the University of London and University of Pittsburgh, USA. Visiting scholar in several institutions: International Peace Research Institute, Oslo, Norway; Institute for Latin American Studies, University of Stockholm, Sweden; Center for Latin American Studies, University of Pittsburgh; Instituto de Estudos Avançados, University of Sao Paulo, Brazil; Centro de Estudos Ibéricos y Latinoamericanos, University of Guadalajara, México; University of Santiago, Chile; Universidad Nacional de Ingeñería, Lima, Peru. Author of *La Política Británica en la Guerra del Pacífico, Sendero Luminoso,* and several papers on the Amazon and the South American Pacific area from the perspective of economic history and international relations.

Patrice Elizabeth Olsen is an associate professor in history at Illinois State University. Her current research focuses on covert operations, foreign intelligence, and collective memory. Her book *Artifacts of Revolution* (Rowman and Littlefield, 2007) received the Michael C. Meyer and Lewis Hanke prizes.

Luis Fernando Ayerbe is a professor in the department of economics and the post-graduate program of international relations at the State University of Sao Paulo (UNESP). He has also been a visiting researcher at the David Rockefeller Center for Latin American Studies at Harvard University and the Autonomous University of Barcelona. In 2001 he received a prize from the Casa de las Americas (Havana) in the category of social/historical essay. His publications include *Estados Unidos e América Latina: a construcão da Hegemonia e Revolucão Cubana.*

Chapter 1

Introduction—The Bush Doctrine and Latin America

Gary Prevost

The Bush Doctrine refers to the revision of U.S. foreign policy by President George W. Bush in the wake of the September 11, 2001 attacks on the United States. The beginning of the policy change came in a speech to the U.S. Congress immediately after the attacks when the president said that the United States "would make no distinction between the terrorists and those who harbor them," a statement that was followed by the U.S. invasion of Afghanistan. Subsequently, the Bush Doctrine has come to be identified with a policy that permits preemptive war against potential aggressors before they are capable of mounting attacks against the United States, a view that was used largely to justify the war against Iraq that began in 2003. The Bush Doctrine is a significant departure from the policies of deterrence that generally characterized U.S. foreign policy during the cold war and the period between the collapse of the Soviet Union and September 11, 2001 attacks. It can also be contrasted with the Kirkpatrick Doctrine of supporting stable dictatorships that was influential during the Reagan administration.

The U.S. policy in Afghanistan was not in itself a significant shift in U.S. policy. The invasion of Afghanistan to remove the Taliban government that had harbored the Al-Qaeda could be seen as an act of self-defense given the direct connection between the Taliban and Al-Qaeda. As a result, the concept of the Bush Doctrine is associated much more with the set of policies unveiled on June 1, 2002, in a speech to the graduates of the U.S. Military Academy at West Point. The initial policies labeled the "war on terrorism" were in many ways simply a reformulation of long-standing U.S. policies in a new context following September 11, 2001. However, the West Point speech took fundamental U.S. policy in a new direction. The speech is elaborated in a Nation Security Council text entitled *National Security Strategy of the United States*, issued on September 17, 2002.

The centerpiece of the new strategy is that the United States will engage in pre-emptive war, should the United States or its allies be threatened by "terrorists" or "rogue states" that are engaged in the production or development of "weapons of mass destruction." The right to self-defense is extended in order to authorize preemptive attacks against potential aggressors before they are able to launch strikes against the United States. The Bush Doctrine also contains the notion that the United States can act unilaterally with military action where multilateral action is not feasible. The policy also includes the notion that the "United States has, and intends to keep military strengths beyond challenge," and will take actions to remain the world's main superpower.

In reality, the Bush Doctrine is not entirely new. Formulations very close to these first appeared in the draft of the Defense Planning Guidance guidelines written by Paul Wolfowitz, the undersecretary of defense for policy in 1992. The policies, when leaked, proved controversial and were formally withdrawn. However, there is no indication that the ideas were actually repudiated and people like Wolfowitz continued to promote them while outside of the U.S. government during the Clinton administration. Preemptive and unilateral military actions, short of full-scale warfare has long been part of U.S. security strategy. In Latin America in the last 40 years there were invasions of the Dominican Republic and Panama. The Clinton administration used preemptive military action in Somalia, Iraq, Sudan, and Yugoslavia. As stated in the September 2002 document, "The United States has long maintained the option of preemptive actions to counter sufficient threats to our national security."

However, independent of the summits' process and much more through targeted bilateral policies the Bush administration has pursued a much more military and security-oriented policy in the post-9/11 period—the application of the Bush Doctrine to Latin America. Of course, U.S. Latin America policy pre-9/11 had an important security dimension especially in the Andean region. Beginning in the 1980s, the United States responded to the growing strength of the rebel movements (SL and FARC) with a significant counter-insurgency program under the cover of fighting drug trafficking. Following the defeat of Sendero Luminoso in 1992, U.S. efforts shifted more to Colombia and passed through Congress during the Clinton administration. They continued unabated since 9/11 but now pursued within the framework of the "war on terrorism." The intensity of Plan Colombia escalated in 2002 with the election of Miguel Uribe to the presidency of Colombia, vowing to "eliminate the insurgency." Uribe has become a vital ally to the Bush administration, the only major Latin American leader to support the United States in its war in Iraq.

However, it is very important to note that a renewed Plan Colombia is not the only evidence of the Bush Doctrine in Latin America. It has also been especially well manifested in bilateral U.S.—Mexican relations, the search for new permanent U.S. military bases in Ecuador and Paraguay, and the renewed contract between U.S. military officials and their Latin American counterparts. The latter has been highlighted by high-profile Latin American trips of U.S. Secretary of Defense Donald Rumsfeld. In addition to these Bush Doctrine based policy initiatives, U.S. policy toward the region's two most revolutionary governments has hardened during the past four years. In 2002, the Bush administration gave its support to a conservative coup that briefly toppled the Venezuelan President Hugo Chavez, and ever since his survival, the United States has stepped up its rhetoric against Chavez, declaring him to be undermining Venezuelan democracy in spite of his repeated victories in elections, which were declared to be fully legitimate by international observers. In the fall of 2005, the U.S. government refused to extradite Luis Posada Carilles to Venezuela to face strong terrorism charges stemming from the bombing of a Cuban airliner off Barbados in 1976. The United States refusal was on the grounds that Posada was likely to be tortured by Venezuelan authorities. This refusal to extradite was especially striking since it was revealed soon after that the United States was sending its own terror suspects to secret prisons in Eastern Europe where they likely faced torture with the full knowledge of U.S. Central Intelligence Agency (CIA) officials.

The U.S. policy toward Cuba also took a different direction in the post-9/11 time period though the shift may have not been directly linked to the terror attacks. On one level U.S. policy toward Cuba has been unchanged for more than 45 years: the removal of the Cuban revolutionary government by whatever means possible. During the Clinton administration this policy was known as "two track." On the one hand, the U.S. embargo/blockade of the island was tightened with the passage of the Helms-Burton Law in 1996. That legislation was aimed primarily at discouraging new foreign investment in Cuba from Europe and Latin America. On the other, the Clinton administration believed that the revolutionary system could be undermined through significantly increased contact between Cuban and U.S. citizens. To this end, permission to travel to Cuba from the United States was extended significantly to include more than the usual quota of scholars, journalists, and Cuban Americans who were permitted to travel to the island from 1977 onward. Colleges and universities were licensed by the U.S. government to conduct classes on the island and a wide range of nongovernmental organizations, especially those engaged in humanitarian assistance, were permitted to organize trips to Cuba.

Initially the Bush administration did not reverse the new travel policies, and by 2005, close to 150,000 U.S. citizens had traveled to the island each year, with the permission of the U.S. government. Tens of thousands more traveled illegally and there was only minimal enforcement of the ban on tourist travel by the U.S. government. In addition, with the support of the Clinton administration, in 2000, U.S. Congress passed a legislation allowing the Cuban government to purchase food and medicine from the United States for the first time since 1962. By 2001, the Cuban government began to purchase food and very quickly trade grew in volume to over $300 million per year and placed Cuba among the top 25 purchasers of U.S. agricultural products.

However, first in 2003 and then more definitively in 2004, the Bush administration began to reverse the policy initiatives of the Clinton era. First, the U.S. government suspended the regular talks that had occurred between the two governments over immigration issues. Second, in 2003, the U.S. government announced that a whole category of legal travel by U.S. citizens to Cuba, people-to-people trips, would be done away with at the beginning of 2004. However, the most significant change occurred with the issuance of the Powell Commission report in May 2004. The report argued that the openings created to Cuba by the previous administration, especially in the travel arena, were benefiting Cuba and therefore not serving the long-stated U.S. policy goal of overthrowing the Cuban government. As a result, a series of policy changes were announced. The category of educational travel by U.S. students to the island was sharply curtailed. Most of the educational trips to Cuba were short-term and those were eliminated completely. Only semester or yearlong enrollment programs were continued and those involved only a few hundred students per year.

However, the most significant change involved the regulations on Cuban-American travel and also the sending of remittances to Cubans on the island. The rules governing both arenas had grown quite liberal during the Clinton years but the Powell Commission recommended changes and as a result Cuban-American travel was limited to once every three years and the amount of money that could be sent on a quarterly basis was reduced. In another significant move, the U.S. Department of Justice began moving with much greater commitment to prosecute U.S. citizens who were judged to have traveled to Cuba illegally. In addition to these new travel rules on U.S. citizens going to Cuba, the flow of Cuban academics and performing artists to the United States was virtually stopped. In the years prior to 2004 such travel by Cubans to the United States had become routine. In the later half of 2004 it slowed to a trickle. The U.S. government had sanctioned the travel in the hope that many such professionals would choose to stay in the United States, embarrassing and destabilizing the Cuban government. However, most professionals returned to Cuba, taking with them significant amounts of U.S. dollars. Since that was not the intended goal of the United States, policies were changed.

In the summer of 2005, considerable attention was focused on Paraguay and the renewal of its security relationship with the United States. In the months that followed speculation focused primarily on a large military base at Mariscal Estigarriba in northern Paraguay, 120 miles from the Bolivian border. The base was constructed in the 1980s by U.S. technicians during the administration of Alfredo Stroessner, the long-term Paraguayan strongman who had close ties with the United States. The base has a 3800–m landing strip, the longest in Paraguay, and is suitable for B-52 bombers and C-5 Galaxy and C-130 transport planes. The base has housing for 16,000 troops and has been maintained by the Paraguayan armed forces in the interim for many years. There was no change in the status of the base but a series of events in mid-2005 led to a serious speculation that U.S. policy makers, in the wake of 9/11 were contemplating a potential permanent use of the base by U.S. forces. On May 26, 2005, the Paraguayan Congress approved a provision that grants a waiver preventing U.S. troops from being prosecuted under the International Criminal Court (ICC) for activities carried out on Paraguayan soil. That the

Paraguayan Congress would pass such a measure is not too surprising given the pro-U.S. leaning of its political leaders and the worldwide effort of the United States to gain such waivers. However, suspicions about U.S. intentions regarding the base were fueled by the fact that the congressional vote was not publicly revealed in Paraguay but rather revealed by a piece of investigative journalism published a month later in the Argentine journal, Clarin. The May 26 vote occurred in the context of several other developments on the security front. On May 5, the Paraguayan congress approved an increase to 400, the number of U.S. troops involved in the annual joint training exercises of the two countries.

On June 10 Paraguayan Vice President Luis Castiglioni traveled to Washington where he met with Vice President Dick Cheney and Defense Secretary Donald Rumsfeld. On July 1, the first contingent of 400 troops arrived in Paraguay to begin the first of 13 exercises that would last until the end of 2006. U.S. and Paraguayan officials stressed the civil affairs nature of the exercises but in reality only two of the missions were related primarily to poverty reduction and health care. Responding to the growing alarm that the troop presence was the harbinger of the establishment of a permanent U.S. base at Marsical Estigarriba, the U.S. embassy in Asuncion issued a communiqué stating that the United States has no intention of establishing a permanent military base in Paraguay. These sentiments were echoed later in the summer by Paraguayan President Nicanor Duarte. "There will be no North American base or other installation with that characteristic, because we are a sovereign country."[1]

Inspite of the denials by both U.S. and Paraguayan leaders that no dramatic developments are in the offing, there has been considerable speculation from Brazilian and Argentine political officials and academics that the United States is focusing on Paraguay as a location from which to pursue its regional interests at a time when it faces less pliable governments in Argentina, Brazil, and Uruguay than it did in the 1990s. There are a number of factors that lead the United States to view Paraguay in a strategic manner. Most important is its position in relation to the so-called Triple Border region of Brazil, Argentina, and Paraguay.

For the past several years since 9/11, the U.S. government has focused on the Triple Border region as the location of a variety of activities viewed as dangerous by U.S. authorities—drug trafficking, human trafficking, and terrorist activities. In regard to the latter, the United States has claimed that the Colombian FARC was active in the area and that there was fundraising for the Lebanese Hezbollah. Clear proof of the latter two activities has never been provided by U.S. authorities. Typical of this U.S. approach was evident during the visit of State Department Western Hemisphere Affairs Senior Advisor for Security Affairs Deborah McCarthy to Brazil in December 2005. At a regular meeting of the 3+1 Group (Brazil, Paraguay, Argentina, and the United States) Ms. McCarthy stressed that the triborder region continues to be a security concern for the United States. According to McCarthy, "all three countries are vulnerable to terrorist attacks." There was no indication that McCarthy provided any specific proof of her claims to the meeting. In response Brazilian diplomats declared that there was no evidence of such terrorist potential.[2]

Many in the region view the U.S. activities in Paraguay as not actually being connected to possible terrorist activities but rather for other reasons. Most commonly cited in such views are possible interventions in Bolivia, the desire to break up MERCOSUR and control of the Guarani aquifer.[3] MERCOSUR is a key Latin American trading bloc that encompasses Argentina, Uruguay, Paraguay, Brazil and Venezuela. Because these countries have been skeptical of the FTAA project, MERCOSUR has been a potential target of a U.S. strategy of divide and conquer to prepare the way for the approval of the FTAA in the future. The Guarani acquifer as Elsa Bruzzone details in chapter 11 is a key Latin American natural resource for the twenty-first century with its large supply of precious drinking water.

The focus on Bolivia was especially strong in May–June 2005 as the popular forces in that country confronted a government that was pressing ahead with unpopular plans to develop newly found natural gas reserves through cooperation with foreign transnational companies. Eventually these protests forced the Mesa government to resign paving the way for the elections that were won in December 2005 by Evo Morales, a leader of the popular forces. At that time there was fear by some that the U.S. troop presence in Paraguay might be used to intervene in Bolivia. It is not clear that such interventions were likely but the temporary resolution of the crisis in June with Mesa's resignation and the promise of elections made such intervention not possible. Morales assumed office in early 2006 promising a strong neoliberal agenda that will challenge U.S. policy in the region. The possibility of a permanent U.S. military presence in northern Paraguay could be seen as a warning to Morales on just how far he can go in pressing his progressive agenda.

The possible connection of U.S. presence in Paraguay being related to MERCOSUR relates to the strategy now being pursued in the arena of trade agreements in the wake of the stalling of the FTAA process during the last two years. With no comprehensive treaty in sight, the United States has pressed ahead with a strategy of regional and bilateral agreements focused in part on smaller, weaker countries such as Paraguay. The strategy has borne some fruit with the completion of the U.S.-Chile Treaty, the near completion of the Central American Free Trade Agreement (CAFTA), and ongoing negotiations with Colombia, Ecuador, and Peru. If the United States were successful in negotiating an agreement with Paraguay it would be especially significant because it would potentially weaken MERCOSUR. This act would be significant because it has been from MERCOSUR, articulated by Brazil and Argentina, that the primary opposition to the FTAA has emanated. In the fall of 2003, the United States was expecting a fundamental breakthrough in the negotiations on the FTAA leading to its triumphal signing in Miami at the November ministerial meeting. Such a success would have allowed the launching of the FTAA in 2005 as had been projected at the Miami Summit of the Americas in 1994. Instead Presidents Lula of Brazil and Kirchner of Argentina held a summit in Buenos Aires in October and formulated a position that became known as the "Buenos Aires Consensus." The leaders did not rule out the eventual completion of the FTAA but laid out a set of conditions from the Latin American perspective that would need to be honored if the accord were to go forward. Primary among the conditions was the necessity that the United States open its own market to more Latin American goods and to reduce its agricultural subsidies. Ever since October 2003, these Latin American conditions have been a barrier to the completion of the FTAA treaty. As a result, during the past two years the United States has pursued its divide and conquer strategy while the Latin American countries with Kirchner, Lula, and Venezuelan president Hugo Chavez in the leadership have sought to strengthen trade ties within the region. One of the most important developments in the Latin American strategy has been the formulation of ties between Venezuela and MERCOSUR.

It is in this context that the overtures for a bilateral trade agreement with Paraguay have proceeded quietly. The first indication that U.S.-Paraguayan trade talks were underway came in a September 11, 2005 article in the Argentine newspaper, *Clarin*. It was the same article that speculated over the possible U.S. military base in the Chaco.[4] In late September, Paraguayan officials denied that they would enter into a bilateral trade agreement with the United States in violation of its treaty commitments to MERCOSUR. Paraguayan government officials refuted the allegations, but they defended the policy of building closer economic and military ties with the United States. In particular, President Nicanor Duarte used the outspoken comments against Paraguay by Brazil's foreign minister Celso Amorin to rally support for his foreign policy agenda. "We want First World nations to buy our goods, especially those goods in which we are competitive," Duarte explained, "we are not corseted in MERCOSUR." These comments only fueled greater speculation that Paraguay could leave MECOSUR for a trade deal with the United States. However, Paraguayan Foreign Minister Leila Rachid rejected accusations that Paraguay would permit a base in the Chaco in return for greater access to U.S. markets. "We won't swap security for free trade." Paraguay is a major exporter of meat with Russia being its largest current customer, receiving 41,000 tons.[5]

U.S.-Mexican relations have also been significantly affected by the events of September 11, 2001. On the eve of the attacks, Mexican President Vicente Fox was in Washington where he addressed a joint session of the U.S. Congress and the primary focus of his remarks was the need for U.S. immigration reform. His pleas to regularize the situation of millions of Mexicans working illegally in the United States was well received by President George Bush who pledged that general immigration reform and guest worker program would be high on his legislative agenda. In the wake of September 11 this issue dropped dramatically in Bush's priorities and has only been revived in 2006 five years later. In the interim, security issues rose to the forefront of U.S.-Mexican relations in a manner that was unprecedented. Over the decades the United States and Mexico had cooperated on security matters but always with a significant measure of caution from the Mexican side based on painful issues stemming back to the seizure of large amounts of Mexican territory following the 1846–1848 Mexican-American War. This wariness was always present in the long years of rule by the Mexican Institutional Revolutionary Party (PRI) from 1928–2000. Only with the election of the pro-U.S. PAN leader, Fox, did the prospects for closer relations in the security arena arise.

The character of the new security relationship was underscored at the March 2004 Summit between Bush and Fox. Bush stated, "In this age of terror, the security of our borders is more important than ever, and the cooperation between Mexican and American border and law enforcement is stronger than ever." The nature of that cooperation is primarily U.S.-financed projects on the Mexican side of the border designed to bolster U.S. security needs. U.S. spending on military and police aid to Mexico has more than tripled in the last five years to more than $57.8 million per year. For Mexico this represents a significant departure from the past and places them third in receipt of such aid in the Western Hemisphere, ranking behind only Peru and Colombia. Migrants who have not committed a crime cannot be legally stopped from entering the United States by Mexican authorities. However, by training and equipping Mexican police and soldiers, the United States is hoping they will be able to stop drug smuggling and terrorists. The aid to Mexico has mainly been equipment to strengthen the Mexican forces, including helicopters, X-ray machines, computers, trucks, motorcycles, and police cars. In December 2005, U.S. Border Patrol taught water rescue techniques and gave equipment to the Mexican military to accept greater assistance and cooperation from their North American counterparts. As a result, in 2005, the Pentagon earmarked $2.5 million for financing Mexico, the first time in recent memory that Mexico has received direct aid from the United States for buying equipment. Such aid has been criticized by Mexican human rights activists given the questionable human rights record of the Mexican military. In addition, the U.S. counterterrorism program spent $450,000 in Mexico, more than the expenditures in Colombia. In 2006, the United States will give Mexico eight more helicopters and other equipment that will be used on the Guatemala border. The United States also plans to help Mexico with the installation of a telephone intercept capability.

The Pentagon is playing a bigger role in Mexico under the banner of fighting terrorism. Setting aside long-standing sovereignty concerns, the Fox government has been publicly tightlipped about its new relationship with the United States, fearing a nationalist backlash. All the details of the new relationship exist within the framework of the March 2005 treaty for Security and Prosperity Partnership of North America signed by the three NAFTA countries.[6]

Notes

1. *Associated Press Bulletin*, August 30, 2005.
2. *O Estrado de São Paulo*, December 8, 2005, p. A10.

3. Good examples of this perspective include Raul Zibechi, "A Wedge in MER-COSUR: The United States in Paraguay," *Alma Latina News* via *Progress Weekly*, September 29, 2005 accessed at www.progressweekly.com and Benjamin Dangl, "US Military in Pragauay: Threatening the Left and Eyeing Gas and Oil in Latin America," *Monthly Review*, October 2005, accessed at www.monthlyreview.org. Published and accessed on February 26, 2006.
4. Clarin (Buenos Aires), September 11, 2005.
5. Intelligence Research Ltd. Brazil Report September 27, 2005. Accessed through www.lexisnexis.com. Accessed on February 22, 2006.
6. For a detailed exposition of the new U.S.-Mexico security relationship see Chris Hawley, "U.S. Pays Mexico to Secure Border," *Arizona Republic*, December 29, 2005, p. 1.

Chapter 2

The United States—Latin America and the Caribbean: From Neopan-Americanism to the American System for the Twenty-First Century

Carlos Oliva Campos

In an essay entitled "The United States—Latin America: From Panamericanism to Neopanamericanism"[1] an attempt was made to analyze the emerging scenario opened for the inter-American relations at the end of the cold war in 1989. Using the history of relations between the United States and the Caribbean as the general context, it is a great parable that has two historic junctures, the development of the First Pan–American Conference, Washington DC, October 1889 and the regional juncture opened exactly a hundred years later, that is to say, 1989. Obviously the intention of connecting both junctures in one historic comparison, consciously assumed numerous risks: the abstraction of a great many events not linked to the subject in between both; the possible involuntary omission of facts and analysis that should be considered; and above all, to offer the necessary arguments to understand why the comparison was made. The main purpose of that exercise was to show, first, how much inter-American relations were transformed with the change of the United States hemispheric position from regional to hemispheric power; and as a result of this, how much it facilitated the international and regional juncture of 1989, the development of new policies and strategies designed by the American government, different from what had happened a hundred years ago. As a basis for comparison, the Pan-American project was chosen; adding to this the clarification that everything related to the so-called inter-American System structured after the end of World War II was intentionally excluded. Among the reasons for such a decision, was the historic comparison of two very different periods for the U.S. relations with Latin America and the Caribbean, pursuing similar objectives, that is to say, the articulation of a new model of economic relations under the U.S. hegemony. The Free Trade Area for the Americas (FTAA) project was launched after the 1989 juncture, but its origin dates back to the beginning of the nineteenth century, when the United States should have answered the invitation to participate in the Panamerican Amphictyonic Congress held in 1826.[2]

The 1989 regional juncture was exceptionally favorable for U.S. objectives and political interests. The new scenario that was being outlined was called Neopan-Americanism, in reference to the American project of continental domination officially implemented a hundred years earlier, under historic conditions that did not allow the United States to meet its objectives. The main arguments of the 1989 regional conjecture are summarized below:

1. The end of the strategic alliance between Cuba and the Soviet Union, understood as the main extra continental threat to U.S. national security and the promotion of what was known as the communist subversion in the hemisphere.
2. The overcoming of the main content in the inter-American security agenda, as a result of a negotiating process in El Salvador and Guatemala that ended with favorable results for U.S. interests. To this we must add the electoral defeat of the Nicaraguan Sandinistas and the American operation in Panama (December 1989) that marked the beginning of a new intervention model, using the new themes of consensus before the international public opinion, namely, the defense of democracy and human rights and the struggle against drug-trafficking.
3. The evident movement of U.S. strategic priorities, from a military and security agenda to another that gave exceptional attention to the new trends that were being imposed on the world economy. The challenges were of different nature: drug-trafficking, the environment, corruption, and democracy, just to mention a few.
4. The construction of a majority consensus among the political elites of Latin American and Caribbean countries with the United States, with the purpose of moving together to face the new economic challenges, expressed in the hemisphere four main themes: response to a neoliberal economic policy, the opening of national markets to the free trade game, the creation of a hemispheric commercial bloc to face the global impact of emerging blocs in Europe and the Pacific Basin, and to facilitate the leadership of great corporation before the new opportunities found in the continent by the geoeconomic approaches. This project that started to be developed with the launching of the Initiative for the Americas (IPA) in June 1990 by George Bush senior is the result of the substitution of the cold war bipolar geoestrategic rivalry by the multipole geoeconomy of the post–cold war.[3]

Also important is the geoeconomy, understood as a reinterpretation of the traditional geopolitical approach, enriched by the activation of the economic dimension to the geographic environment. Under this new global approach, the big industrialized countries, resolve their conflicts of power to determine their leadership options, on the basis of a new strategic vision of the world defined through the broad spectrum of economy and not of the war. Through the use of nonwarlike mechanisms (in strict military terms), a game of competition is followed by new market concepts, the decisive role of technology leadership, and the productive control of consumer goods for society. It is the expression of the interests of big multinational corporations and state institutions together that decide the foreign policy of great powers, from which a new strategic conduct derives according to the international commercial and economic predominance.[4]

As it has been correctly explained, the deep changes revealed in the new strategic relations among the emerging great powers from the international system in the post–cold war scenario, show a re-dimensioning of geography as a global strategic factor. Regions such as the Persian Gulf, the Caspian Sea Basin and the South China Sea acquired strategic importance due to the new emphasis on the protection of vital resources such as oil and natural gas.[5] In addition other resources like water and biodiversity can be added to ensure a high standard of living for developed countries and their citizens.

Regarding the re-dimensioning that the global economy suffers, we must stress that the new developments of industrial capacities and the technological development substitute for the past war scenarios in relations between powers. Rivalries are expressed in a world repositioning of markets and natural resource niches for their industries and in the great speed they can accomplish to contact and articulate other markets to gain competence. Like never before the great lords of war see themselves turned into the guardians of great capital and are left trapped in a process of redefining their own corporate identity.

At first impression one could think that the identification of a new hemispheric scenario was enough to go deeper into the subsequent developments that occurred: The Initiative for the Americas (IFA), the promotion of the North American Free Trade Agreement (NAFTA) until its implementation in January 1994, and the First Summit of the Americas in Miami, in December that same year, that opened the road to the development process of the Free Trade Area of the Americas (FTAA). Nevertheless, when reflecting on the unavoidable transformations that the U.S. global foreign policy still suffers from, with the transition period of the cold war to post–cold war, it was pertinent to review the historic assumptions that had determined the role and place occupied by Latin America and the Caribbean and its possible alterations in the light of a new conjuncture. The first thing to be reviewed was the basic assumption, namely, the double strategic function of the region; on the one hand, it functioned as a geographic area where the U.S. domination system was established, and on the other, it acted as an operative platform to plan American foreign policy. Before the conditions were created, this assumption competed and became stronger, with the progressive implementation of all things related to the American economic bloc, FTAA, and the free trade. Another assumption has to do with the historic role of Latin America and the Caribbean as a laboratory to test new policies. It calls our attention as to how the progressive reemergence of scenarios were perceived as threats to the U.S. national security, Colombia with the subsequent extension of all the Andean area, new economic, political, and military intervention models are tested as a supplement to the always useful old instruments like the increase of security assistance, military advisors, arms sales, and intelligence covert operations among others. What would be missing is the inclusion of a new assumption to identify the region as a direct supplier of strategic resources such as oil, drinking water, and biodiversity to the United States.

This analysis leads to the following working hypothesis: the new international and hemispheric conditions of the post–cold war compete with the old historic assumptions that have consolidated the inter-American relations by incorporating new ones that impose greater challenges to Latin America in order to maximize its margins of independence before the new American global domination project.

The United States Facing a Different World: The Old Themes and the New Challenges

An unquestionable architect of U.S. foreign policy in the last quarter of the twentieth century, Henry Kissinger, referring to the new period in world history affirmed:

> The end of the Cold War has created what some observers have called a "unipolar" world or a "superpower." But actually, the United States is not in a better position to impose unilaterally the world agenda of what was there at the beginning of the Cold War. The United States is more predominant than what they were 10 years ago, however, ironically speaking, power has become vaguer. In this way, the US capacity has really decreased to apply it to shape the rest of the world.[6]

Despite the fact that in these lines one may find some hard words to discuss the new global scenario, there is one particular point that we analyse and summarize as follows: if the United States were able to succeed, supported in different factors in the breaking of the bipolar conflict of the Cold War, it is also true that they had to face the change by assuming the price of the effort made and the lack of an alternative strategy to go into the new global scenario. The price is well known—the weakening of a political-military leadership that gave way to the reconditioning and additional efforts throughout the Cold War period. A second idea linked to the previous one, indicates that if the United States survived the post–Cold War as a political-military leader of the international system, in economic terms the situation is changing notably due to the development witnessed by the economies of Germany and Japan. As was affirmed by Richard Barnet, those defeated in World War II emerged as the great winners of the post–Cold War.[7]

The new global scenario opened with the post–cold war facilitated international conditions so that projects such as the Trilateral Commission, headed by Zbifniew Brzezinski in times of Détente[8] found new spaces of realization for some of their main theses. The idea of understanding the new international power schemes, after the interaction between the three big poles the United States, Europe, and Japan, economically speaking was

stated. Despite the fact that there were better conditions to defend democracy and human rights, the price of that division of power was greater and
irreparable for the United States. Add to this the debatable criterion, though
it should not be disregarded all together, the emergence of the European
Union (EU) in 1992, meant the end of the American capacity to extend its
influence throughout the world.[9]

A third idea refers to the articulation of the new global strategy with
the components that were applied in the final period of the cold war.
Among the ideas were the defense of human rights and democratic
regimes. The role played by the strategy should not be forgotten, first
against East European socialist countries and then with a global projection, through the Democracy Project and one of its most active mechanisms the National Endowment for Democracy.[10] Nevertheless, the fact
that the ideological confrontation of the political system of East
European socialist countries or the search for the return to democracy of
societies controlled by military dictatorships should not be disregarded,
they were phenomena of a very different nature to the establishment of a
democratic project, than the tasks of eradicating hunger and poverty as
causes of new armed conflicts.

Therefore, as Kissinger correctly pointed out, the United States was facing a new and more diffused world, among other reasons because they
were going deeper into it but lacking definitions. The history of American
foreign policy reveals the constant search for a position of power toward
the goal of world hegemony. Together with the Soviet Union and the
Berlin Wall, all traditional paradigms that supported U.S. leadership during the cold war had collapsed. An analysis on this theme from the beginning of the 1990s to the present administration of George Bush shows a
revealing lack of definitions, conflicts, and interrogation, dealing with how
to understand and project national security and U.S. leadership in the
post–cold war.

In the document entitled National Security Strategy of the United States,
dated August 1991,[11] many of the ideas stated are self-evident. As it was logical to imagine for that period, there were still doubts and concerns about the
countries that were moving away from what the Soviet Union had been.
Russia was carefully observed for its deep economic and political crisis, and
above all, for the maintenance of their nuclear capacity to destroy the United
States. That document also reveals other very interesting aspects. In one of
the parts, it affirms, "We are facing new challenges not only for our own
security, but for our lines of thoughts around that security," alluding to the
lack of clarity on how to define the new concept. On the other hand, the
topic of the U.S. leadership could not be outside the debate. Hence, the real
concern about Europe, without the Soviet threats, was obvious and the
demand for new answers on the nature of the transatlantic alliance.
Nevertheless, a special value to be recognized from the document was the
international inventory on regions and themes in which the new global
scenario was taking shape.

Five years later, the National Security Strategy of 1996,[12] defines a global projection that combines measures aimed at ensuring the American security and military supremacy with others that aimed at favoring the free market as well as the values of Western democracy. In the document, attention is given to technological development, recognizing that new technologies favor the American economic development, but they could also fall in the hands of terrorists and organized crime and drug-traffickers thus creating new possibilities of insecurity for the country and its citizens. With this reflection, threats to the national security were no longer perceived with a transnational character alone, rather stating an increase of concern for what could happen in the territory of the United States.

In 1998, under the presidency of William Clinton, the document on the National Security Strategy for a new century was made known, and among its strategic objectives it stated the following:

1. The protection of the sovereignty, the territory and population of the United States.
2. Prevention of the emergence of hostile rivals.
3. Guarantee of access to decisive markets and to the strategic resources, particularly energy resources.
4. Defeat of aggressions against the United States and/or its allies.
5. Free circulation in seas, air, and space routes and the security of vital communication.[13]

The first element that calls the attention to this set of objectives is the explicit mention of the U.S. defense of the national territory with a more domestic approach than international, evidencing a greater concern for the internal threats. In the second place, it is another example of the lack of definitions about the enemy to be confronted; while a third very important element, the guarantee of both the access to the so-called decisive markets as well as the strategic resources, particularly energy.

In this discussion framework, there were no doubts on the key role played by the "national interest" of the United States and how to understand it with the new global perspective. The attention to this topic by many of the important theoreticians of the U.S. foreign policy and international relations stemmed from a revision of the traditional concept of "national interest," to identify its new contents. According to the classic concept defined by Hans Morgenthau, the "national interest," among other matters, should be similar to the general guidelines of the U.S. Constitution (like the general well-being of the population) but it was also marked by the political traditions and the general cultural background in which the foreign policy was framed. Nevertheless, the real definition of the concept is found in its perception of the wider world that presupposes a permanent state of conflict and war that should be confronted by the coordination of all actors and domestic interests.[14]

It is interesting to call attention to the rich debates that took place in important American journals such as *Foreign Affairs* and *Foreign Policy* during the 1990s addressing the subject of "national interest." In the center of the debate, different approaches that allow the recovery of the necessary consensus of the nation on crucial topics were discussed. Many of these approaches were variably designed. Arguments were used on the need to impose on Iraq, a post–First Gulf War "active restrictions" policy that would allow the U.S. armed forces to maintain operational control over the Baghdad government. On the other hand there were the ideas of Samuel Huntington who spoke of the "clash of civilizations" and Anthony Lake who spoke of "rogue states."[15] These ideologically charged perspectives were challenged and criticized by Stanley Hoffman in Lake's case creating a "shopping list" of U.S. objectives that lacked a coherent strategy.[16]

Perhaps American politicians were not ready to accept more pragmatic formulas like the proposal of Kissinger,[17] who, by rethinking the theory of the balance of power as an indispensable resource for American leaders, envisioned the need to build alliances to maintain the balance in several regions of the world and the view that these partners could not always be chosen only on the basis of moral considerations. This is nothing new for the United States foreign policy, as Horaio Cagni reminds us:

> Saddam Hussein was created and armed by the West as a containment wall to face the Islamic revolution in Iran. For years he fought the Ayatollah's regime using the chemical weapons that the democratic West was supplying. After the Kuwait invasion, Iraq served, knowing it or not, as the challenger of the coalition headed by the United States. They were militarily destroyed because they threatened the geo-strategic and geo-economic Western interest, but they were not defeated because the state rational prevailed, and it is better that the Iraqi leader crushes the Kurds and Shiites than a Kurd or Shiite rebellion succeeds. The respect for the self-determination process of the peoples ends where money begins.[18]

Saddam Hussein's final fate is well known. But today the United States is paying for its grave error of judgment, for after overthrowing and arresting Saddam, its occupation troops face an uncontrolled resistance to date, in which the Sunnis appear in the protagonist role. Something similar happened with Osama Bin Laden. Being a man of the United States, trained and supported to act against the Soviet troops in Afghanistan; or the case of Manuel Antonio Noriega in Panama, well known by Bush senior when he was the CIA director. And not to forget its indissoluble alliance with the United States, protected and guarded by the powerful Israeli lobby. Kissinger was aware his proposal did not go beyond the previous practice of the United States.

Beyond all the attention paid by politicians and intellectuals of notable experience and acknowledged capacity, it was not until the traumatic events of September 11, 2001, that the articulation of a new national consensus was imposed. Here we must only point out in this part of the analysis that the knowledge of what was historically defined as national interest for the country had reached its best expression in the field of foreign policy, identifying an enemy capable of becoming a real threat to that society. The conventional enemy that was buried with the Soviet Union was substituted with a new enemy under totally different norms. The United States was left with a real threat that cannot be faced under traditional approaches of the U.S. foreign policy, despite the fact that the first reaction, the total war against terrorism, responds precisely to those approaches questioned.

A well-known article signed by the Adviser of National Security Affairs of the White House, Condoleezza Rice, stresses this important aspect very well:

> For the United States it is extremely difficult to define its "national interest" in the absence of Soviet power. Continuous reference to the "period after the Cold War" is proof that no one can think about what comes after the confrontation between the United States and the Soviet Union. Nevertheless, these transition periods are important because they give strategic opportunities. In such changing periods it is possible to influence the confrontations of the coming world.[19]

With the terrorist attacks of September 11, 2001, the answers that had not turned up until then appeared, adding directly a new internal dimension to the concept of national security. This new domestic dimension, as a result of the terrorist attacks, articulated the concept of homeland security. The framework of limited power of the state, promoted by the neoliberal agenda of the 1990s, contrasted with the new concentrations of state power needed to fight the "war on terrorism" under the presidential leadership of George Bush.[20]

Internationally, September 11 provided the necessary enemy against which to unleash a global offensive to articulate alliances and commitments. But as previously discussed, the ethereal nature of the new enemy did not overcome but rather rivaled and complicated the diffuse character of the threats to be faced. Ultimately, and perhaps regrettably, the United States chose a very handy option: war in Afghanistan and Iraq.

The United States emerged in the post–Cold War as an undisputed political-military leader of the international system and has put up with the huge costs of that leadership. This topic could not escape a debate in the intellectual and political environment of the country. Hypotheses were advanced on how the nation should perform under those terms. The Wilsonian internationalism or its Roosveltian version, expressed in the promotion and defense of democracy and of human rights, was to a great extent linked to multilateralism supported by the main international institutions like the United Nations (UN). This approach was taken in an attempt to ensure an international collective security system. Kissinger's new balance of power, with a viewpoint not without risks of what was the "strategic deployment" of the years of Détente, was among the main variables discussed. History is known. If during the first five years of the 1990s, the United States raised the UN's international role, (its interpretation of the *peacemaking-peacekeeping* operations), they however, did not overcome their traditional unilateralism, and Somalia in 1993 was another good historic example of how wrong it is to implement the interventionist patterns of the past in a different world. David Hendrickson made a very sharp reflection on these events when he affirmed that Somalia had remained an "acid test" for the United States and exposed the limitations of the policy of "crime and punishment."[21] With September 11, 2001, they moved to an open unilateralism with the articulation of the selective alliances and the explicit adhesion of all the allies to their international military actions.

> The results of the "global crusade" against terrorism were not the expected ones. Far from allowing the withdrawal of American troops from Iraq, the situation seems bogged down; and the unavailability of the present government of Iraq became obvious. Despite the threats to other countries like Syria, Iran and North Korea, it doesn't seem rational for the United States to get involved in another war, with the present battle fronts still open. To this we must add the internal problems of the present Administration particularly in the South of the country, with the results of Hurricane Katrina; and the changes generated by the behavior of its citizens as a result of life "post 9–11" This is a reality that has been extended to main US allies, also victims of terrorist activities. (Spain 2003 and Great Britain 2005)[22]

Today, U.S. international relations are based on the project of global domination that seems to have two main axis, defense at all cost of its political-military leadership in the world, as a balancing factor against the economic coleadership with the European Union, Japan, and emerging China, and its strategic repositioning to control the sources of renewable and nonrenewable resources that the country is urgently demanding as the largest consumer on the planet. In this second axis, Latin America is trapped, with its huge oil and gas reserves, its abundant reserves of drinking water, and its rich biodiversity. The confrontation is and will be unavoidable, if the present imperial logic does not change.

Latin America in the Post–Cold War Era

With the beginning of the post–cold war era, Latin America saw its economic panorama undergoing rapid transformations. On the one hand, the limitations of neoliberalism became evident, an economic policy that brought traumatic consequences for many countries in the region. On the other, responding to a prioritized objective for the United States, a greater emphasis was given to the economic-commercial relations. In the years previous to the post–cold war, the United States had signed a Free Trade Treaty with Canada in 1986 followed by another more polemic one with Mexico in 1989. This allowed for the articulation of a hemispheric economic bloc, led by the United States, responding to the new bloc created in the Old continent, the European Union (1992). NAFTA came to be the hard core of the American hemispheric strategy, being a better footing than the ambitious FTAA project that tried to unify a set of actors as different as is undoubtedly the mosaic of countries that make up Latin America and the Caribbean.

It should be no surprise then that NAFTA, as an original project, served as the pattern for economic policy decisions that the United States approved for its relations with the rest of the countries in the hemisphere. Hence, it is not strange that during the first years of the 1990s there were talks were about a "naftalization" of their Latin-American policies.[23]

Despite the big differences between what a process of regional integration should be and a free trade area, and beyond language barriers, both concepts have intermingled in the broad writing on the theme. However, it is not an original event for the history of inter-American relations. The very concept of Pan-Americanism is taken from Bolivar's idea at the Amphictyonic Congress held in Panama in 1826.

In this scenario of the post–cold war era, emerging trends were imposed internationally in which a new triad of power was established and consolidated that comprised the great transnational corporations and neoliberal governments as indispensable control and regulation instruments and international organizations following the style of the World Bank (WB), the International Monetary Fund (IMF) and for the region, the Interamerican Development Bank (IDB) and so on. This new international power faces a huge impact—support and subordination to the large Latin American capital and subjection to new politics.

Compared with this emerging power, the normal reaction of society that was pressured by the new challenges and threats they had to face, were found to have reached levels of mobilization, organization, and articulation never experienced before throughout the international system. Such is the case of the widespread global justice movement, with branches in all continents and for the case of Latin America that it is nurtured with other contents like the struggle against neoliberalism and against the FTAA project. Different organizations of the continent, like the Continental Social Alliance, linked themselves to other networks in the region and abroad, organizing many fora to present their positions and denounce the consequences of globalization, neoliberalism, FTAA, and the new U.S. domination strategies on the peoples of the region. There were organized mobilizations against the summits of the governments in Seattle (1999), Cancun (2003), and Miami where protests limited many of the results that those countries intend to obtain.

Therefore, in the framework of the new neoPanAmerican scenario, cracks started to appear, as an expression of the normal reaction of those "on the bottom." First, these cracks appeared in a spontaneous and disorderly way but gained gradually in organization and political clarity of their determination. So in that very same year of 1989 the so-called Caracazo took place in Venezuela, which was the collection of popular expressions that though did not represent the existence of an organized political movement, did challenge the bases of the old Venezuelan oligarchic regime. Precisely the nonsolution to the serious social problems existing in Venezuela brought about the military coup attempt of Colonel Hugo Chavez, a figure who had succeeded in the 1998 national elections, hardly three years later.

The reaction of the popular forces was also expressed in other countries of the hemisphere. Such was the case of the Zapatista National Liberation Army (EZLN) that moved the Mexican society at the beginning of 1994, opening new paradigms of struggle against the system. The EZLN who were intelligent enough, moved from the armed confrontation to an original model of political confrontation, which although went through successes and failures, has succeeded in placing itself in the political discussion of that nation. It should also be stated that with the EZLN a new chapter of the popular struggle was opened. It placed native rights in the economic, political, and social realm on the hemispheric agenda. This has had a great impact on countries with notable indigenous populations such as Ecuador, Bolivia, and Peru, where indigenous groups are moving forward in their own internal organization. To understand the extent of that impact, suffice to remember that the Ecuadorian indigenous people acted decisively for the displacement from power of two presidents in that country (Jamil Mahuad in 1999 and Abdala Bucaram in 2001). In the case of indigenous movements in Bolivia, after their demanding struggle, they were able to overthrow President Gonzalo Sanchez de Lozada in 2003 and his successor Carlos Mesa (2005).

Parallel to these ethnic movements, the economic crisis generated by neoliberalism in Argentina unleashed a broad popular movement in December 2001, bringing about the fall of successive presidents unable to halt the crisis, opening the national scenario to political forces originally not included in the options for power. Nestor Kirchner, the beneficiary was a Peronist secondary figure who was able to win the minimum consensus to defeat Carlos Menem and his commitment to neoliberalism. From that convulsive scenario two social actors came together, the beaten middle class of Argentina and the unemployed, known for their actions during the crisis as "picketers." The latter, became outstanding by the incorporation of new forms of social struggle, from the organization at the neighborhood level, assemblies, and communities contributed with new formulas to the popular struggle theory. A key theme for the movement is the territory, reinterpreted from the crisis scenario they face. In this sense, we believe it is important to relate the following reflection by Daniel Campione:

> The territory, the "local" . . . has risen to and directly question the social and political domination model. A social reproductive microcosm is formed expressing a different territorial articulation to the one implemented by neoliberal capitalism, destroying environment and links, promoting the isolated and insulated individualism.
>
> To occupy the territory is a strategic imperative; to occupy it with people linked by solidarity . . . the critique of unemployment is not the axis . . . but the critique of capitalist work and the society that supports it. From there the global is questioned, there is no struggle against "exclusion," to go back to "inclusion," it is against the alienating and exploiting society in its totality.[24]

A third social actor, the Landless Movement (LM) becomes likewise outstanding, gaining in organization and clarity about its objectives. It finds its main environment of intervention in Brazil, but it has similar expressions in other countries of the Southern Cone. How to define them? As dispossessed agricultural workers? As unemployed workers? Perhaps it is a mix of one and the other, since it summarizes the man with hunger, with no means of production and whose only option is working the land. According to Joao Pedro Stedile, founder of the Landless Movement, the occupation of lands in Brazil is a historic problem of such relevance that the challenge included hits at the very concept of property.[25]

More recently (April–May 2005) this original group of landless actors was enriched by the incorporation of the ones who called themselves Fugitives of Ecuador, an adjective given by the then president Lucio Gutierrez to the informal trading sectors of Quito, who made him run away from the country and forced Vice President Alfredo Palacios to take over the presidency.

The analysis of these four actors, expression of what very correctly Carlos Vilas calls institutional challenges to constitutional governments,[26] gives us valuable information on how much the impact of neoliberalism and globalization have been for our countries, bringing about the inclusion of new social sectors in the great mass of dispossessed, as a result of the increasing gap between rich and poor. The new political movements that have emerged in Latin America are clearly important but it is not yet clear that they are capable of fully transforming the region and its relations with the United States. They must be understood as actors with an important potential performance, when that alternative can be brought to fruition. They are undoubtedly factors of the political and social change but they need to be socially articulated, gaining in political consciousness and uniting with those forces that already have political institutions to develop the social change.

Why do these indigenous organizations not achieve greater political importance? The results of their actions demonstrate their shortcomings. In the first place the experience that the Ecuadorian indigenous organizations went through grouped in the Confederation of Indigenous Nationalities of Ecuador (CONAIE) and its political wing Pachakutik should be carefully analyzed. Lucio Gutierrez used the prestige and the social pressure of indigenous movements to take power and then caused divisions inside their organizations, politically damaging them. This does not mean that alliances of the indigenous movements with political sectors with coinciding interest and aspirations cannot be viable. On the contrary this is an indispensable factor, if a political change is intended that will lead to a new project of nationhood. This interpretation is very important not only for the Ecuadorian indigenous movement but for the indigenous movements in other countries such as Bolivia, Peru, and Mexico. The true demand of the rights of native peoples goes through a necessary articulation with other social sectors equally marginalized and socially exploited by capitalism. We are a wide variety of ethnicities and races thanks to the inheritance of the times of the conquest and European colonization. If this diversity is not considered, without discrimination and respecting the rights of each individual, one cannot think on the making up of our nations. Any political option disregarding that reality hardly has any chance to succeed.

The case of Argentinean Picketers also shows important aspects for the analysis. It is a very heterogeneous movement, and though it has sectors with a clearer political horizon, they have been beaten by the ruling system and its rejection of the government, and in particular, its police machinery is a factor not easily overcome. This has made them vulnerable to political manipulations, falling consciously or unconsciously in the conflict for power where the current President Kirchner and his predecessor Eduardo Duhalde took a leading part. They helped to bring down De La Rua and others but they had no national political alternative to offer.

Regarding Ecuador, it is significant that after playing a decisive role to the ousting of Gutierrez, the indigenous organization were not so effective some months later with the popular demonstrations convened to protest against the evident commitment of Palacios to the traditional oligarchy linked to the transnational capital.

Unlike the above-mentioned new social movements, we must point out the emergence of another group of actors, organized through long-standing political parties, Peronism in Argentina, Labor Party of Brazil and Broad Front of Uruguay, which have, as a defining feature, access to power through the ballot box. A second initial characteristic of these political actors is that their victories were the result of deep national situations of crisis, an expression of the failure of traditional parties that had ruled previously. Of course, the sociopolitical links between both groups of actors is acknowledged. For example, the political support of the Landless Movement to Lula in Brazil and of some picketers sectors to Kirchner in Argentina, but they were not decisive factors in the electoral rise of these governments.

Perhaps, regarding the economic crisis, Brazil may be presented as a different case because with the previous government, Fernando Henrique Cardoso, the economic indicators did not reveal the terrible results that were observed in Argentina, Venezuela, and Uruguay. But the social indicators were decisive for the gaining of power by the Workers Party (PT) in January 2003. Theotonio dos Santos illustrates this reality when he reminds us that in 2001 the Gross Domestic Product (GDP) growth was 1.5 percent in a country in which the population grew at 1.3 percent with the market of national work absorbing annually only 2.3 percent of the young working population of the country. Following this reasoning, every year an incredible mass of unemployed is generated, an unavoidable source of social violence, a topic of paramount urgency in Brazil.[27]

Another feature to mention is the fact that all these new governments were placed by the public opinion inside the left arena evidencing a superficial analysis of the subject. Lula and Vazquez have negotiated with sectors of the center and right wing. Kirchner is an emerging figure of traditionally populist Peronism, and should not be placed inside the broad spectrum of the Argentinean left. Chavez may be a different case who does clearly belong within the framework of the Left. He has aligned himself with Cuba and has launched ambitious programs aimed at Venezuela's majority poor. It was these sectors that came to his rescue during the attempted coup in April 2002 by the members of the right wing. As the alliance with Cuba strengthens it is proper to characterize Chavez as a leftist and radical populist.[28]

There are no doubts about the precedent set by these democratically elected governments in a region whose history is characterized by fast covert operations or direct coups d'etat to overthrow them. Perhaps it would be good to point out that these governments, besides being favored by the loss of credibility of their traditional political opponents and having the majority popular support, also benefit from an international context in which the themes of democracy, governance, and human rights were favored by the great centers of world power.

Nevertheless, the complexity and relevance of the subject demands some reflections. Trying to go beyond the essence of the problem to useful theory about the Left, Beatriz Stolowicz reminds us that "the identity essence of the Left is the quest for human emancipation, which is not possible without social equality. From the second half of the 19th Century, that quest is associated with a critique of capitalism and to the intention of building a society without exploitation nor domination by a minority over the majority."[29]

The collapse of the so-called real socialism, the demobilization of the great majority of armed movements, the many interpretations of the political reality that emerged from different Left political parties at the beginning of the 1990s made it necessary to create a new regional space to prevent greater disarticulation of the forces identified with that political position. The Sao Paulo Forum has played an important historic role in the difficult juncture within which it had to act, but it could not prevent the emergence of the political differences mentioned alone, which have, consciously or unconsciously, played the game of the prevailing neoliberalism. One of the results of that trend has been what some have called "the whitecollar left" or "constitutionals," alluding to those forces that establish levels of coexistence with capitalism. On this issue Marcelo Colussi stated the following:

> Are they "traitors" who "sold out to capitalism"? That is a slogan of a beginner, nothing more than a moving speech lacking an in-depth analysis. The constitutional Left does what it can: and today, in the framework of the post Cold War, with the victory of the capitalism and the present unipolar position, more so in the Latin American region, the historic "backyard" of the hegemonic superpower, has very little ahead. If the foreign debt is not paid, if they think in expropriations and popular power platforms and they dare to arm the people, their days are numbered. But Kirchner, Lula, Vazquez or (Ricardo) Lagos, did they talk at any moment about the socialist revolution in their election campaign? Did any one of them raise the same slogans that were proposed three decades ago by the armed movements, that with no fear or complex, spoke about communism and confiscations, the ones they directly or indirectly belonged to or supported? Without any doubts, no."[30]

A selective analysis reveals other interesting elements that begin to establish a difference between the social class components articulated in each of these forces. In Venezuela, a country in which social reactions against the present system have their background way back in time, like the Caracazo or the military coup attempt by Chavez, a political movement is forged around the figure of a former military offiical, in a scenario where the levels of poverty got out of control and the great dispossessed, unemployed, and marginal masses have given decisive support to the president. In this case, Chavism is supported in this poor sector of the population, in some segments of the farmers, and in the labor movement; and especially in the armed forces, thus facilitating the Bolivarian government arguments on the importance of the political-military alliance as an essential factor to safeguard the changes assumed by the Venezuelan government.

The case of Uruguay also has its peculiarities. As it is known, the Broad Front was founded in 1971 by General Liber Seregni. But the road traversed until the electoral victory in October 2004 has been long and difficult. For the 2004 elections, the Broad Front responded to the 1999 elections, when the right wing united to defeat General Seregni by organizing a policy of alliance which proved decisive in the victory. In 2004 Encuentro Progresista and Nuevo Espacio joined the Broad Front, along with the trade union— PIT-CNT— the Federation of University Students of Uruguay (FUSU), as well as different business, retired persons, and communal organizations. Tabare Vazquez was the candidate of Encuentro Progresista—Broad Front— Nueva Mayoría, obtaining the presidential victory in the first round and obtaining a majority in the parliament.

The national situation the new government inherited was critical. An essay drafted by Tabare Vazquez himself revealed challenging figures. Almost one-third of the population, about 1 million of Uruguayans, live in poverty; 100,000 of them under abject poverty. Sixty percent of the youth below 18 are in poverty, contributing to social violence. Almost 1 million men and women are unemployed or underemployed. Almost half of the economically active population, around 750,000 people, is not covered by social security. Over 300,000 Uruguayans do not have any public health protection, much less private. Barely 20 percent of the students that enroll in secondary education become graduates. Over 100,000 Uruguayans have left the country as emigrants.[31]

The third case, Brazil, caught the attention of the world because for the first time in the history of a country, a trade union leader was able to become the president of the nation with convincing popular support. Brazil is among the top ten economies of the earth and its extensive geography is full of great contrasts. There is no doubt that this factor existed in the strategy of Lula's government that established alliances with important sectors of the great financial interests, for example the nomination of Jose Alencar, a tycoon of Brazilian textiles and leader of the Center Liberal Party for vice president of the republic. This controversial pact was regarded by Alencar as "a new political society . . . where Lula represents the labor and I represent capital."[32]

In Lula's logic, who stated his intention of putting an end to hunger and malnutrition of over 20 million Brazilians, the economic and political support of sectors of big national capital was something indispensable. This decision brought about important criticism from the beginning of this term. The well-known sociologist Francisco de Oliveira wrote about Lula's managerial style, referring both to the alliance with capital as well as the continuation of many of the policies that Fernando Henrique Cardoso initiated.[33]

The criticism of Lula and his team was transformed into a political crisis in the summer of 2005, when the revelation of payments to conservative deputies by the PT to ensure the votes in favor of the government proposals came to light. Although it was known that this kind of illegal action is nothing new in the Brazilian politics, the connotations that it has for Lula exceeds all the previous scandals. As the first Left wing party in power, its discredit may lead to an unprecedented division of the national Left. Whether it directly affects Lula, the PT government is in a crisis, and the few accomplishments shown by Lula in his presidential term have not much likelihood of being continued if Lula is succeeded by a government of the Right.

Nevertheless, despite the sharp political crisis, there is a great base of the Left that continues to see Lula as the best option. This has been understood by the president, and he has embarked upon a reunion with the bases of the PT. If he is credible and convincing, he may keep some reelection options for 2006; but there is no doubt that the right wing forces, particularly the social-democracy of Fernando Henrique, have become stronger with the crisis.

As it can be noticed this amalgam of actors, an expression of a new regional sociopolitical shaping, although very diverse in itself, reflects the broad spectrum of problems that our region has accumulated throughout its history. Corresponding with this, one cannot expect that just one formula will work, because each national case entails its own dynamics and peculiarities.

Nonetheless, there are some factors that call the attention and demand further analysis:

1. The need to establish a difference between the social actors that are capable of developing until they become movements with definitions and political goals, including the seizing of power from those who do not meet those demands and remain only at the level of resistance to the established system.
2. The construction of a political culture capable of visualizing everything related to the access of political power: a comprehensive and all-encompassing vision of all the problems to be faced; the structuring of an organized political force; the definition of a governmental program, enough clarity to identify possible political alliances; the knowledge of all those internal and external factors that have an impact on the national government; to draw every possible experience from previous mistakes; the defense of the legitimacy and democratic credibility of the new government; and above all, not to lose the feedback channels with the social basis that support it. In summary, to raise as a viable political alternative to face the preestablished order.

3. The enormous challenge of having lived alienated for centuries or in the political opposition for a long time and all of a sudden finding oneself before the opportunity of being part of a new emerging political order. This entails deep changes in the political psychology of individuals and in their own cultural policy, which is not accomplished overnight.

4. The capacity to consolidate a new political alternative beyond the conjuncture, aware that to change such a huge historic accumulation of problems the national voters must be convinced of the need for at least a middle-term project, to deal with the maneuvers of the internal opposition regarding this delicate subject, and above all, to resist the attacks of the United States and the controlled world of the media.

Which are the margins in which the Latin American Left moves today? At least three lessons must be drawn up from the recent history to find an objective answer. The first one, the demobilizing effect caused by violence generated by a triad of military interventions by the United States, Latin American military dictatorships and American covert operations. The results were tens of thousands of persons dead, missing, or displaced, etc, a factor to take very much into account. The second lesson, the progressive loss of credibility in the traditional political parties, both from the Right as well as from the Left, giving way to massive disappointments and desertions. The third lesson has to do with a crucial theme, the stability and consolidation of democratic regimes. The history of Latin America shows a high democratic deficit, initially explained through the direct impact formulated by the first lessons but there are many more thorny problems. The very construction process of the nation-states in our region has reached the present period with quite a few unresolved issues and cracks. Many countries are very vulnerable economically and subordinated to the market and foreign capital of, mainly, the United States. They are politically dependant on the United States and under the risk of suffering the already known effects: accumulation of social problems as time passes. Such a situation has generated a set of problems that, far from being solved, have become worse under the conditions imposed by globalization and neoliberalism, like management corruption, political fraud, and social violence. The latter has today become not only a problem of national security for our countries, but also one of the great regional challenges to be faced.

During the past years in which diverse resistance movements have been identified and with the emergence of new political forces, the question has been what is the political alternative for the existing evils? On this theme the lack of a defined and coherent alternative has been one of the big criticisms of the forces against the change. Many meetings and international fora have only remained as declarations. The challenge of meetings such as the World Social Forum and the Social Forum of the Americas is that the participants in such international and regional gatherings are challenged to develop agendas for social and political change that can work in their own countries.

A great historic deficit that has undermined many of these forces has been the little or no capacity to unite themselves according to national interest with other similar forces by disregarding prominence. It cannot be denied that the Right wing has a historic advantage. Tabare Vazquez and the Broad Front suffered the effects of that practice during the 1999 elections, when the Blancos and Colorados became allies to defeat him in the second round of elections; and that same electoral horizon is threatening Lula, if he runs for the next elections without any political allies.

Of course, the level of consolidation to be attained by the new political alliances contained in concrete governmental programs is another factor derived from the above-mentioned. The great risk, and we have already seen it with Lula, is searching for the indulgence of key economic sectors so as to capture most of the required votes at the expense of further concessions. Franck Gaudichaud summarizes such a regretful outcome as follows:

> Two years after his coming into power, President Lula became the spoiled child of both financial means and agribusiness. And during recent months, just like previous executives (so much criticized by Lula when he was still a consistent militant), the Brazilian government embarked on a widespread network of corruption. Undoubtedly, that this resulted from a gradual transformation of the PT which began more than twenty years ago. And if the left is incapable of implementing alternatives in that continent-country, no wonder we are witnessing the same script in small countries."[34]

From this "mare magnum" of events we can conclude that there were new political trends with well-defined characteristics. Let us begin examining what seems to be turning into an "emergent political leadership," when it was already a government or was progressively going in that direction. Under that assumption, two examples are discussed, Nestor Kirchner in Argentina and Andres Manuel Lopez Obrador in Mexico. The first, president of his country and the second the strongest candidate in the still premature Mexican electoral arena. Other names can be added too: for example, in Brazil, Jose Serra or Fernando Henrique Cardoso figures still waiting for the final outcome of Lula, the Chilean socialist president Michele Bachelet, and Tabare Vazquez himself.

What do these politicians have in common?

1. They are politicians who know that their national context is marked by the effects of neoliberalism and, therefore, they have (Fernando Henrique did it already) to develop their governmental programs within that reality since they feel incapable of doing so or because they do not intent to change that reality.
2. They are exponents of power sectors defending certain national interests (financial, commercial interests) who are aware of their limitations with the large transnational capital and have understood that they must work in that sphere in order to preserve their domestic spheres.

3. They have gained support both within the most moderate right and the less radical left. This has resulted in the minting of terms like center-right and center-left with all ambiguities demanded by such definitions.
4. They represent an anticrisis option and as such they have a certain social consensus against the serious problems accumulated by their countries.
5. Kirchner's leadership can be taken as an example, or the more speculative example of Lopez Obrador. These are politicians who are aware of the fact that they should develop skills to defend spaces of national independence spaces vis-à-vis the United States, the International Monetary Fund, the World Bank, and the World Trade Organization without creating ruptures with those institutions.

Far from accepting or not the existence of this new political leadership, which can be interpreted as a detachment or expression of the so-called third track, the common denominator of this group of politicians is that they are not trying to replace the existing system and, to this end, they resort to a conciliation between the less radical interests of both groups. However, in order to better understand the above-mentioned phenomenon, we must pay attention to the following considerations by Beatriz Stolowicz:

> This is a new political and ideological strategy aimed at preserving capitalism in an attempt to separate it from the bad prestige associated with neoliberalism and to preserve it from social and political crisis. Its objective is to neutralize the possibility of achieving the alternative projects devised by the partisan and social left.
> It is the strategy of dominant sectors to neutralize a growing social and electoral left in order to "modernize it as center," that is to say, to "moderate" its purposes. The ideological efficacy of this strategy lies in the fact that it masks the moderation of its purposes as an objective under the moderation of its means, which is introduced as "realism."[35]

The warning signals are already activated without leaving aside the great expectation for the changes that might take place. As always, the role to be played by organized popular movements must be decisive. Venezuela, with the required consolidation of its political process and its Bolivarian Alternative (ALBA) as a regional tool of great value for the multilateral and regional activity, constitutes a factor to take into consideration so as not to let the anxiously awaited alternative to the current system turn into nothing as it has already happened on so many occasions in the past. The debate is still open.

The New Social and Political Configuration of Latin America: A Threat to the U.S. National Security?

Nowadays it is very common to read or listen to the mass media, the political media and academicians speak about fundamentalism as an expression of religious fanaticism, extremism an even terrorism. But beyond the ideological sense given to the term, it has an undisputable political root. That is why

Aurelio Alonso affirms "heavily underlined" that politics is an important matrix to be considered in fundamentalist movements.[36]

Further on, the writer states that

> the Puritanism found in pilgrims responded to an ethic code and a doctrine that fairly fits into the fundamentalist qualification. Persecuted by both Anglicans and Catholics, searching for a new land where they could live and worship God in their own way, they believed they were dragged by the divine Providence to colonize New England. Their spirituality survived in Christian religion and became a founding element of the political ideology of the United States of America[37]

In turn, Kissinger, in its work entitled *The Diplomacy*, states the following:

> No nation has been more pragmatic in the daily conduct of its diplomacy, or more ideological in its search for its historical moral convictions. No country has been more reluctant to venture abroad, while creating alliances and commitments of unprecedented scope and dimension.
>
> The singularities attributed to the United States throughout its history have given birth to two contradicting attitudes concerning foreign policy. The first one is that the best way in which the United States can serve its values is by perfecting domestic democracy, by acting as the lighthouse for the rest of mankind; the second one is that the nation's values impose the need to launch crusades on their behalf across the world.[38]

Theology, mysticism, messianism, pragmatism, and fundamentalism are some of the concepts that might come to mind when reading previous bibliographical quotes. A strict Christian religiosity as the founding element of a political ideology provides the option of resorting to "crusades" with all its historical and religious connotation as tools to defend that ideology and the "universal nature" of its values.

We all remember that the key element in the confrontation between the United States and the Soviet Union was the cold war in the so-called third world. Their political and ideological arguments included the "communist threat," the "domino theory" or the "axis of evil." The "axis of evil" has strongly survived the cold war into the post–cold war period. In the American political discourse at international level, the "axis of evil" is formed by a group of countries considered as enemies—Iraq, Iran, Libya, Syria, North Korea, and others left "in rest" and then mentioned again—and believed to be an active threat to the United States.[39] Under the current Bush administration, the term "axis of evil" has reached very dangerous dimensions. Lee Feinstein and Anne-Marie Slaughter state:

> The use of the "axis of evil" term by this government indicates a more severe version of the statement made by the government of Bush senior. It leaves almost no margin to diplomacy and forces the United States to select between promoting a change of regime or doing nothing.[40]

As it happened during the 1980s, Cuba was charged with promoting subversion in Latin America. In the past, it was accused for its support to Central American guerrillas and now for its close alliance with Chavez in Venezuela. In the past, the so-called Santa Fe I document stated:

> Should we let Grenada, Nicaragua and El Salvador to become new Cubas, new outposts for Soviet fighting brigades? Will the Moscow-Havana axis next step be to head to the north of Guatemala and then to Mexico and the south of Costa Rica and Panama?[41]

Now, the Santa Fe IV document states:

> Fidel Castro, the Cuban chieftain, closed the G-77 Conference held in April 2000 in Havana stating that the Third World should assume the international leadership because wealthy nations are incapable of governing the world . . . populist democracy is dominating Latin America from Cape Horn to Rio Grande and is now penetrating Seattle, Washington DC, Toronto and Millau, France.[42]

Evidently, the geopolitical approach has not changed the axis of evil and the domino theory. What radically changed was the pretext. Yesterday, it was the threat posed by armed movements, now the threat comes from "populist democracies" headed by the "inflammatory Venezuelan President Hugo Chavez" as Peter Hakim described him.[43]

Previously, it was the Central American crisis, today it is the Andean area with an exceptional record to be qualified as "hotbed." Chavez in Venezuela; native movements in Ecuador, Peru and, especially, in Bolivia, with Evo Morales, as the newly elected president, with a project aimed at nationalizing hydrocarbons; and Colombia, for a long time now living under a counterinsurgency Plan Colombia that serves as a platform for any subregional military operation.

Felipe de la Balze describes the geopolitical implications and threats to American national security as follows:

> Worrying signs can be seen in the new alliances between guerrilla movements and drug traffickers with the emergence of populist authoritarian regimes in countries like Venezuela and the weakening of the rule of law in the northern Andean region. The restlessness in afflicted countries could propagate and reach other countries. The political and economic influence by Washington in South America would decrease and, as a result of this, the US political, corporate and security interests could be affected.[44]

The American System for the Twenty-First Century

In an essay devoted to examine the current dynamics of the world power game and its central axis, hegemony and domination, the Mexican researcher

Ana Esther Ceceña, stated the following:

> The capitalist world, its expansion and limitations, is built on the basis of competition. Competition and constant increase of profits, struggle for power, unlimited appropriation of resources of every kind and permanent confrontation with political and civilizing horizons constitute the driving force which encourages the persistent development of productive forces and all required mechanisms to establish the rules and limits of this game of power and to enter the world under winning conditions. In this regard, the possibilities, content and scope of shaping the world system and its vulnerabilities stem from this competition and its resulting conflict situation.[45]

World system, competition and vulnerabilities are the three main concepts used by the author that, based on the hegemony-domination axis, constitute the key basis for analysis in this chapter. To this end, they will be placed in context by taking the United States as the main reference together with its hemispheric and territorial perspective—or similarly for the purpose of this work—that is, the proposed American System for the twenty-first century. Ana Esther Ceceña and other researchers have already dealt with these issues with all scientific rigor, therefore, in our specific case, the main issue of interest would be to discern which are or could be the Latin American and Caribbean participation scenarios in the U.S. global strategic repositioning of the world. We attempt to present some ideas concerning both conscious and structured participation in the region as part of the geostrategic hemispheric project validating old assumptions that historically support inter-American relations. In this sense, an interesting aspect within the analysis to be made will be the actual participation level of Latin American and Caribbean corporate and political elites in this project. Let us start by defining the main concepts that will be used.

The world system of the cold war era, understood as the group of state actors who interact in different scenarios already known, namely, bilateral, intraregional and extraregional, and conditioned by a global power structure based on the United States-Soviet Union bipolarity. This system was supplanted due to many reasons; first, the substitution of this bipolar axis by a unipolar one represented by the United States. A second factor to be mentioned is the fact that the traditional nature of the system was altered by the inclusion of new nonstate actors. We are speaking about nongovernmental organizations of different nature: agricultural, communal, craft, religious, ethnic, environmentalist, and cultural organizations, as well as other first-class actors, the multinational corporations. The first ones came to light by forcing their way within the system; the second ones imposed themselves as a power over states. Nongovernmental organizations, through their several ways of intervention, occupied certain spaces within the system and gradually increased their influence in international relations. The big multinationals took possession of current management and control dynamics in the world economy. As a result, we must say that this actor became decisive in the current physiognomy of the international system and was even capable of changing the political and military priorities prevailing during the cold war into new trends in the global economy and market. As Samuel Huntington affirmed when paraphrasing Daniel Bell, if before the war it was the continuation of that policy through other means, now economy is the continuation of war, but through other means.[46]

The United States, Germany, and Japan from the individual point of view, and later on the emerging economic blocs, as the European Union and the NAFTA, without forgetting the gradual and patient growth of China, now mark the economic direction of the international system. According to Ceceña, these are the main competitors trying to constantly maximize their economic power capabilities and minimize their vulnerabilities. This confrontation is waged on two main areas of power: technological development and the better use and control of available natural resources, especially the nonrenewable ones. In the sphere of technological development, a great revolution has taken place in the sphere of communications with implications for the main economic sectors. But the sphere of natural resources is decisive and is the subject of the following thoughts.

Another important issue today that has generated multiple studies is sustainable development. Malthus, with his well-known research, was among the first ones who called the attention on the need to establish a balance between the world population growth and global food production and human costs derived from the disproportion between both, and concluded that the most developed societies would be the ones capable of finding solutions to this challenge. His thesis constitutes an important starting point for any analysis.[47] This kind of selection and, perhaps better to say of exclusion, of those populations with less capacity to produce foodstuffs and at the same time with less birth control, and the greater options of developed countries characterize the scenario for the sustainable development we want to stress. Because it expresses an essential relationship between nature and economy, nature and market, nature and power.

Of course, the road taken does not lead to a validation of the importance of sustainable development as defined by the main international organizations and underdeveloped countries, but to warn on the fact that since the post–cold war period there is an increasingly stronger idea from the system-leading powers to achieve a sustainable development through the new strategic repositioning of the main natural resources they need to preserve their power at global level. This is a new kind of economic war between the big powers, while the military war is considered to be an option to snatch those resources from the "Third World."

The war in Afghanistan and the second war launched against Iraq are just two irrefutable examples of this thesis and the result of an evaluation process of the capability limits of the United States in terms of domestic reserves of the main strategic resources, especially oil. This goes without saying that it faces an accelerated increase in the domestic energy consumption and that it has the opportunity, under the post–cold war conditions, to get control of the main oil deposits in the Middle East by giving access to big transnational corporations to those resources thus guaranteeing a geographic balance between the different resource providers in the world. In other words, this is war seeking a new global redistribution of natural resources.

In an interesting article, already mentioned, devoted to an analysis of what is considered "the new geography of world power" in the post–cold war era, Michael Klare states the following:

> During the Cold War the concern for resources is frequently subordinated to the political and ideological dimensions of the rivalry between the United States and the Soviet Union. But now, once the Cold War ended, access to vital raw materials has gained once more its key position when planning American security.[48]

Available statistics on U.S. oil consumption and its importing demands are multiple, but they all indicate a high consumption tending to increase, while domestic reserves are experiencing a reduction. In 2003, the population in United States accounted for 6 percent of the world total, but it consumed over 25 percent of its oil production (1 billion tons yearly) and an estimated annual growth of 1 percent due to the high demand concentrated in the transportation sector (40 percent of the country's final energy consumption). The United States imports 45 percent of the oil it consumes, twice the figure consumed 30 years ago. Out of these imports, 65 percent come from the Middle East where its main allies, Turkey and Israel, have no oil at all.[49]

Obviously, oil accounts for a vital resource for such a highly consumer economy as that of the United States. In the National Energy Policy document published in May 2001, there are statistical tables revealing that while the daily consumption estimate of oil barrels can increase in 6 million in the coming 20 years—in the year 2021, according to the date indicated in the report—domestic production can decrease, during the same period, by 1.5 million barrels daily.[50]

President George W. Bush, during his second week in power, ordered the creation of the National Energy Policy Development Group. Michael Klare reminds us, in his above-mentioned article, that during the 2000 debates when George W. Bush was a candidate to the presidency, he demanded the need to explore the existence of oil and natural gas in still-virgin territories of the United States in order to reduce the country's dependence on foreign providers. When he took power, one of the first decisions he made was to meet with the Mexican President Vicente Fox to discuss an increase in oil imports from that neighboring country.[51] Such information is very important due to the well-known interest of the United States to have energy producing sources in its territory in order to reduce the impact of potential conflicts in producing countries, as in the case of the Middle East.

This document on National Security Strategy dated September 30, 2002 states the following:

> "Improving energy security. We shall strengthen our own energy security and shared prosperity from world economy by collaborating with our allies, trading partners and energy producers in order to enlarge sources and the kind of world

energy to be provided, especially in the Western Hemisphere, central Asia and the Caspian Sea region"[52]

According to statistical data from January 2003, out of the first 15 countries that exported crude oil to the United States, 6 were from the Western hemisphere, namely Canada, second place after Saudi Arabia; Mexico, third place; Venezuela, seventh place; Colombia, tenth place; Trinidad and Tobago, fourteenth place; and Ecuador in the fifteenth place. While within the first 15 oil exporting countries to the United States, at that same date, 6 were from the Western hemisphere, namely, Canada in the first place; Mexico still in the third place; Venezuela still in the seventh place; the United States Virgin Islands in the twelfth place; Colombia in the fourteenth place and Argentina in the fifteenth place. It means that in January 2003, the United States imported oil from eight countries in this hemisphere, when adding those indicated in both tables.[53]

Excepting Canada, which is the United States' natural ally, Mexico, Venezuela and Colombia account for the main oil providing countries in Latin America and the Caribbean. The incorporation of Mexico into NAFTA has undoubtedly implied a reinforcement of its subordination to the United States. It is worthwhile mentioning the increase of dependence to the United States experienced by the Mexican economy, as well as its close alliance with the big American capital that precipitated the rupture of the traditional political system controlled by the Partido de la Revolución Institucional (PRI), defeated by the Partido Acción Nacional (PAN) during the last elections held in the year 2000. To this we must add the fact that, in the sphere of international relations there is an increasing consensus in diplomatic agendas of both countries on democracy and human rights. This has caused a rupture from the Mexican traditional nationalistic and independent policy now facing unexpected crisis before its incorporation to NAFTA, as the ones experienced in the Cuban-Mexican relations.

Regarding Venezuela and Colombia, these are two countries located in the Andean region that, due to different reasons, are characterized as national security cases for the United States. Colombia, because of the direct involvement of the United States in the Colombian internal conflict through its military support to the government against the guerrillas and its strategic struggle against drug trafficking. In the case of Venezuela, the government headed by President Chavez is now in an open political confrontation with the United States and oil is one of the key elements in the bilateral agenda. According to Venezuelan sources, citing Petróleos de Venezuela (PDVSA) company, the country has a 78-million-barrel reserve equivalent to half the oil existing in the Western Hemisphere. It occupies the fifth place in reserves at world level and the sixth place in natural gas (148 trillion cubic feet of natural gas). According to the same source, the United States receives 15 percent of its oil imports from Venezuela, a figure that might increase to 25 percent in 2015.[54] Beyond the strict accuracy of data provided, it is undeniable that oil is a priority issue for the national security of the United States.

The United States is not interested in oil only. Natural gas, found in large reserves in South America, water resources, and biodiversity are also items defined as strategic by American analysts. Regarding the latter, Raul Ornelas points out that

> biodiversity is emerging as a new key element in capitalist production. As information technology and digital telecommunications have already created a new production apparatus; the industrialization of life is now both possible and profitable.
>
> Unlike energy resources, biodiversity is a resource whose economic consideration is quite recent. Besides, the great spaces of biological diversity are located in underdeveloped countries.[55]

In that same article, Ornelas includes a statistical table—in which he mentions a report by the World Resources Institute in 2001—which illustrates the geographic location of biodiversity in the world. Out of the 12 countries included in the table, 10 are Latin American countries. The other 2 are the United States and Indonesia. This data alone contains the explanation for the great interest to control that biodiversity that is symbol and pride of our region.[56]

At this point, it is necessary to guide the reader through the road being paved by Ana Esther Ceceña and other authors as Ornelas himself whose research insist on how the hemispheric strategy of the United States is articulated so as to get control of the main natural resources in the Latin American region. In stricter terms, it could be debatable whether this is a new project or a new stage of the plunder and exploitation suffered by southern peoples since the United States imposed its hemispheric hegemony. Suffice it to think about the arguments used by U.S. administrations to attack and invade Latin American and Caribbean territories to understand that these plundering practices are not new. What really seems new within this globalization scenery, the "philosophic mutation" between past and present, is that resources were extracted before as part of an hegemonic exercise aimed at gaining higher benefits for the American nation and its main actors (that is, companies, government, inter-American System mechanisms, inter alia). Therefore, the region was considered as the "historic backyard" of the United States. Today, natural resources are indispensable because the nation's survival is at stake, a nation that has paid the historical price of a world leadership demanding these guarantees even at the risk of losing and falling, as others, within the concord of big nations. Nevertheless, this must be done through a transnational agreement between the "corporation" made up by U.S. multinational enterprises, different agencies and departments in the U.S. administration in charge of establishing policies for the region, international organizations such as the World Bank and the Inter-American Development Bank, nongovernmental organizations financed by U.S. funds, the mass media and the corresponding military commands (the South Command and its several branches) as guarantors of this project. This "corporation" needs a similar counterpart in the region with a similar physiognomy, capable of meeting the goals pursued. From another perspective, Ana Esther Ceceña summarizes the problems in the following terms: "The framework for the total redefinition process of domination relations both in the sphere of inter-capitalist competition and in the sphere of class relation is the restructuring of the technological basis of the general organization of the system which took place in the 1970s and 1980s."[57]

Obviously, the United States has no opposition to its military leadership, nor does anyone seem interested in opposing it because of the cost implied in doing so. The revenge of yesterday's allies and enemies is in the economic field resulting in U.S. military adventures and benefits derived from such adventures, but its bet does not traverse the military road. Strictly speaking, we can affirm that the American economic bloc, the most reliable and controllable by the United States, is NAFTA. Because the FTAA implies an articulation with different actors, the question marks concerning the cost of commitments to be met by the United States cannot be set aside. That is why there is a generalized encouragement for FTAs and the conclusion of a free trade agreement with Central America, not for economic reasons, but for geopolitical reasons. In order to achieve its goals, the United States is promoting bilateral FTAs or articulating others with selected groups of countries, as the recent FTA proposal with Colombia, Ecuador, and Peru with the purpose of isolating countries such as Venezuela or exerting pressures against Brazil and the MERCOSUR.

It is precisely at this point of the analysis that we must include the issue concerning ways found in the FTAA, meaning the macroprojects for the hemispheric subregional articulation searching for the new positioning of the United States. This is the Puebla Panama Plan (PPP) for the area including Mexico and Central America to be geographically articulated with the following projects for South America: splitting the Colombia Plan in the Amazonian Andean Plan; access to the large Guarani Water System which, at the same time, partly coincides with the strategic zone of "Triple Frontier" (Brazil, Argentina, and Paraguay) and the Antarctic zone—all of which have huge natural resources: energy, water, and biodiversity just to mention the well-known ones.

How feasible could be the completion of such an important project? We are asking a question with multiple short-term, middle-term, and long-term answers and a question that implies the reaction of multiple stakeholders, from peoples to governments in countries where these resources are found that, in this case, is almost like saying the whole region. This could be the fate held for Latin America by the new century. Could it be the "American system of the 21st century?"

The Puebla Panama Plan

Officially disclosed in 2001, after the visit paid by the Mexican President Vicente Fox to El Salvador, this is a proposal formulated from both the Mexican and American interests emerging from initiatives like the Development Plan submitted during Ernesto Zedillo's government and the Plan on the

Mesoamerican Biotic Corridor sponsored, among others, by the World Bank and the Inter-American Development Bank. It is worthwhile mentioning, among its many objectives, the linkage of the eastern coast of the United States with the main urban and rural centers of the south-southeast region of Mexico through a set of large interoceanic corridors with immediate access to all natural and human resources of the region and top-quality operational conditions for the U.S. Armed Forces. Ricardo Cifuentes described the project and indicates its immediate consequences for the region:

> By serving the Puebla Panama Plan, governments in the region are already devising several partial programs. And so, this concept of corridors will end incubating fiber optic networks, roads, cities, ports, new railroads and airports in a zone which will become a strategic zone for international trade and whose functions and contributions to ecological balance and biodiversity will be degraded as a result of the presence of a tangle of businesses and enterprises— and their several polluting and subjugating effects to biological diversity.[58]

The Amazonian-Andean Project

We must begin by saying that under this name there is no definitive project. What happens is that when considering the interests already projected in the Plan Colombia and, above all, the Andean Regional Initiative, this region is then connected, not only geographically but also strategically, with the Amazonia. In both subregions a high percentage of the hemispheric natural resources is concentrated.

The Plan Colombia, disclosed by the government of the United States in the year 2000, stemmed out from an initial idea, to fight against drug trafficking, but has become a generalized intervention in the Colombian internal conflict that goes beyond its frontiers and which is now projected as a regional problem. In its original conception, the Plan included $7 billion ($3 billion offered by the United States and the rest by Colombia through an external borrowing and other tax adjustments).[59]

There are many unclear questions on the real interest of the United States to put an end to drug trafficking due to the economic benefits received by the big American transnationals, especially the main banks of that nation. According to Diego Delgado Jara, when quoting Antonio Geraldi, a commercial bank executive in the United States:

> The 500 billion dollars from illegal origin coming into the main American banks and circulating among them exceed the net income of all computer companies in the United States and, of course, their benefits. This annual income exceeds all net transfers made by the main oil and military companies and aircraft manufacturers. The largest banks in the United States—the Bank of America, J.P. Morgan, Chase Manhattan and, above all, the Citibank—receive a high percentage of their banking benefits from services provided to these accounts of criminal dirty money. The large banks and financial institutions in

the United States support the global power of the United States through their laundering operations and management of illegal foreign funds.

The Citibank, the first money laundering bank, is the largest bank in the United States, with 180,000 employees across the world distributed throughout 100 countries, 700,000 well-known deposits and over 1 billion deposits of private individuals in secret accounts and carries out private bank operations (investment portfolio management) in more than 30 countries thus turning it into the bank with the largest global presence compared with all financial institutions in the United States.[60]

To this we must add that today the Andean region includes a population of some 30 million inhabitants distributed throughout eight countries, namely, Brazil, Bolivia, Colombia, Ecuador, Guyana, French Guyana, Venezuela, and Suriname. Before the arrival of the white man, thousands of ethnic groups lived in the region, however today there are only 370 recognized ethnic groups. "The combined regimes of economic expansion (mining, agriculture, tree cutting) encouraged by different "development plans," plus the anxious intervention of hundreds of corporations, can make the Brazilian forest disappear in fifty years. This destruction has already started, is vertiginous and increasing. In the year 2000 alone, 20,000 square kilometers of forests were destroyed."[61]

In the Western hemisphere, the Amazonia and the Antarctic are the main areas associated with climate change, the greenhouse effect and their obnoxious consequences for human life. In the case of the Amazonia, Brazil is the most responsible country in the region due to geographical reasons. During his first mandate, President Fernando Henrique Cardoso granted maximum priority to this issue.[62] In turn, the Brazilian minister (Itamarati) handles it with a lot of political and diplomatic prudence, and debates concentrate in the creation of a "multilateral regime of climate change." Brazil has had a very active participation, since the United Nations began promoting an international reflection on climate change and its effects for humans, due to its own responsibility in the deterioration of environment. As Everton Vargas and María Rita Fontes Farías warn:

> The evolution and expansion of knowledge on climate change do not necessarily mean the creation of common interests or the reduction of conflicts of interests between the parties to the regime. On the contrary, the better the knowledge, more complex will be the distribution of charges to mitigate and adapt ourselves to the impact of climate change.[63]

Unlike Brazil, the United States is reluctant to assume commitments on this issue as, for example, the signing of the Kyoto Protocol and its position during the 1992 Rio Conference and other meetings on this topic.

> There is still a long way to go in order to reach a genuine global agreement on climate change. The opposition by the United States government to ratify the Kyoto Protocol is a clear proof that the interests behind the creation of a development model based on the indiscriminate use of energy do not allow it to give

up its advantages in the sharing of responsibilities to fight against global warming in keeping with the negotiated regime.[64]

But the Amazonian issue has more dangerous angles revealing the connections among all countries in the region. In its above-mentioned article, Ignacy Sachs acknowledges that the Amazonia, not only for its adequate physiognomy but also for its geographic location, has become an important route for drug trafficking linked with Colombia and, therefore, the object of interest for the antidrug struggle in the United States.[65]

Diego Delgado Jara goes beyond and states that at the beginning of the 1990s, the then commander of the Superior School of War in Brazil, General Oswaldo Muñiz Oliva, defended the urgent need to train the Brazilian armed forces to protect the sovereignty of the Amazonian region. Delgado Jara, quoting Guillermo Navarro Jiménez, states that such concern stemmed from a number of public statements made by leaders in developed countries like the then vice president of the United States, Albert Gore, and the French president, Francois Mitterand, who denied the Brazilian national sovereignty over the Amazonian region and defended the application of the "limited sovereignty" and "right to interfere" doctrine.[66]

At this point, it is adequate to cite information published in a book entitled *Introduction to Geography* by David Norman used in junior high schools in the United States. On page 76, to the right of the map of South America, the author states that in the mid-1980s "the most important forest in the world became a responsibility of the United States and the United Nations . . ." And further on he describes the Amazonia as "one of the poorest regions of the world surrounded by irresponsible, cruel and authoritarian countries. It was part of eight different countries which are mostly kingdoms of violence, drug trafficking, ignorance and primitive and unknowledgeable peoples."[67]

Aside from the political and philosophical arguments instilled in American children, this is another example of the thinking that, since the origin of inter-American relations, has been instilled in that country about Latin American countries.

The Guarani Water System (The Triple Frontier)

The Guarani Water System is one of the largest underground reservoirs in the world. According to Dr. Jorge N. Santa Cruz, national coordinator of the Guarani Water Project in Argentina, this reservoir extends from the El Pantanal zone in Brazil (850,000 km^2, 9.9 percent of the territory); Argentina (225,000 km^2, 7.8 percent of its territory, especially the well-known Argentinean Pampas); Paraguay (70,000 km^2, 17.2 percent of its territory); to Uruguay (45,000 km^2, 25.5 percent of its territory). This accounts for an estimated total of 1,190,000 km^2 at different depths (between 50 and 1500 m); Argentina being the country where the system is located at more steady depths (below 900 m). The waters are mainly used by Brazil that supplies, totally or partially, some 300–500 cities. Paraguay has some 200 wells mainly for human use. In Uruguay there are 135 wells for public water supply, some of which are used for thermal exploitation. In Argentina there are 5 thermal perforations of fresh water and one of salt water under exploitation in the Entre Ríos province. Also there is a complete ignorance and lack of general exploitation in the rest of the zones within Argentina.[68]

Certainly, the fact that the most coveted important natural resources as oil (concerning national reserves in the United States) or fresh water with a limited durability are under analysis by specialists increases the offensive launched by the big powers to guarantee these supplies. In the case of fresh water available data are highly significant:

> A little more than 70% of the land is covered by water. Of that total, some 90% accounts for salt water present in oceans and seas and less than 3% is fresh water. Out of that 3%, 79% is practically unusable, enclosed in polar ice caps, glaciers and perennial snows; 20% accounts for underground waters and only 1% is surface water. Out of that 1% of surface water, 52% is found in lakes, 38% as soil humidity and 8% atmospheric humidity and only 1.75% in rivers with different types of pollution and, therefore, its consumption is dangerous for the health.[69]

To this dramatic statement we could add that, according to the United Nations, in the year 2025 drinking water consumption will be 56 percent above available supplies and, in the year 2015, an annual investment of $180 billion to reduce half the number of persons without access to drinking water in the planet, a figure that would be more easily devoted to war and space industries than to water. More than investments we are seeing privatizations of water since governments sell exploitation rights over this precious liquid. La Suez (French origin), Bechtel, Coca Cola, and Pepsi Cola, from the United States, are aggressively operating in South America to get control of this resource as much as possible. Likewise, there are other methods applied through international organizations. This is the case of the Guarani Water System with a project sponsored by the Global Environmental Fund, the World Bank, the OAS, the International Atomic Energy Agency, the governments of the Netherlands and Germany and the four MERCOSUR member countries at a cost of some $27 million.

> This four-year project is structured in seven areas: (1) Knowledge and use (expansion of scientific knowledge); (2) Management (joint implementation of the management framework); (3) Participation (promotion of participation of the society); (4) Education and communication (educational campaign on the need to protect the environment); (5) Pilot project (development of measures for the management of underground waters and mitigation of damages); (6) Geothermal energy (evaluation of the water geothermal potential); and (7) Coordination (administration work and project management).[70]

The main concern that emerges after realizing the project content is the great bulk of information required that will go to the hands of water transnationals thus facilitating their penetration process and territorial control. With the support of the project sponsors, the big transnationals will have more freedom of access to the huge water reservoirs of the system.

The Antarctic

The Antarctic has been a zone of great historical conflicts. It should be remembered how in the past the United States tried to create the Organization of the South Atlantic Treaty, a proposal that, though it did not prosper, showed the strategic interests in conflict. The Malvinas War, in April–June 1982, is another evidence in this regard proving that the United States is capable of sacrificing Latin America, as it did, in order to preserve its global strategic alliance with Great Britain. In his memoirs on this issue, the Chilean ambassador Oscar Pinochet de la Barra states the importance of the Antarctic, a mass of 30 million km^3 equivalent to 70 percent of the planet's fresh water. In the current period of gradual melting, this huge mass will be reduced and the largest water drinkers are the big industries located in the Northern Hemisphere. That is why it is not necessary to believe in a world war to realize that a time will come in which the Antarctic countries, especially, the Antarctic neighbors, will have to carefully regulate the exploitation of this wealth.[71]

Likewise, the Antarctic contains huge oil and natural gas reserves coveted by the United States, Great Britain, Russia, and Norway, among others, an issue placed under the control of the 1991 Treaty signed in Madrid, Spain, prohibiting the oil exploitation there for 50 years. Another attractive resource is the krill, a highly nutritive crustacean with a very high demand in the world market.

Then, how can we visualize such an important project? Probably with the use of tools and mechanisms like the following:

1. Development of research projects to identify the best options to exploit natural resources.
2. Investments with regional or foreign partners (this is more probable with oil since studies carried out indicate a submarine platform with technological complexities).
3. Creation of required communication networks to guarantee both access and exploitation of resources. Those are projects to articulate water networks, using the numerous and important existing rivers, especially in South America, the South American Regional Initiative, which attempts to connect Venezuela through the Orinoco with Buenos Aires through La Plata River, the opening of new oceanic maritime routes (with the articulation of the numerous Central American ports with the Caribbean islands, or the South Americans in the Pacific Ocean) and the interoceanic, through the Panama Canal or other alternative projects (the Colombian Chocó); the implementation of IDB projects to improve and

establish new terrestrial communication routes (the Manaus–Caracas road project) or the so-called Marginal Road to the Forest to interconnect Peru with Suriname); among others.

4. Creation of safety conditions in every area with identified strategic resources, such as the oil zone known as "five frontiers" (Colombia, Ecuador, Peru, Venezuela, and Brazil), with large trans-Andean pipelines reaching the Tumaco ports in Colombia and San Lorenzo, in Ecuador. For this purpose, the sites of some American military bases are noticeable, like those located in Liberia (Costa Rica), Sotocano (Honduras), Aruba and Curacao (Netherlands Antilles), Tres Esquinas, Larandia, and Puerto Legizamo (in the Colombian Putumayo), Manta (Ecuador), and Iquitos (Peru) with the support of the sophisticated radars from Guaviare and Leticia (Amazon River) and the satellite bases in Tabatinga (Black River).

Some Final Considerations

Today, relations between the United States and Latin American and Caribbean countries show very significant changes that must be stressed. First, the new international conditions opened within the framework of the post–cold war period revalidate the essential content that, in the light of the original American political thought, resulted in the search for and construction of these relations. Among the challenges faced today by Latin America and the Caribbean, after the traumatic effects of neoliberalism, is the real possibility of the absorption of their economies, the expropriation of their natural resources, and the complete disarticulation of their national sovereignty and independence. This is the price to be paid if the strategic repositioning project of the U.S. government takes place. In view of its budget, an American System for the twenty-first century will be defined and this project will reduce to unforeseen margins the existence itself of the community of nations south to the Rio Grande.

Second, we must also recognize that Latin America and the Caribbean are experiencing significant changes implying a new regional social and political configuration that is generating new conflict scenarios with the United States. This issue must be dealt with in the short-term by Latin American political leaders now emerging and within the level of tolerance admitted by the new perception of threats to U.S. national security.

Finally, the FTAA has not yet been implemented as projected and this has resulted in bilateral and selected negotiations. This has generated a new division of influences for the United States with the NAFTA, the Central American Free Trade Agreement (CAFTA), and the projected Free Trade Agreements with Ecuador, Peru, and Colombia. In contrast the rest of the Latin American nations headed by Brazil, Argentina, and Venezuela have embarked on a path of seeking alliances and trading relations not just with the European Union but with other international actors, especially the People's Republic of China, Russia, South Africa, and the Arab world. Within South America, the new political context also allows for Hugo Chavez to pursue his Bolivarian vision for Latin American unity built around plans for the sharing of Venezuela's vast reserves of oil and natural gas.

Notes

1. Gary Prevost and Carlos Oliva Campos, eds. *Neoliberalism and Neopanamericanism: The View from Latin America* (New York: Palgrave Mcmillan, 2002).
2. "The Free Trade Area for the Americas: The Historic Background," from *Integration to Subjection*. Summary of Papers Submitted at the FTAA International Seminar: Historic Roots, Regional Impact and Perspectives. La Tierra Edition No. 22, Quito, Ecuador, pp. 25–34.
3. M. Delal, "North American Free Trade," *Foreign Affairs* (Fall 1991): 140.
4. Paul Aligica, "Geo-Economics as a Geo-Strategic Paradigm: An Assessment," *American Outlook and Hudson's E-Zine, Hudson Institute*, USA, August 9, 2002.
5. Michael Klare, "The New Geography of World Conflicts," *Foreign Affairs in Spanish*, ITAM (2001): 152.
6. Henry Kissinger, "La Diplomacia," Simon and Shuster, 1994, reimpreso por el fondo de Cultura Económica. Traducido por Mónica Utrilla, México, D.F., 1996: 806.
7. Luis Maira, "Latin America and the New International Scenario," *Mexican Magazine on Foreign Policy*, year 8, no. 31, Mexico, Summer 1991, p.17.
8. Diana Johnstone, "Trilateral Commission: The Transnational Bourgeoisie Is Consolidated," Economic Diffusion, Economic and Political Research Institute, year 15, no. 2, Guayaquil, August 1977, pp. 77–89.
9. Joseph S. Tulchin, "The United States and Latin America in the World, United States Policy in Latin America: A Decade of Crisis and Challenge," in John D. Martz, ed. (Lincoln, NE: University of Nebraska Press, 1996), p. 325.
10. Carl Gersman, "The United States and the World Democratic Revolution," *Washington Quarterly*, USA (Winter 1989–1990): 127–139.
11. http://www.fas.org/man/docs/918015-nss.htm. Accessed on November 6, 2006.
12. "A National Security Strategy of Engagement," *The White House*, February 1996.
13. Raúl Ornelas, "Latin America: Territory for the Construction of Hegemony," *Magazine of Venezuela on Economy and Social Science*, Caracas, 2 (May–August 1993): 119.
14. J.A Vázquez (Compiler), Limusa Noriega, ed. *International Relations: The Thinking of New Clasics* (México D.F.: Prentice Hall, 1994), pp. 169–170.
15. Samuel P. Huntington, "The West and the World," *Foreign Affairs*, USA, (November–December 1996): 26–46; Anthony Lake, "Confronting Backlash States," *Foreign Affairs*, USA (March–April 1994): 45–55.
16. Stanley Hoffman, "The Crisis of Liberal Internationalism," *Foreign Affairs*, USA (Spring 1995): 167–172.
17. Kissinger, "Diplomacy," p. 808.
18. Horacio Cagni, "The Fallacy of Collective National Security," *Disenso*, Buenos Aires, 15 (Autumn 1998): 74.

19. Condoleeza Rice, "The Promotion of National Interest," *Foreign Affairs in Spanish*, ITAM (Spring 2001): 127–146.

20. "National Security Strategy," *United States, State Department, International Information Programs*, September 30, 2002 (5 Parts).

21. David C. Hendrickson, "The Recovery of Internationalism," *Foreign Affairs*, USA, (September–October 1994): 38.

22. Stephen John Stedman, "The New Interventionism," *Foreign Affairs*, USA, 72, 1 (1993): 6.

23. Tulchin, "The United States and Latin America," p. 323.

24. Prologo de Daniel Campione En: Miguel Mazzeo, piqueteros. Notas para una tipología, Fundación de Investigaciones Sociales y Políticas Ed. Manuel Suárez, Buenos Aires, Argentina, 2004 : 16.

25. Interview with Joao Pedro Stedile by Bernardo Mancano Fernandez, "Brave People, the Landless Struggle in Brazil," *Caminos Editorial*, Havana, 2001, p. xii.

26. Carlos M. Vilas, "Golpes de Pueblo contra el neoliberalismo," Análisis de Coyuntura. Ed. Mario Molina, AUNA-Cuba, Edición Especial, septiembre de 2005, La Habana, Cuba, 2006. pp. 3–12.

27. Theotonio dos Santos, "From Terror to Hope. Boom and Decline of Neoliberalism. Ideas & Letters" (Brazil, 2004), p. 486.

28. Otto Reich, "Latin America's Terrible Two," *New National Review*, Cover Story, April 11, 2005.

29. Beatriz Stolowicz, "Uruguay: Triunfo de la izquierda o del centro," Uruguay. de la utopía al poder. Fundación Vivian Trías Ediciones de la Banda Oriental/Ediciones La Tierra, Quito, Ecuador, 2005 : 171.

30. Marcelo Colussi, "United States-Latin America Relations," *Rebellion*, www.rebelion.org., España. September 19, 2005. Accessed on July 10, 2006.

31. Tabaré Vázquez, "Social Uruguay," *Uruguay from Utopia to Power*, p. 103.

32. Roger Burbach, "The Brazil of Lula: Washington's Challenge?" Trabajaores, Worker University of Mexico Vicente Lombardo Toledano, year 6, no. 33, November–December 2002, p. 57.

33. Francisco de Oliveira, "New Social Class Rules in Lula's Government," *Folha De Sao Paulo*, September 22, 2003, p. 11A.

34. Frank Gaudichaud, "The Latin American Volcano: Bets and Realities of the Left, South to the Rio Bravo," *Rebellion*, www.rebelion.org, Spain, September 23, 2005, Accessed on July 11, 2006.

35. Stolowicz, "Uruguay: Victory Left or Center?" pp. 173–174.

36. Aurelio Alonso Tejada, "El Fundamentalismo de aquí y de allá," Caminos, Centro Memorial Martín Luther King, Jr., La Habana, Cuba, 23, (2002): 7 (Revista cubana).

37. Tejada, "Fundamentalism," p. 8.

38. Kissinger, "Diplomacy," p. 12.

39. Victor D. Cha, "Korea's Place in the Axis," *Foriegn Affairs*, USA (May–June 2002): 79–92.

40. Lee Feinstein and Anne-Marie Slaughter, "The Obligation of Preventing," *Foreign Affairs in Spanish*, ITAM (Spring 2001): 93–94.

41. Francis L. Bouchey, Roger W. Fontaine, David C. Jordan, Gordon Summer, Lewis Tabs, ed., "Interamerican Relations: Shield of the New World Security and Sword of the United States Global Power Projection," *Half-Yearly Notebooks* Cide, no. 9, First Semester of 1980, Mexico D.F., p. 305.

42. Documento Santa Fé IV, América Latina frente a los planes anexionistas de los Estados Unidos, Prólogo Fernando Bossi, Proyecto Emancipación–Comité Permanente Congreso Anfictiónico Bolivariano, emancipa@infovia.com.ar, www.qgocities.com/proyectoemancipación: 29–30. Accession Date: July 11, 2002.

43. Meter Hakim, "Restlessness of the Americas," *Foreign Affairs in Spanish*, ITAM, 1, 2 (Summer 2001): 130.

44. Felipe A.M. de la Balze, "Searching for Allies in the Backyard: The TLCAN and the Southern Cone," *Foreign Affairs in Spanish*, ITAM, 3 (Autumn–Winter 2001): 70–71.

45. Ana Esther Cecena, "Domination Strategies and Construction Plans of the World Hegemony," *Globalization Dossier*, Mexico DF, February 6, 2001, p. 1.

46. Samuel P. Huntington, "Why international Primacy Matters," *International Security*, USA (Spring 1993): p. 72.

47. Thomas Robert Malthus, "*Essay on the Beginning of the Population*" (Madrid: Akal S.A. Editions, 1990).

48. Klare, "Geography of World Conflicts," p.153.

49. Orlando Caputo, El petróleo en cifras. TelepolisviveInternet .Distrito.Política Internacional, www.alainet.org. (S.F.)

50. Report of the National Energy Policy Development Group U.S., Government Printing Office, May 2001, p. x.

51. Klare, "Geography of World Conflicts," p. 153.

52. Document on "National Security Strategy," 2002, p. 4.

53. "El nacionalismo petrolero aterra a Estados Unidos," por Vicky Peláez, El Diario/La Prensa, 27 de junio de 2006, EE.UU.,: 1–2.

54. William E.Izarra. "Venezuela: USA Target," *Sovereignty, Caracas*, January 13, 2004, p. 2.

55. Ornelas, "Construction of Hegemony," pp. 126–127.

56. Ibid., p. 129.

57. Ana Ester Cecena, "Latin America in the Geopolitics of Power," *Free America*, 21, Buenos Aires (September, 2003): 151.

58. Ricardo Cifuentes, "The Global Attack Centered on Natural Resources," *Latin American Observatory of Environmental Conflicts*, Argentine, (s.f.).

59. Diego Delgado Jara, "Manta Base, Colombia Plan and Domination of Amazonia," *Ecoalternative Network*, January 22, 2004, p. 4.

60. Guillermo Navarro Jiménez, "*Colombia Plan: Abc of a Tragedy*," Zitra Editions, Quito, Ecuador, February 2001, pp. 134–135.

61. Cifuentes, "Global Attack Natural Resources," p. 8.

62. Ignacy Sach, "Amazonia and the Solution," *Foreign Policy*, Brazil (September–November 2000): 67–71.

63. Everton Vargas Maria Rita Fontes Faria, "Climatic Change and the Perspective of Brazil," *Diplomacy*, Santiago de Chile, 9 (January–March 2002): 19.

64. Ibid., 23.

65. Sach, "Amazonia," p. 64.

66. Jara, "Manta Base," p. 8.

67. Aníbal Ortiz Pozo, "USA. Oil Today, water tomorrow and then . . .," *Koeyu Latin American Magazine*, Venezuela, March 20, 2004, pp. 1–4.

68. Jorge N. Santa Cruz, "The Project of the Guarani Aquiferous System," *MERCOSUR. Water National Institute*, Argentina, April 2004, p. 1.

69. Ricardo Luis Mascheroni, "International Water Day and the Importance of Guarani Aquiferous," *Environmental Management*, March 31, 2004, p. 1.
70. Nelson Fernández, "Guarani Aquiferous," *Prodiversitas*, Uruguay, May 27, 2003.
71. Oscar Pinochet de la Barra, "Memories of the Antarctic Environmental Protection Protocol," *Diplomacy*, Santiago de Chile, 85 (October–December 2000): 14.

Chapter 3

The Axis of Misunderstanding: The Bush Administration, Intelligence, and Hemispheric Security after September 11, 2001

Patrice Elizabeth Olsen

As we know, there are known knowns. There are things we know we know. We also know there are known unknowns. That is to say we know there are some things we do not know. But there are also unknown unknowns, the ones we don't know we don't know.

Secretary of Defense Donald Rumsfeld, February 12, 2002,
Department of Defense News

At first glance, the above quote from Defense Secretary Donald Rumsfeld may appear to be little more than a mind-twisting play on words, defying the best efforts at clarification. Web-based pundits have had a fine time turning the secretary's odd phrases into poetry and limerick; journalists, scholars, and the public are left to wonder at his meaning. And there is meaning within. Rumsfeld's circuitous phrasing contains a fundamental truth for the intelligence community and the foreign policy establishment. No nation possesses the faculty of making foreign policy decisions with absolute certainty. That is, there will always be "unknowns"—in terms of capabilities and intentions of allies and foes alike, as well as likely outcomes and the perils of "blowback"— the unintended or unanticipated consequences of covert actions.[1] Indeed, the "unknowns" are the reasons for the intelligence community's existence: to uncover, interpret, and analyze those vague, gray, and potentially dangerous issues and to disseminate the resulting product to intelligence consumers in a timely fashion. This awareness of the existence of "unknowns" was certainly present in the Bush administration following 9/11. Yet the new National Security Policy, presented in September 2002, is predicated on a "perfect" intelligence process; that is, the precise and accurate development of requirements, collection of all relevant information, thorough processing and analysis, and timely dissemination to policy makers.[2]

This chapter discusses changes in the U.S. government's conception of security following the attacks of September 11, 2001, and the impact of this changing agenda upon the conduct of foreign intelligence agencies. It provides an analysis of key alterations with attention to the revision of cold war–era doctrines of deterrence in George W. Bush's National Security Strategy of the United States. Moreover, as identification of threats to the region posed by what the Bush administration labels "international terrorism" is operationalized, an increased role for intelligence agencies such as the Central Intelligence Agency (CIA) and the National Security Agency (NSA) is promoted. Such action negates important reforms enacted in the 1970s meant to support accountability and oversight. Given the various flaws in the conceptualization of hemispheric security, as well as a tendency toward unilateral action, this chapter argues that the removal of such restraints and the implementation of Bush's National Security Strategy pose serious challenges to civil liberties and human rights within the United States and throughout the hemisphere.

On the Bush National Security Strategy—General Comments on Its Introduction

In accordance with Section 603 of the Goldwater-Nichols Defense Department Reorganization Act of 1986, an amendment to the National Security Act of 1947, presidents must submit an annual report on national security to the U.S. Congress. On September 20, 2002, President George W. Bush released a document titled "The National Security Strategy of the United States." At 31 pages, at first look it appears to offer a comprehensive definition of threats, and a multilevel approach to countering grave challenges to U.S. national security. As "Defense *LINK*," a website of the U.S. Department of Defense assures citizens, "what America stands for is at the heart of the new National Security Strategy."[3]

It is apparent that such sweeping revision was not entirely in response to 9/11—the antecedents lie in the controversial Defense Planning Guidelines first proposed by Dick Cheney in 1992.[4] It may be argued that such an assessment was long overdue. For the past 50 some years, U.S. national security had been a distinctly cold war product, embodying the calculus of deterrence as expressed by George Kennan in his famous 1947 *Foreign Affairs* article. Kennan's writing detailed the dangers of Soviet expansionism and the need to "contain" it via diplomatic pressures and "the adroit and vigilant application of counterforce at a series of constantly shifting geographical and political points, corresponding to the shifts and maneuvers of Soviet policy."[5] In the 1950s and 1960s, with the acceleration of the nuclear arms race with technological developments such as the hydrogen bomb, gave rise to improved targeting and delivery systems—developments apparently matched by the Soviet Union at each stage. A new vocabulary emerged as well—powerful and tough—throw weights, circular errors of probability, first strike, massive retaliation, and launch-on-warning. The doctrine simultaneously induced fear, as a generation of Americans learned to "duck and cover," taught that the bomb could fall at any time—and complacency, as presidents from Eisenhower to Reagan assured the public that the United States would never use such weapons first. The underlying presumption, amidst the muscular rhetoric of counterforce and countervalue targeting, of new weapons systems and basing modes borrowing names from the awe-inspiring deities Nike, Poseidon, Thor, and Titan was that of rationality. Neither side was willing to risk the annihilation of the planet. Neither side believed the other sufficiently mad to do so.

The Bush document is not written in the scary language of the deterrence theorists of RAND, the Pentagon's hired think tank and other cold war think tanks. Here there is no Herman Kahn, "thinking about the unthinkable" or mutually assured destruction. But the Bush document does contain a duality: warm, almost folksy language, apparently written for mass consumption given its simplistic analogies and oversimplification of complex dynamics of international and bilateral relations, and the message of ubiquitous threats and imminent dangers, the promotion and manipulation of fear. Four years later, we have the opportunity to reflect on the operationalization of this strategy.

To be sure, Bush's projected enemy as announced in the introduction to the strategy statement is more slippery. The enemy is not a single, easily identifiable proper noun, as in the Soviet Union,—but terrorism—the enemy that "can bring great chaos and suffering to our shores for less than it costs to purchase a single tank." Perhaps this document is not the place to discuss complexities such as misperceptions of the 1980s, in which these very terrorists [e.g., the Mujahideen] were seen as assets to be used in the greater struggle against the Soviet Union,[6] and the unintended consequences or "blowback" of U.S. covert actions in the Middle East and elsewhere in recent decades. Instead, this document simplifies the discourse and controls it: the issue is simple—a free society, versus the enemies of freedom. Indeed, as he said on November 7, 2001 in a joint news conference with French President Jacques Chirac: "Over time it's going to be important for nations to know they will be held accountable for inactivity. You are either with us or against us in the fight against terror." His introduction strikes chords intended to resonate with the majority of U.S. citizens, and assumes universality of the means to achieve and protect values. Complexities are made easy to comprehend, reduced to 30-second sound bites:

> People everywhere want to say what they think; choose who will govern them; worship as they please; educate their children—male and female; own property; and enjoy the benefits of their own labor. These values of freedom are right and true for every person, in every society—and the duty of protecting these values against their enemies is the common calling of freedom-loving people across the globe and across the ages.[7]

Yet the next paragraph presents concepts of American exceptionalism that are ultimately more worrisome than even the darkest cold war scenario on nuclear war created by RAND or the Office of Technology Assessment.[8]

In this introduction we learn that "today, the United States enjoys a position of unparalleled military strength and great economic and political influence."[9] This statement is a little too close for comfort to the boldness of Secretary of State Richard Olney's 1895 interpretation of the Monroe Doctrine and U.S. power during the Venezuela boundary dispute with British Guiana: "Today the United States is practically sovereign on this continent and its fiat is law upon the subjects to which it confines its interposition. . . . its infinite resources combined with its isolated position render it master of the situation and practically invulnerable as against any or all other powers."[10] While the attacks of September 11 diminished this sense of invulnerability, they did not similarly reduce the aspirations of dominance. While the administration assures the U.S. public "in keeping with our heritage and our principles, we do not use our strength to press for unilateral advantage,"[11] the world envisioned here is of one dominant power, the United States, promoting free markets as panacea for the world's ills. Such actions will liberate the world and at the same time protect the United States from the scourge of terrorism. Indeed, throughout this document, "freedom" is most often mated with "markets" and "trade." So too is hemispheric security. Freedom is thus linked with consumption, and marketed as such.

Ideals expressed in this preamble's 11 paragraphs have been gravely compromised by the conduct of the administration since 2002, particularly in the war in Iraq, and the uses and misuses of intelligence. Thus U.S. strength will presumably be used in a manner consonant with traditional democratic principles. "Good relations among the great powers" would be promoted, as well as "a balance of power that favors human freedoms: conditions in which all nations and all societies can choose for themselves the rewards and challenges of political and economic liberty." All this is highly laudable and in consonance with rights of national sovereignty and freedoms expressed in the UN Charter and enshrined in international law. Alliances are central to the maintenance of world peace, the document states: "No nation can build a safer, better world alone." Thus U.S. commitments to the UN, WTO, OAS, and NATO are reaffirmed. Moreover, "coalitions of the willing can augment these permanent institutions." Skeptics can rest easy, as the document promises, "in all cases, international obligations are to be taken seriously.[12] They are not to be undertaken symbolically to rally support for an ideal without furthering its attainment." Perhaps footnotes would have helped to clarify this last point that is so conceptually vague. It is in this area that some of the document's most glaring inconsistencies appear. To this point, "the gravest danger our Nation faces lies at the crossroads of radicalism and technology. Our enemies have openly declared that they are seeking weapons of mass destruction, and evidence indicates that they are doing so with determination. The United States will not allow these efforts to succeed. We will build defenses against ballistic missiles and other means of delivery. We will cooperate with other nations to deny, contain, and curtail our enemies' efforts to acquire dangerous technologies."[13]

Unfortunately, the "good relations among great powers" is not evidenced in the ever dwindling "coalition of the willing" and the labeling and shunning of "Old Europe," and other states, as well as the United Nations.[14] The document does not mention the Nuclear Non-Proliferation Treaty, or the Biological Weapons or Chemical Weapons conventions, mechanisms for preventing the spread of WMDs to terrorist or "rogue states." Nor does it address the Kyoto Protocol, a significant measure in promoting environmental security. The specter of terrorist attacks also provides the opportunity to abrogate treaties, particularly the Anti Ballistic Missile Treaty (ABM) of 1972, itself a potentially destabilizing action (intentions to abrogate the treaty were announced by Bush on December 13, 2001). A certain recklessness is evident as well, as the Bush administration proceeded beyond the best counsel of scientists, as seen in the 2003 *Nuclear Posture Review*, committing billions of dollars to weapons systems of dubious feasibility, such as cyber-, laser-, and electronic-warfare capabilities. Indeed, it is a frightening new world, as evidenced in the document, rather than a brave new one. U.S. diplomatic history over the past one hundred years reveals considerable initiative and purposefulness, if not always with the desired outcomes. Echoing the wise counsel of the Pearl Harbor Hearings as well as countless admonitions of select committees on intelligence, the document's authors inform us, "So we must be prepared to defeat our enemies' plans, using the best intelligence and proceeding with deliberation. History will judge harshly those who saw this coming danger but failed to act."

Later segments, particularly section III, "Strengthen Alliances to Defeat Global Terrorism and Work to Prevent Attacks on Us and Our Friends" offer further platitudes but little clarification. A new enemy is identified: "the enemy is terrorism—premeditated, politically motivated violence perpetuated against innocents." The scope is by extension, immense and the struggle, epic: "the struggle against global terrorism is different from any other war in our history." There has been some success. Afghanistan has been "liberated," and "coalition forces continue to hunt down the Taliban and Al-Qaeda." But Afghanistan "is not the only battlefield on which we will engage terrorists. Thousands of trained terrorists remain at large with cells in North America, South America, Europe, Africa, the Middle East, and across Asia."[15] In sum, the war against terrorism is a global crusade. The implications of this expansion for the intelligence community, particularly the CIA and NSA, are immense. Whether the conflict is portrayed as the "war against terrorism" or as Rumsfeld attempted to redefine it, the "Global Struggle Against Extremist Violence" (GSAVE), the scope of intelligence collection and demands on analysts have grown exponentially. So too have the opportunities for misperceptions and errors.

Bush and Latin America

The Bush administration has sought the support of Latin American states "to take up a coordinated effort that isolates the terrorists." Aid is promised, as "once the regional campaign localizes this threat to a particular state, we will help ensure the state has the military, law enforcement, political, and financial tools necessary to finish the task." It is in this regard that the ahistorical approach of the Bush administration is apparent given the stress on Latin American security. As Adam Isacson notes, "Terrorism . . . is a term that is easily abused and can easily come to mean both everything and nothing. If the definition of 'terrorist' is not rigorously applied, the region's security forces may end up applying it far too broadly." Moreover, various security forces have readily perceived the "enemy within" as the true threat to national security—witness actions in Chile, Uruguay, Brazil, and Argentina in the dirty wars against "subversives" (including labor organizers, students, campesinos leaders, human rights activists, journalists, leftist intellectuals, among others) in the 1960s, 1970s, and early 1980s.[16] Given financial and other incentives by the U.S. government, what protection exists at present against similar linguistic expansion? As Isacson asks,

> "are Bolivian coca growers who blockade roads, terrorists? Coca-growing campesinos whose booby traps kill or maim eradication forces certainly deserve jail, but do they (as well as the union they belong to, the political party affiliated with it, and allied labor and indigenous movements) really merit the terrorist label? Are Honduran peasants who stage roadblocks to stop over-logging, terrorists, as some in Honduras claim? . . . Are Mapuches who damaged plantation property to press for land claims, terrorists, as Chilean prosecutors have argued? When Colombian President Álvaro Uribe calls human rights groups 'defenders of terrorism' in a speech before a military audience, is he engaging in rhetorical exaggeration or a veiled threat?"[17]

The occasions for selective use of intelligence to support affirmative answers, or "cherry-picking" are plentiful. So too are the opportunities for misperception. While only Colombia's Revolutionary Armed Forces of Colombia (FARC), National Liberation Army (ELN), United Self Defense Forces of Colombia (AUC), and Peru's Sendero Luminoso appear on State Department lists of foreign terrorist organizations, counterterrorism is used "as a justification for military aid in all 16 of the Western Hemisphere country narratives in the State Department's congressional presentation document for foreign aid programs."[18] And indigenous groups are not the only suspects. Patrick Hénault reports administration concerns that the tri-border area of Argentina, Brazil, and Paraguay "could, in fact, serve as an entry point for terrorist organizations wishing to attack the US or its interests in the region." As Hénault states,

> "according to the U.S. State Department, Hezbollah, al-Gamaa al-Islamiya, and Hamas have financing and recruitment operations in the area. The Argentine intelligence services have reported that members of Al-Qaida have used the area to conduct training and coordination with Shia extremist groups and that fleeing terrorists have transited through the area. The Brazilian security services have indicated, moreover, that Osama bin Laden and Khalid Sheikh Mohammed, identified by the United States as Al-Qaida's treasurer, spent time in the tri-border area in 1995."[19]

What are the repercussions of those affirmations? Might 9/11 be employed by Latin American security forces as an opportunity to "justify their anti-subversive fight"—a struggle so "misunderstood by many sectors of society, and an opportunity to gain institutional space within the state"?[20] Might assistance or support for counterterrorism detract from Latin American states' abilities to develop and implement a distinct national security policy, relevant to their own perceptions of threats? If the goal of national security policy is not solely to guarantee political survival but also to assure citizens a decent quality of life, as Vicente Fox has argued, then threats may be from transnational actors, deindustrialization, debt, deforestation, drugs and narco-terrorism, destabilization, and migration. As Farid Kahhat points out, "These are not necessarily military threats, nor do they jeopardize the territorial integrity of the State. Thus, military means are not always the most effective responses to these threats."[21]

From Deterrence to Preemption

Against the elusive enemy, terrorism, deterrence is bound to fail. "Traditional concepts of deterrence will not work against a terrorist enemy whose tactics are wanton destruction and the targeting of innocents; whose so-called soldiers seek martyrdom in death and whose most potent protection is statelessness." This is the assumption underlying the document's Section V, "Prevent Our Enemies from Threatening Us, Our Allies, and Our Friends with Weapons of Mass Destruction." The document's authors promise that this government will "constantly strive to enlist the support of the international community," and "will not hesitate to act alone, if necessary, to exercise our right of self-defense by acting preemptively against such terrorists."[22]

New enemies are identified—terrorists and rogue states—though we are assured that there are a "small number" of the latter. The document states quite confidently that "at the time of the Gulf War, we acquired irrefutable proof that Iraq's designs were not limited to the chemical weapons it had used against Iran and its own people, but also extended to the acquisition of nuclear weapons and biological agents."[23] The passage is misleading, and easy to misread: omit "designs" and retain "extended to the acquisition of nuclear weapons." The impact is chilling. Given the document's statements that "other rogue nations seek nuclear, biological, and chemical weapons" a clear threat to all nations exists. Hence the Bush administration offers a "comprehensive strategy to combat WMD." This includes "proactive counterproliferation efforts," and "strengthened nonproliferation efforts to prevent rogue states and terrorists from acquiring the materials, technologies and expertise necessary for weapons of mass destruction." Further, the Bush administration pledges to "enhance diplomacy, arms control, multilateral export controls, and threat reduction assistance that impede states and terrorists seeking WMD, and when necessary, interdict enabling technologies and materials. We will continue to build coalitions to support these efforts."[24] Could the International Atomic Energy

Agency (IAEA) be a more effective mechanism for such? The agency is not mentioned here, nor are the various United Nations Special Commission (UNSCOM) inspection efforts—apparently, arms control and limitations on proliferation of WMDs is possible only with U.S. initiative and leadership.[25] A case may be made that there already exists various international bodies dedicated to non and counterproliferation of WMDs and the creation of temporary coalitions is not necessary. Indeed, permanent, stable mechanisms might enjoy greater legitimacy throughout the world, particularly the developing world, not just the previously mentioned "great powers."

The document's authors make an argument that preemption is condoned by international law: "For centuries, international law recognized that nations need not suffer an attack before they can lawfully take action to defend themselves against forces that present an imminent danger of attack."[26] Here the concept of "imminent threat" must be adopted to meet modern exigencies. Threats must be identified, the case for taking "anticipatory action" made. Yet this calculation of "imminent threat" is highly problematic. It relies heavily on intelligence—relevant, timely, and profoundly accurate. The opportunities and incentives for "cooking the books" are immense—that is, for intelligence estimates to be skewed to fit preconceived ideas and desired outcomes, and policy makers' predispositions. Indeed, as James Bamford argues in relation to WMDs in Iraq,

> "what is now clear is that the original justification for the invasion—that the United States was in imminent danger from the threat of Iraqi weapons of mass destruction—was fraudulent, as many in the CIA and other intelligence agencies were quietly warning. Instead, it was simply a pretext for a war long advocated by a small group of hardline neoconservatives with their own agenda. The man who might have made a difference was George Tenet, but rather than fight or resign in protest, he chose instead to simply go along. It was a 'slam dunk' decision."[27]

If the "comprehensive strategy" is to be realized, then accurate, apolitical intelligence is essential. But this linkage is not seen in the document. Assurances that the United States will "not use force in all cases to preempt emerging threats" are compromised by other statements such as "in an age where the enemies of civilization openly and actively seek the world's most destructive technologies, the United States cannot remain idle while dangers gather."[28] These are somewhat hollow assurances, given the events of the past three years: "We will always proceed deliberately, weighing the consequences of our actions," and Defense Secretary Rumsfeld's repeated statement: "The absence of evidence is not evidence of absence," claiming proof of Iraq's record of lying on its weapons declarations over the past several years. The presence of threats is a prevalent theme throughout this document. Yet the process for identifying what these threats are is not clear.

The Intelligence Community Transformed

Having identified the threats, outlined the responses, altered the doctrine from deterrence to preemption, the document proceeds to detail the desired transformations of the intelligence community sought. Revisions have been proposed numerous times since the passage of National Security Act of 1947. Central flaws, such as the "dual hatting" of the DCI (inability of the DCI to both direct the CIA and the Intelligence Community as a whole) were noted in 1955 by the Commission on Organization of the Executive Branch of the government. Similarly, problems of overcollection, accountability, and control were detailed by the Senate Select Committee to Study Governmental Operations with Respect to Intelligence Activities (Church Committee, 1976) and the House Select Committee on Intelligence (Pike Committee, 1975).[29]

Yet few far reaching reforms were enacted; presidential initiatives in covert action eroded congressional oversight, while advances in technology drove collection to ever higher levels. The document's Section IX, intending to "Transform America's National Security Institutions to Meet the Challenges and Opportunities of the Twenty-First Century" begins with the recognition that "the major institutions of American national security were designed in a different era to meet different requirements. All of them must be transformed."[30] The need to strengthen the U.S. military is made clear in this section. Sentiments of exceptionalism are prevalent. The strength of the U.S. armed forces is "unparalleled." The prose reads as if borrowed from Alfred Thayer Mahan and Theodore Roosevelt: "the presence of American forces overseas is one of the most profound symbols of the U.S. commitments to allies and friends. Through our willingness to use force in our own defense and in defense of others, the United States demonstrates its resolve to maintain a balance of power that favors freedom. To contend with uncertainty and to meet the many security challenges we face, the United States will require bases and stations within and beyond Western Europe and Northeast Asia, as well as temporary access arrangements for the long-distance deployment of U.S. forces."[31]

The specific security challenges are not mentioned, nor are the costs of constructing or maintaining these bases. Further, innovation in military forces is essential; that is, "experimentation with new approaches to warfare, strengthening joint operations, exploiting U.S. intelligence advantages, and taking full advantage of science and technology." The document expresses the government's intent to reform the Department of Defense, particularly in the areas of "financial management and recruitment and retention."[32] Only a few lines are devoted to the intelligence community specifically. Yet serious change is implied throughout the document, and necessitated by the new policy.

The document correctly points out that the essential target of U.S. intelligence activities—the Soviet Bloc—has changed. The targets are now multiple, complex, and elusive. Hence, like the Department of Defense (DoD), the intelligence community must be transformed; its techniques of operating against a fixed target are of little value in this new age. Intelligence is essential: "We must transform our intelligence capabilities and build new ones to keep pace with the nature of these threats. . . . Those who would harm us also seek the benefit of surprise to limit our prevention and response options to maximize injury."[33]

Yet this is hardly a new concept in the art of war, nor is it unique to terrorism. The element of surprise is key to successful attacks. This document, as well as the subsequent 9/11 investigations, made the imperatives to improve analysis and intelligence collection very clear—as well as the need for greater cooperation among intelligence agencies."[34] The document states, "we must strengthen intelligence warning and analysis to provide integrated threat assessments for national and homeland security." Such activities would necessarily be carried out overseas, given the terrorists' theaters of operation. Yet the attacks of 9/11 brought in a new dimension to the intelligence agencies' labors. "Since the threats inspired by foreign governments and groups may be conducted inside the United States, we must also ensure the proper fusion of information between intelligence and law enforcement."[35]

What could be this "proper fusion," and how could it be achieved? Congressional intelligence committees of the mid-1970s and since have been reluctant to advocate increased domestic collection without sufficient safeguards on civil liberties. The Bush administration apparently has had few such reservations. It is right to pause and consider the operational restraints on the CIA and NSA. The agencies' charters prohibit them from conducting operations and monitoring communications within the United States. Programs such as CHAOS, SHAMROCK, MINARET, and other surveillance operations, the creation of watch lists, and the targeting of U.S. citizens during the 1950s and 1960s violated basic constitutional rights and civil liberties, particularly freedom of speech, assembly, press, and rights to privacy. While the document promises new initiatives including the establishment of "a new framework for intelligence warning that provides seamless and integrated warning across the spectrum of threats facing the nation and our allies" and the development of "new methods of collecting information to sustain our intelligence advantage"[36] there is no mention of protection of civil liberties. Indeed, the balance between liberty and security has shifted.

This section, and policies emanating from its reasoning, also assume efficiency in relation to intelligence collection, analysis, and dissemination. Typically the intelligence cycle is depicted in flow charts as an orderly process, from generation of requirements to collection, to analysis, evaluation, and dissemination.[37] The reality is not so tidy. The U.S. intelligence community's abilities to collect information have increased exponentially over the past two decades. Yet comprehension of this material—the laborious, careful processing of raw into finished intelligence is not always possible. The shortage of translators is well noted; decryption of encoded, enciphered material may not always be possible. Added to these technical problems is the sheer volume of what has been collected. According to James Bamford, "with tens of millions of communications continuing to be vacuumed up by NSA every hour, by 2001 the system had become overwhelmed as a result of too few analysts."[38] Indeed, since 2001 the abilities to collect information from e-mails, cell and satellite phones, and other sources have increased dramatically, further compounding this problem.

More problematic is the processing of raw intelligence. In order for preemption to work—that is, to "forestall or prevent such hostile act,"[39] intelligence must be perfect. Not only must capabilities be known beyond reasonable doubt, but also intentions. And such insights into intentions are often absent. Collection via machines, regardless of their sophistication, will rarely illuminate intentions. Such is the realm of HUMINT, of the often cumbersome, dangerous spy net operating in hostile territory, penetrating the target and discerning this vital information, as so many CIA case officers have made clear. Most recently Robert Baer in *See No Evil* concludes,

> The CIA doesn't have a choice but to once again go out and start talking to people—people who can go where it can't, see what it can't, and hear what it can't. . . . And until we have that CIA—one with thousands of human ears and eyes, out listening where the ones who will do us harm hatch their evil schemes—I don't think any of us should feel safe again.[40]

Furthermore, as former National Intelligence Officer for the Near East and South Asia Paul Pillar wrote in March 2006,

> The most serious problem with U.S. intelligence today is that its relationship with the policymaking process is broken and badly needs repair. In the wake of the Iraq war, it has become clear that official intelligence analysis was not relied on in making even the most significant national security decisions, that intelligence was misused publicly to justify decisions already made, that damaging ill will developed between policymakers and intelligence officers, and that the intelligence community's own work was politicized.[41]

For preemption to truly serve as an element of national security, bias and prejudice have no place in these calculations, nor should policy makers influence intelligence analysts to skew their interpretation in a particular direction. This is no mere academic exercise, nor a simple blurring on a flow chart of responsibilities and linkages. Politicized intelligence leads to poor outcomes, and "blowback." Moreover, it is a violation of the trust citizens place in their government, and gravely undermines security.

Conclusion: The "Unknown Unknowns"

Since the initial statement of the new national security policy four years ago, a great deal has changed: war in Afghanistan and Iraq, terrorist attacks in Bali, Madrid, London, the passage of the USA PATRIOT Act and Homeland Security Act, and extensive testimony in congress on the 9/11 attacks and intelligence failures. There has also been extensive commentary on the administration's magnification and distortion of threats, beginning in the fall of 2002. Early criticism, and warnings on doctored intelligence such as by Dana Milbank (*Washington Post*) and Paul Krugman and James Risen (*New York Times*), were borne out by events and revelations in the last three years.

Notable in this respect are the words by James Bamford, James Risen, and Joseph Wilson on the fallacy of Niger's yellowcake uranium transfers, the slanting of National Intelligence Estimates to fit a particular agenda, and the rise of domestic surveillance.[42]

From the Intelligence Reform and Terrorism Prevention Act, signed by President George W. Bush in December 2004, there is the new position of Director of National Intelligence (DNI), now held by John Negroponte, charged with creating the mechanisms for coordinating true national strategic intelligence. Significant problems continue for the DNI. The Department of Defense still controls 80 percent of intelligence budget, and thus Negroponte has scant ability to control it. He has implemented changes in the production of the Presidential Daily Briefs and National Intelligence Estimates, but there are few safeguards in place to prevent future politicization of intelligence. Further, there is little accountability to the American public, in terms of opportunities for open discussion on the practice and use (or misuse) of intelligence. Their elected representatives, too, are denied such opportunities, given congressional rules that ban disclosure of classified information, limited briefings, and a lack of power to examine and amend intelligence agency budgets.[43]

The public, in sum, has been asked to accept such limitations in order to protect national security, while programs such as the short-lived Terrorism Information and Prevention System (TIPS) encouraged citizens to spy on each other, and fear of the "unknown unknowns"—a fresh attack upon the United States—was used by the administration to justify expanded, covert NSA wiretapping programs. To argue that wartime curtailment of civil liberties (as seen in precedents such as the Sedition Act of 1789, the Espionage Act of 1918, and the internment of Japanese Americans in World War II) is warranted is, as a *New York Times* editorial stated in 2002, "to draw exactly the wrong lessons from history."[44] Finally, as the new National Security Policy states "while we recognize that our best defense is a good offense we are also strengthening America's homeland security to protect against and deter attack."[45] The policy has not had that effect to date, according to the report card released on December 5, 2005 by former members of the National Commission on Terrorist Attacks Upon the United States. Thomas Kean and nine others from the bipartisan panel gave 1 A (for efforts blocking terrorist financing), 12 Bs (for protection of civil liberties), 9 Cs (private sector emergency preparedness), 12 Ds (cargo, luggage screening), and 5 Fs (almost no progress made in coordinating communication for first responders). In sum, we are not more secure.[46]

More recently, on March 16, 2006, the Bush administration released its second National Security Strategy document. Attempting to distinguish it from the first document, President Bush offered the following explanation in his introduction: "This is a wartime National Security Strategy required by the grave challenge we face—the rise of terrorism fueled by an aggressive ideology of hatred and murder."[47] This document closely resembles his first National Security Strategy document. It retains the same chapter headings, and offers a brief summary of what was contained in each in the original, and also summarizes what has been accomplished since 2002. Preemption is muted by new statements as to "effective multinational efforts," and the emphasis on "transformational diplomacy." Free markets are still a panacea; "economic freedom is a moral imperative." This may explain his logic in relation to Western Hemisphere security, as the document states,

> Countries in the Western Hemisphere must be helped to the path of sustained political and economic development. The deceptive appeal of anti-free market populism must not be allowed to erode political freedoms and trap the Hemisphere's poorest in cycles of poverty.[48]

What is notable about this document, is its reluctance to engage in critical analysis, or to engage diverse opinions on the formulation of national or hemispheric security such as those expressed at the World Social Forum or the Defense Ministerial of the Americas meetings. Instead, the document is replete with self-congratulatory if not fully accurate statements: Congress and the administration have come together "to adopt and implement key reforms like the Patriot Act which promote our security while also protecting our fundamental liberties."[49] Concerning the significant issue of intelligence, the document assures that "the President and the Congress have taken steps to reorganize and strengthen the U.S. intelligence community." Significant problems within the intelligence community are being resolved, as "a single, accountable leader of the intelligence community with authorities to match his responsibilities, and increased sharing of information and increased resources, are helping realize this objective."[50] Yet as noted earlier in this chapter, the creation of a new office, the DNI, will not resolve the decades-long problem of the lack of coordination among intelligence agencies. Nor does the DNI possess sufficient authority over the budget to control how resources for intelligence collection, analysis, and dissemination are allocated.

Furthermore, there is no discussion here of the demonstrated hazards of politicized intelligence, nor of the difficulty of collecting and analyzing vast amounts of disparate data. Only faintly does the document address the issues of flawed or misused intelligence, and offers a parallel to the 1991 Gulf War, claiming that analysts had underestimated WMD threats, hence "there will always be some uncertainty about the status of hidden programs."[51] Yet understatement in one case does not justify overstatement, or "cooking the books," creating a "slam dunk" for an invasion of Iraq.

Addressing this issue in part, the document states, "the Iraq Survey Group also found that pre-war intelligence estimates of Iraqi WMD stockpiles were wrong—a conclusion that has been confirmed by a bipartisan commission and congressional investigations. We must learn from this experience if we are to counter successfully the very real threat of proliferation."[52] It is not at all clear how this learning will be facilitated or promoted. Instead, the loose language of this document allows for continued hedging by policymakers, rather than increased accountability to Congress and the American people.

While the new document addresses regional issues, Latin American nations receive little direct attention. In Section VIII, with the objective to "Develop Agendas for Cooperative Action with the Other Main Centers of Global Power," the Western Hemisphere merits two paragraphs stressing unity of goals and values. "Our goal remains a hemisphere fully democratic, bound together by good will, security cooperation, and the opportunity for all our citizens to prosper. Tyrants and those who would follow them belong to a different era and must not be allowed to reverse the progress of the last two decades." Partnerships with Latin American states will "advance our four strategic priorities for the region: bolstering security, strengthening democratic institutions, promoting prosperity, and investing in people."[53]

Yet such laudable ambitions are undermined by statements made earlier in the document under the rubric of "Work with Others to Defuse Regional Conflicts." Here complex regional issues are rendered in black and white: "in Colombia, a democratic ally is fighting the persistent assaults of Marxist terrorists and drug-traffickers." More troubling still, "in Venezuela, a demagogue awash in oil money is undermining democracy and seeking to destabilize the region." And to maintain a consistent policy stance, "in Cuba, an anti-American dictator continues to oppress his people and seeks to subvert freedom in the region."[54] A demagogue, a dictator, and a democratic ally. If the objective of this foreign policy is to halt constructive dialog between Venezuela and the United States, or perpetuate misunderstanding between the United States and Cuba, or render absurdly simple the continued violence in Colombia—and provide a justification for expanded military aid, then the statement will serve its purpose well. If the objective is to ease hemispheric tensions, it is difficult to imagine official policy statements less likely to do so.

Enhanced hemispheric security means more resources devoted to the military and to intelligence, a trend made clear by the DoD in the *Quadrennial Defense Review Report*, released on February 6, 2006. The impact of the new national security policy on intelligence agencies throughout the hemisphere has been remarkable, with the potential to create significant distortions in economics and politics. As Patrick Hénault notes,

> In most countries in the region, funding allocated to the armed forces, police, and intelligence services had been inversely proportional to democratic advances. After all, one of the obstacles to the development of democracy in the Americas is the nature of civil-military relations. In several countries, armed forces' subordination to civilian control is not enshrined, and the military continues to exercise undue influence in political and economic affairs. There is concern that increasing the military's resources and the role it plays fighting terrorism will put it back at centre stage, thereby slowing the region's demilitarization.[55]

In sum, the repercussions of the Bush administration's National Security Strategy on democratization, human rights, and civil liberties—throughout the hemisphere—are perhaps one of the most troubling of the "unknown unknowns."

Notes

1. See Carl Boggs, *Masters of War: Militarism and Blowback in the Era of American Empire* (New York: Routledge, 2003).
2. For a discussion and schematic of the intelligence process, see Mark M. Lowenthal, *Intelligence, from Secrets to Policy*, 3rd ed. (Washington, DC: CQ Press, 2006), pp. 54–67.
3. http://www.heritage.org/Research/HomelandDefense/WM149.cfm accessed November 13, 2002. The absence of a mandate to define "what America stands for" considering the 2000 presidential election is conspicuously absent from this discussion. The article "U.S. National Security Strategy Based on American Values" by Jim Garamone of the American Forces Press Services was reprinted by the American Forces Information Service, Washington, DC, October 11, 2002.
4. Defense Planning Guidance for the 1994–1999 Fiscal Years (Draft); Defense Guidance for the 1994–1999 Fiscal Years (Revised Draft); Defense Strategy for the 1990s; Defense Planning Guidance for the 2004–2009 Fiscal Years— as cited in David Armstrong, "Dick Cheney's Song of America, Drafting a Plan for Global Dominance," *Harper's* 305 (October 2002): 76. See also R.C. Longworth, "The Cheney Doctrine: U.S. Asserts 1st-Strike Option," *Chicago Tribune*, September 29, 2002. Perspectives, 1.
5. X, "The Sources of Soviet Conduct," *Foreign Affairs*, 24, 4 (July 1947): 576.
6. See George Crile, *Charlie Wilson's War* (New York: Atlantic Monthly Press, 2003).
7. "National Security Strategy of the United States," September 2002, http://www.whitehouse.gov/nsc/nss/pdf, accessed December 12, 2005, p. 3.
8. See, for example, Samuel Glasstone and Philip J. Dolan, eds. *The Effects of Nuclear Weapons*, 3rd ed. (Washington, DC: U.S. Department of Defense, 1977); United States Congress, Office of Technology Assessment, *The Effects of Nuclear War* (Washington, DC: U.S. Government Printing Office, 1979).
9. "National Security Strategy of the United States," p. 3.
10. Lars Schoultz, *Beneath the United States: A History of U.S. Policy toward Latin America* (Cambridge, MA: Harvard University Press, 1998), p. 115.
11. "National Security Strategy of the United States," p. 3.
12. Ibid., pp. 3, 5, 7.
13. Ibid., p. 4.
14. According to GlobalSecurity.org, "As of July 1, 2005, there were 26 non–U.S. military forces participating in the coalition and contributing to the ongoing stability operations throughout Iraq. These countries were: Albania, Armenia, Australia, Azerbaijan, Bosnia and Herzegovina, Bulgaria, Czech Republic, Denmark, El Salvador, Estonia, Georgia, Italy, Japan, Kazakhstan, South Korea, Latvia, Lithuania, Macedonia, Mongolia, Netherlands, Norway, Poland, Romania, Slovakia, United Kingdom, and Ukraine." Countries that have pulled out of Iraq include [from 2004–2005] Nicaragua, Spain, Dominican Republic, Honduras, Philippines, Thailand, New Zealand, Tonga, Hungary, Portugal, and Moldova. Furthermore, Bulgaria, and Ukraine will withdraw their troops by the end of December 2005. Other nations have reduced the numbers of their troops in Iraq, including Norway (from 150 to 10), Netherlands

(1,345 to 4), Italy (300 less?), and Poland (700 less). See http://www.globalsecurity.org/military/ops/iraq_orbat_coalition.htm. Accessed December 2, 2005.

15. "National Security Strategy of the United States," p. 11.

16. Further dangers exist. According to Aldo Marchesi, "In Uruguay and Argentina as elsewhere in Latin America's Southern Cone, there has been a heated debate on the characteristics on the dictatorships that affected the region during much of the 1970s and 1980s. Controversies persist not only about the factors that caused dictatorships to emerge but also about the nature and enduring significance of human rights violations committed under military rule. Struggles over memory of repression have been a key aspect of redemocratization processes throughout the region, as the military, political parties, social movements, human rights organizations, and various cultural actors have all taken part in the conflicts of 'memory against memory.' " See Marchesi, "Old Ideas in New Discourses: 'The War Against Terrorism' and Collective Memory in Uruguay and Argentina," *Social Science Research Council*, "After Sept. 11," http://www.ssrc.org/sept11/essays/marchesi.htm. Accessed November 5, 2005.

17. Adam Isacson, "War on Terror, Target: Americas—Closing the 'Seams': U.S. Security Policy in the Americas," *NACLA Report on the Americas*, 38 (May–June 2005): 13. For further discussion of the problems posed by vague definitions of terrorism, particularly "indigenous terrorism," see Janette Habel, "US Demands a Secure, Compliant Hemisphere," *International Development Economics Associates*, "Political Economy," http://networkideas.org/themes/political/jan2002/po10_Latin_America.htm. Accessed November 4, 2005. She also cites Nobel peace laureate Adolfo Perez Esquivel, the president of the Justice and Peace Service (SERPAJ), who "believes the US is pushing for 'a remilitarisation of Latin America in antici-pation of a growing number of social conflicts connected with the extension of free trade agreements.' "

18. Isacson. See also Frida Berrigan and John Wingo, "The Bush Effect: U.S. Military Involvement in Latin America Rises, Development and Humanitarian Aid Fall," *Arms Trade Resource Center*, November 5, 2005, http://www.worldpolicy.org/projects/arms/reports/MilitaryAidLA110405.html. Accessed March 1, 2006.

19. Patrick Hénault, "Regional Trends: Latin America and the Caribbean," *DND Policy Group* (Canada: Department of National Defense, 2003) http://www.forces.gc.ca/admpol/eng/doc/strat_2003/sa03_12_e.htm. Accessed November 5, 2005.

20. Marchesi, *Old Ideas*.

21. Farid Kahhat, "Hemispheric Security after September 11," *Social Science Research Council*, "After Sept. 11," http://www.ssrc.org/sept11/essays/kahhat.htm. Accessed November 5, 2005.

22. "National Security Strategy of the United States," p. 12.

23. Ibid., p. 18.

24. Ibid., p. 18.

25. As Scott Ritter points out, a pattern of this sort of manipulation existed before September 11, in relation to UNSCOM inspection of alleged Iraqi violation of UN sanctions. Ritter states, "UNSCOM was simply not operating from the same play book as the CIA was. UNSCOM wanted the facts as they pertained

to our disarmament mission. The CIA wanted the perception as it sustained their regime change mission. Facts are a valuable asset, but only when they are accompanied by a perception that recognizes the facts as such. If perceptions are formed void of facts, or in spite of facts, then the perception becomes the reality, not the facts." Ritter, *Iraq Confidential: The Untold Story of the Intelligence Conspiracy to Undermine the UN and Overthrow Saddam Hussein* (New York: Nation Books, 2005), p. 132.

26. "National Security Strategy of the United States," p. 18.
27. James Bamford, *A Pretext for War, 9/11, Iraq, and the Abuse of America's Intelligence Agencies* (New York: Anchor Books, 2005), p. 423.
28. "National Security Strategy of the United States," p. 19.
29. Alfred Cumming, *The Position of Director of National Intelligence: Issues for Congress,* (Washington, DC: Congressional Information Service, Library of Congress, 2004), pp. 19–20.
30. "National Security Strategy of the United States," p. 32.
31. Ibid.
32. Ibid., p. 33.
33. Ibid.
34. Ibid.
35. Ibid.
36. Ibid.
37. Mark M. Lowenthal, *Intelligence, from Secrets to Policy* (Washington, DC: CQ Press, 2006), p. 34.
38. Bamford, *A Pretext for War*, p. 111.
39. "National Security Strategy of the United States," p. 19.
40. Robert Baer, *See No Evil, the True Story of a Ground Soldier in the CIA's War on Terrorism* (New York: Three Rivers Press, 2002), p. 271.
41. Paul E. Pillar, "Intelligence, Policy, and the War in Iraq," *Foreign Affairs*, 85 (March–April 2006): 15.
42. See for example, Paul Krugman, "Dead Parrot Society," *New York Times*, October 25, 2002, p. A35. James Risen, "C.I.A. Rejects Request for Report on Preparations for War in Iraq," *New York Times*, October 3, 2002, p. A1.
43. Helen Fessenden, "The Limits on Intelligence Reform," *Foreign Affair*, 84, (November–December 2005):106, 116–117.
44. "The War on Civil Liberties," *New York Times*, September 10, 2002, p. A24.
45. "National Security Strategy of the United States," p. 12.
46. Dan Eggen, "U.S. is Given Failing Grade by 9/11 Panel: Report Card Blasts Progress on Counterterrorism Measures," *Washington Post*, December 6, 2005, p. A1.
47. George W. Bush, letter to the American people, "Introduction," The National Security Strategy of the United States of America, March 2006, http://www.whitehouse.gov/nsc/nss/2006. Accessed March 17, 2006.
48. "National Security Strategy of the United States," p. 37.
49. Ibid., p. 8.
50. Ibid., p. 24.
51. Ibid., p. 24.
52. Ibid., p. 23.
53. Ibid., p. 37.
54. Ibid., p. 15.
55. Hénault, "Regional Trends."

Chapter 4

The Summits of the Americas: Continuities and Changes in the Hemispheric Agenda of William Clinton and George W. Bush

Luis Fernando Ayerbe

This chapter examines the foreign policy of the United States during the governments of Bill Clinton and George W. Bush, aimed at establishing continuities and changes, regarding both the global strategy of the country and in relation to Latin America and the Caribbean. Concerning the latter, the analysis refers to presidential/summits diplomacy, considered by the last two administrations as a privileged place when constructing a new architecture of hemispherical relationships. We refer to the period of the summit meetings in Miami, Santiago, Quebec, and Mar del Plata, between 1994 and 2005, as well as the extraordinary summit in Monterrey in 2004.

The conceptions that guide the international positioning of the United States by the Democratic and Republican governments express strong elements of continuity. Substantial disagreements with regards to the definition of interests, challenges, and threats, especially in relation to Latin America and the Caribbean have not been verified. The unfolding of events following September 11, 2001, basically reinforce the differences that were already present in the initial period of Bush's term in office, making its imposing character more explicit in reaching essentially similar objectives.

The New Lineaments of Foreign Policy

As the first elected government in the period subsequent to the cold war, the Clinton administration had the important task of formulating a new foreign policy regarding the country's international positioning, in a process that implied a wider debate concerning the establishment of national interests and strategic goals.

Although there is not much divergence in the fundamental orientation during the two presidential terms, we consider that in the second term, under the direction of Madeleine Albright in the Department of State, guidelines of foreign policy have been consolidated, with the clear definition of short, medium, and long-term objectives.

In his address at the John F. Kennedy School of Government, at Harvard University, Warren Christopher, the Secretary of State in the first term, analyzing his administration, highlights two aspects that he considers fundamental in his mandate: first, the country's ever-increasing international involvement, attempting to respond to an agenda of new challenges; second, the cut in the international affairs budget.

> When our Administration took office in 1993, we faced an array of challenges that required urgent attention. Russia's democracy was in crisis; its economy was near collapse. The nuclear arsenal of the former Soviet Union was scattered among four new countries with few safeguards. The war in Bosnia was at the peak of its brutality and threatening to spread. North Korea was developing nuclear weapons. The Middle East peace process was stalemated; negotiations were stymied. Repression in Haiti was pushing refugees to our shores. NAFTA's passage was in serious doubt, threatening our relations with the entire hemisphere.[1]

In Christopher's evaluation, the new world order requires a more engaged posture from the United States: "Because of our military and economic might, because we are trusted to uphold universal values, there are times when only America can lead."[2] In order to meet the requirements of this leadership, it is necessary to count on adequate resources. However, according to the data presented by the secretary, based on 1985, there was a reduction of 50 percent in the amount spent on international affairs.[3] In relation to the programs of foreign aid, the expenditure was reduced by 37 percent.

When criticizing budget cuts, especially aimed at the supporters of isolationism, the Secretary synthesizes the relevance of the (United States) foreign policy to overcome the problems that affect the internal order of the country:

> Americans are proud that we are the world's leading nation and they know leadership carries responsibilities. They see the evidence that isolationists miss: that the security of our nation depends on the readiness of our diplomats as our first line of defense; that the safety of our streets depends on our fight against drugs and terror abroad; that our jobs at home depend on the health of the global economy.[4]

In contrast with the limited resources faced by Christopher, Albright highlights the 17 percent increase obtained in her administration, leaving her successor the most favorable budgetary situation since the 1990s.[5]

The reversion of this declining trend concerning the attribution of governmental resources for international affairs was considered one of the main priorities in Albright's administration. The argument presented to the U.S. Congress regarding the need to increase the budget for the year 2001 concisely reveals the main lineaments of the foreign policy in the Clinton period.

Although our economy is strong and our military unmatched, there remain serious dangers to our interests. These include terrorists, possible conflicts in key regions, the risk of another financial crisis, drug trafficking, and the spread of nuclear, chemical, and biological weapons.

In addition to the threats, there are opportunities to serve U.S. interests by bringing nations closer together around basic principles of democracy, open markets, the rule of law and a commitment to peace.[6]

In consonance with these lineaments, there is a change of approach in relation to foreign aid. Expenditure on global involvement is not accounted for as lost funds in causes whose impact in the quality of life of the country's citizens is uncertain. By justifying each program formulated by the Department of State, national interests are clearly defined.

The proposed budget for 2001 shows good examples of the accounting for loss and profit that characterizes the new posture, articulating in the same course of action themes such as the promotion of trade agreements and exploitation of labor that is considered inhumane.

In relation to free trade,

Since President Clinton took office, we have negotiated more than 300 agreements to help reduce tariffs on the sale of American goods and services. Today, trade is responsible for more than 11 million U.S. jobs. U.S. exports to the developing world—our fastest growing trade partner—totaled $275 billion in 1997 alone.[7]

Concerning the topic of promotion of democracy,

A key objective of U.S. foreign policy is to promote values that reflect the interests, character, and ideals of the American people. We do this because it is right, but also because it is smart. Compared to dictatorships, democratic nations are more likely to be stable, better able to cope with financial stress, more reliable trading partners, and less likely to generate refugees or contribute to other global problems.[8]

Linked to this theme in the agenda, we highlight the combat against inhumane labor conditions:

We have also taken the lead in a global effort to ban the worst forms of child labor, and to establish core standards to prevent the exploitation of workers overseas, while giving American workers a more level playing field on which to compete. We continue to argue that labor impacts should be considered when trade agreements are negotiated.[9]

The increase in the attraction of budgetary resources is a fundamental component in a bigger strategy of valuing the role of the Department of State in the defense of the "American way of life."

In the next section, we analyze documents of the USAID (United States Agency for International Development), attached to the Department of

State, which illustrate the main lineaments in the Albright administration, especially in relation to the "transition countries," which includes Latin American and the Caribbean.

Governance and Foreign Aid

In her address in the conference *Promoting Democracy, Human Rights, and Reintegration in Post-Conflict Societies*, promoted by the USAID, in October 1997, Secretary Albright divides the world into four categories of countries:

> those that participate as full members of the international system; those that are in transition and seek to participate more fully; those that reject the rules upon which the system is based; and finally, the states that are unable—for reasons of underdevelopment, catastrophe, or conflict—to enjoy the benefits and meet the responsibilities that full membership in the system entails.[10]

In parallel with the fears, when situations of conflict in the countries in "transition and development" arise, there is a positive perception associated to the potential of expanding business. In this aspect, foreign aid meets a variety of the country's interests:

> We have an economic interest in opening new opportunities for American commerce and in preventing new demands on the sources we have available for emergency relief and refugees. We have a budgetary and social interest in helping the people of other countries to build a future for themselves at home. . . . We have a political interest in helping post-conflict societies to embrace democracy and to become part of the solution to global threats such as proliferation, pollution, illegal narcotics, and transnational crime. Finally, we have a humanitarian interest in helping those who have survived the cauldron of war or—in a case such as Haiti, the cruelty of repression—to revitalize their societies.[11]

USAID's Strategic Plan, formulated in 1997 and updated in 2000, seeks to give an answer to the combination of interests and foreign aid commitments defined by Albright, which had seven goals associated with the promotion of sustainable development: (1) encouraging economic growth, with an emphasis on agriculture, the main livelihood for the population of poor countries; (2) the strengthening of democracy and good governance; (3) human qualifications based on education and training, stimulating change in the distribution of public funding in basic education; (4) stabilizing the world's population and protecting human health; (5) protecting the environment, considering long term sustainability; (6) humanitarian assistance to victims of natural disasters or violence; (7) maintaining the USAID as the main bilateral agency for assisting development, providing it with an adequate infrastructure.

We analyze the programs related to the second goal, given the relevance attributed to democracy in the global engagement policy of the Clinton administration, which is one of the pillars (together with free trade) of the agenda for the development of the "transition" countries.

The work surrounding the strengthening of democracy and good governance is based on four objectives, which are related to the applied initiatives:[12] (1) the rule of law and respect for human rights, especially of women, with initiatives aimed at the strengthening of institutions of the justice system, making the access of citizens to justice possible; (2) encouraging political processes guided by credibility and competitiveness, with initiatives that support electoral reform, including education programs for voters and strengthening of political parties; (3) development of a politically active civil society, with initiatives toward the rise of citizen participation in the political processes, control of public institutions, institutional and financial strengthening of civil society organizations, and incentives to the free circulation of information and to a democratic political culture; (4) encouraging transparency and responsibility in government institutions, with initiatives that promote the decentralization functions and decision making processes, strengthening the legislative bodies, government, unity, and the civil-military relationships.

In Latin America and the Caribbean, the positive evaluation of the changes made in relation to the political and economic liberalization, the emphasis of USAID is on the reforms of the "second generation" that are focused on deepening democracy. In relation to politics, the focus is on four aspects: the rule of law, the decentralization of the decisions and democratic practices adopted by the local governments, the creation of conditions to strengthen the civil society, and freedom of the press. These actions are considered strategic to the national interests of the United States in the region.

To reduce pressure of the LAC (Latin America and the Caribbean) region's poor to seek refuge and better opportunities in the United States, and to enhance political stability and economic prosperity in all of the Americas, it is critical that the U.S. government ensure that LAC countries continue in their transitions from conflict to peace and reconciliation, from dictatorships to democracy, and from controlled economies with massive inequity to open markets and determined efforts to alleviate poverty.[13]

Thus, three priority actions are proposed: (1) the strengthening of the regional mechanisms to promote human rights and the rule of law, especially through the Inter-American Institute for Human Rights (IIHR), in which the Inter-disciplinary Course on Human Rights is offered;[14] (2) promoting a regional approach in favor of the legitimacy of the public service; strengthening mechanisms of transparency, state administration accountability, and decentralization of decision-making in municipal governments;[15] (3) strengthening of regional mechanisms in favor of pluralism.

The development of these actions does not happen in a unilateral way, since there is a concern to link them to the collective decisions of the Summits of the Americas. The Second Summit of the Americas in Santiago culminated a yearlong effort of presidential engagement in hemispheric affairs. At the summit, the

Heads of State of the 34 democracies in the region set forth certain regional initiatives that could be accomplished over the next three to five years. These initiatives focused on a "second generation" of reforms aimed at deepening the trend toward democratic governance in the region and removing the barriers to the participation of the poor in the national life of their countries.[16]

Next, we analyze the importance of the summits in the process of the elaboration of the hemispheric agenda of the United States, especially in the themes related to governance, comparing the predominant orientations of the Clinton and Bush governments.

The Architecture of Hemispheric Relations

As pointed out in the previous section, in the United States' view of foreign policy, the Western Hemisphere presents itself as a region in transition, in which peace among the nations, political democracy, and free market economy emerge as unquestionable trends. In terms of the consolidation of this trajectory, as Luis J. Lauredo, the representative of the United States in the OAS, affirms, the problem is in the details:

> is in the details of democracy, in the details of human rights, and in the details of a free market economy that we all must work to ensure the Western Hemisphere does not slip back into the precipice into dictatorship and ultimately, war.[17]

Concern regarding the details in the transition process goes toward a redefinition of the parameters that guide hemispherical relations, leading to the construction of a new architecture whose main stage is the Summit of the Americas, inaugurated by the Clinton government in 1994.

The Summit of the Americas, which began as an informal gathering of heads of state in Miami in 1994, has evolved into a valuable forum for participants to resolve common political, economic, and social issues in an environment of mutual respect and cooperation. In a nutshell, it embodies the leaders' hemispheric agenda for the future. It is the new architecture of hemispheric relations based on common values of democracy, free trade, and on the shared responsibility to be proactive in defending these values.[18]

The affirmation of such community values among the Summits' participating countries presents itself as the main argument in favor of the institutionalization of negotiation mechanisms, formulation of policies, follow-up, and control of this joint trajectory. The pursuit of national interest transcends the Democrat or Republican origin of the administration in power. Although there are differences of approach between the Clinton and the Bush administrations, there is no great discrepancy in the definition of the basic pillars that should rule the hemispheric convergence: liberal democracy and free market economy.

Stemming from the establishment of a basic consensus among the Summit participants regarding these two aspects, the process of negotiations involving the details of a new architecture works with a wide agenda:

> we are developing policies to make governments across the hemisphere more transparent, accessible, and less corrupt. We are looking for ways to promote the administration of justice, increase respect for human rights, and strengthen the rule of law. We are looking at ways to improve countries' abilities to prepare and respond to natural disasters and to improve people's access to quality health care and to a quality education. We are looking for ways to improve labor and environmental conditions in the hemisphere. We are also discussing ways to bridge the digital divide within our hemisphere and ensure that the promise of information technologies benefits our peoples.[19]

In the expectation of identifying the arguments that make the perception of Latin America and the Caribbean more explicit, the main themes of the agenda are grouped around two issues: economical governance, which especially involves the proposal for the creation of Free Trade Area of the Americas (FTAA), and political governance, associated with the negotiation of collective mechanisms of follow-up and control in the transition.

The proposal for the creation of the FTAA by 2005, a date which was ratified in the Summit of Quebec in April 2001, gives continuity to the Americas Initiative, formulated in the 1990s by President George Bush. In terms of national historic antecedents, the starting point asserted by the government is the proposal of the Secretary of State James Blaine in the first Pan-American Conference in 1989 for the creation of a Customs Union.

In March 1998, during the preparation of the Summit of Santiago, Secretary Albright presented an important historical milestone that incorporated, in the foundations of the hemispheric identity, Hispano-American references:

> Simon Bolivar wanted the Americas to be measured not by her vast area and wealth, but "by her freedom and her glory." Today, that vision is closer to reality than it has ever been. For as we meet, with one exception,[20] every government in the hemisphere is freely elected; every economy has liberalized its system for investment and trade.[21]

However, between the two cited references, the Pan-Americanism started by Blaire is the one that points out the initiative of the United States. As the Trade Representative of the United States Robert Zoellick, in George W. Bush's government states in his address at the Council of the Americas, in which he draws his conclusions regarding the Summit in Quebec: "Today, as I look at the Americas, I see a driving purpose: a belief in democracy and freedom, and a rediscovery of the vision that motivated those who called for the first Pan-American Congress over 100 years ago."[22]

Referring to the change of strategic perspective in the relationship between the great powers and their neighbors, Zoellick highlights the contrasting reality of the nineteenth to twenty-first centuries:

> In the 19th century, many strong countries wanted weak neighbors that they could dominate. In the 21st century, strong countries will benefit from healthy, prosperous, and confident democratic neighbors. Troubled neighbors export

problems like illegal immigration, environmental damage, crime, narcotics, and violence. Healthy neighbors create stronger regions through economic integration and political cooperation.[23]

The regional example stressed by Zoellick is the North American Free Trade Agreement (NAFTA) that promoted an increase in trade between the United States and Mexico from $81 billion in 1993 to $247 billion in 2000 and increased the volume of exports to Canada to a level that is the equivalent of the exports to Europe (respectively $179 and $187 billion in 2000). In this process, 2.2 million jobs were created in Mexico, 1.3 million in Canada, and 13 million in the United States.[24] In relation to the economic projections associated with the creation of FTAA, the outlook is extremely favorable. According to the data presented by the Bureau of Hemispheric Affairs from the Department of State, since 1995 the exports to Latin America have risen at an annual rate of 10 percent, twice as much as in relation to Europe.[25]

Referring to the internal critics of the FTAA, who fear a loss of jobs in the United States, Lauredo is emphatic when defending the initiative:

> Latin American countries have some of the world's highest tariff rates—on average, 4 times higher than U.S. tariff rates. The FTAA will eliminate most tariffs, making it more profitable for American companies to export to the region. More American exports mean more American jobs. Second . . . Latin America is our fastest growing export market, accounting for two-thirds of U.S. export growth worldwide and 40% of total U.S. merchandise exports. Third, as growth rates increase and inflation falls, the demand for products and services amongst consumers in Latin America is increasing. . . . If the U.S. doesn't take advantage of the growing Latin market, our competitors in Europe and Asia will. Fourth, free trade has non-economic benefits to the United States. Trade promotes ties between our people and stable regional economies work against the drug trade and migration because people can find legitimate jobs in their countries.[26]

In relation to the fourth aspect mentioned by Lauredo, the consensus in the governmental analysis is that the deepening of the economic interdependence contributes to governance. As Zoellick points out,

> Trade agreements such as NAFTA and the FTAA promote good governance by creating obligations for transparency in government and adherence to the rule of law. . . . Similarly, trade fosters political cooperation. . . . Indeed, we have seen throughout Latin America that growing economic integration has led to a lessening of old regional suspicions and tensions, whether between Chile and Argentina or between Peru and Ecuador. Trade also spurs improvements in education. As people start businesses, and foreign companies invest their capital, standards for education rise to meet the demands of the new economy.[27]

The data concerning the potential impact of FTAA in the growth of exports and the level of employment in the United States leave little doubt regarding the role of Latin America and the Caribbean in the viability of the economic prosperity goals of the Department of State's Strategic Plan 2000. In addition, there is the recognition that the liberalization process may contribute to the onset of situations of instability in a region in transition. As Secretary Albright makes explicit,

> Neither democracy nor prosperity can endure unless they are broadly based. The policies of free markets and open investment, which are the keys to sustained growth, are vulnerable to challenge if too many people feel shut out or left behind and as we have seen in parts of Asia, a booming economy can shift rapidly into reverse if problems of cronyism, corruption, and lack of accountability are not addressed.[28]

This concern was present in the summits in Santiago in April 1998, in Quebec in 2001, and in the Extraordinary Summit of Monterrey in January 2004, in which, parallel to the discussions regarding the implementation of FTAA, initiatives toward the adjustment of the political governance agenda were defined. In the area of education, targets were set regarding the access and attendance of 100 percent of the children in primary school and 75 percent in secondary school, up to 2010. In the area of preservation and strengthening of democracy, justice and human rights, we can highlight the initiatives established toward local development, through the strengthening of the municipal and regional administrations, stimulating the participation of society in the processes of decision-making; the combat against corruption, with the adoption of OAS programs that encourage administrative honesty and legal action against money laundering; prevention and control of consumption and traffic of illegal drugs; combat and elimination of terrorism and fostering trust and security amongst the states, institutionally strengthening the inter-American system. In the area of discrimination and eradication of poverty, the fomenting of micro, small, and medium enterprises can be highlighted; the respect for labor rights based on the ILO; gender equality, promoting judicial equality between women and men.

In the Extraordinary Summit in Monterrey, in which 13 new heads of state participated, although the main objectives defined in the previous meetings were reaffirmed, the agenda of discussions incorporated new international and regional realities that happened between 2001 and 2003. In this perspective, three themes gained special emphasis: (1) the combat against terrorism, which had become a priority in the global agenda of the United States after the September 11, 2001 attack, being incorporated as the central element in the so-called new regional threats; (2) political governance, especially in the sequence of crisis in the last two years, involving the events that led to the resignation of the elected presidents of Argentina (2001) and Bolivia (2003); (3) the process of implementing FTAA, regarding the deepening of divergences between Brazil and the United States about deadlines and the scope of economical liberalization, following the rise of Lula's government.

In the final declaration of the meeting, the agreements reached concerning these themes are made explicit. In the issues connected with security, among the main regional and global threats, the problems of terrorism and production of weapons of mass destruction are highlighted, which are also the two central arguments for the invasion of Iraq in 2003, together with the tyrannical character of Saddam Hussein's government.

This is our first meeting since the tragic events of September 11th 2001. We reiterate that terrorism, as well as the proliferation of weapons of mass destruction, are serious threats to international security, to institutions, to democratic values in the States and to the well-being of our peoples. We have resolved to intensify our cooperation and face these threats.[29]

Concerning governance, the document explicitly defends representative democracy as a basic unit of principles regarding the government system that should guide the hemispheric community, emphasizing the combat against corruption as an effective way of reaching transparency, efficiency, and optimization of economic resources in favor of social development:

We recognize that political pluralism and solid political parties are essential elements of democracy. We stress the importance of norms that ensure transparency in their finances, avoid corruption and the risk of improper influences, and stimulate a high level of electoral participation. Therefore, we will promote the conditions that allow political parties to develop in an autonomous way, without government control.[30]

Concerning the FTAA, the document incorporates the agreements that were sealed in the eighteenth ministerial meeting in Miami in November 2003. After previous understandings between Brazil and the United States (both presiding at this stage of the negotiations) a conclusive common position was reached in the negotiating process in 2005, with the creation of an area of free trade. The new proposal, ratified in Monterrey, and nick-named FTAA Light, is less ambitious than the original project. Although it does not question the wider perspective that should guide the integration agenda, it aims to guarantee increased flexibility in the recognition of the diversity of situations that involve the economies of the region, enabling countries to establish different levels of commitment.[31]

On different dates, yet in the same place, the Council of the Americas (officials from the Department of State from both the Clinton and Bush administrations) enunciates the main consensus reached in the hemisphere through the diplomacy of presidential summits. Referring to the decisions of the Summit of Santiago, in May 1999, Madeleine Albright stresses the following aspects:

There were initiatives . . . to strengthen local governments and thereby broaden opportunities for political participation. There were strategies to formalize property rights, including the assets of the poor, such as houses or farms. There were programs to reinforce the rule of law, including creation of hemispheric justice studies centers. There was support for the Inter-American Convention Against Corruption[32] . . . And there were proposals, in which USAID is actively participating, to increase support for micro enterprise, which is particularly important to the economic empowerment of women.[33]

Weighing up the decisions at the Summit of Quebec, in May 2001, Bush's Secretary of State, Colin Powell, emphasizes the combination of initiatives that aim to tackle the most urgent regional situations, especially in the Andean area and in the Caribbean—considered as a third border jointly with Canada and Mexico—affirming the two central pillars of the Inter-American agenda, democracy, and free market:

> Some of what we did in Quebec was regional. We did some preventive medicine to help Colombia's neighbors defend themselves against the spillover of narco-guerilla activity. We did this by announcing and giving our support to an Andean regional initiative . . . not just to focus on narco-trafficking in Colombia but to see the problem as a regional problem and to invest in human rights activities, to invest in infrastructure development, to invest in economic opportunities that will encourage people to move away from narco-trafficking. . . . And we passed a strong initiative on HIV-AIDS and other issues related to the Caribbean island nations . . . What we have taken to describe here in the United States as a third border initiative . . . But all of these regional initiatives took place within the context of a much larger vision . . . That open markets and good government are closely linked, and that even as we generate investment and create jobs, we need to work toward accountable democratic institutions and democratic practices.[34]

In a speech that presented the agenda of discussions in the Summit in Monterrey, in January 2004, the Assistant Secretary of the State Department for Western Hemisphere Affairs, Roger Noriega, recognized the economic problems faced by the majority of the population in Latin America and the Caribbean, revealing a loss of credibility of countries that promote liberalizing reforms, though making it clear that the direction, regarding both politics and the economy, should follow the lineaments collectively defined in the context of the presidential summits: democracy, the rule of law, the fostering of free enterprise, and free trade.

> Unless women and men from all walks of life have a stake in economic growth in Latin America and the Caribbean, the gap between rich and poor will widen, and genuine prosperity may prove illusive or unsustainable. We know the answer: democracy and the rule of law are essential to global development and trade, because they empower individuals to share the costs and the blessings of prosperity.[35]

In August 2005, Noriega left his position in the State Department; he was substituted by Thomas A. Shannon Jr. inaugurating his performance in the private initiative as Visiting Fellow in the American Enterprise, he analyzed the challenges that president Bush had ahead of the IV Presidential Summit to take place in November in Mar del Plata, Argentina.

Aware of the negative climate to take up the agenda of the Washington Consensus, which is associated with the combined effect of economic and political difficulties of the region, with the fall of governments that defend the liberal reforms in Argentina and Bolivia, and the promotion of Left leadership like Lula, Kirchner, and Chavez, he recommends that the U.S. Government take a firm attitude in the defense of the objectives that speed up the process initiated in Miami in 1994.

At the summit, President George W. Bush pressed his colleagues to reemphasize their commitments to defend democracy and the rule of law, deepen economic reforms, and expand trade as a recipe for sustained, equitable growth. But there were a significant number of Latin leaders who tried to scuttle this work plan and served up sympathetic rhetoric to cynically court the poor.[36]

Noriega's fear was confirmed at the meeting. Despite the United States Government's efforts to continue with the commercial negotiations, there was a strong resistance from the MERCOSUR countries and Venezuela who opposed the inclusion of FTAA in the discussion guidelines, defending to keep the theme that convened the meeting, "Creating decent job opportunities, sustained economic growth; Fighting poverty; and Strengthening democratic governance and institutions."

That position prevailed, despite the strong pressure exerted by the United States, Mexico, and Canada. On the other hand, the opposition to the resumption of commercial negotiations by the five South American countries does not involve the consensus on the future of the FTAA project, since the positions vary from the open rejection of the Venezuelan head of state to the undefined postponement proposed by the other countries.

Despite the differences expressed at the meeting of presidents, bilateral relations of Argentina, Brazil, Paraguay, Uruguay, and Venezuela with the United States flow smoothly. A theme privileged by Kirchner at his meeting with Bush during the Summit was to obtain support in the negotiations of Argentina with the IMF on the foreign debt. One of the positive results of Mar del Plata highlighted by Bush was the investment bilateral agreement signed with the president of Uruguay, Tabare Vazquez. In a visit to Brazil after the Summit Meeting, Bush strongly praised the economic effort of the government of Lula and his positive leadership in the region, thus confirming the favorable moment of bilateral relations. After the official visit to Paraguay in September by Defense Secretary Donald Rumsfeld, there was a strengthening of military bonds between the two countries. Despite the confrontational speeches of Chavez and Bush, bilateral trade continues to be expanded and Venezuela stays as the third largest commercial partner of the United States following Mexico and Brazil.[37]

The Bush Government
and Security—a Pre-9/11 Priority

If we observe the differences between the governments of Clinton and Bush in relation to the value of the way of life as the main basis of a hemispheric community, there are different emphases in the definition of priorities. These priorities are not determined by the circumstances after September 11, 2001, as shown below and drawn from documents previous to the attacks.

In his presentation of the proposed budget for International Affairs for 2002, in May 2001, Powell requested an increase of 2 percent in relation to the previous year, arguing that there is a perception of greater levels of instability in the world in transition. The proposal defines the following priority areas: reform of USAID; bilateral economic assistance; international control of narcotics and the rule of law; assistance to migration and refugees; nonproliferation, antiterrorism, and clearance of minefields; military assistance; and multilateral programs of economic aid.

In the analysis of the document, we highlight the change of approach in relation to Albright's administration showing the main items related to political governance in Latin America and the Caribbean. Concerning the restructuring of USAID, presented as the main theme in the justification of the new budget, there is a redefinition of the focus of action of the Agency, which assumes globalization and prevention of conflicts as core points of international assistance, directing resources and activities to three main programs: economic growth and agriculture, global health and prevention of conflicts, and support development.

The two first points maintain essentially the same orientation of the former administration. In the case of agriculture, besides its key role as an economic activity to which the majority of the poor population in most developing countries is linked, most of the conflicts in these regions are rooted in the rural areas. Therefore, the main objectives of the program are to increase economic opportunities, stimulating the expansion of property, the improvement of productivity and the efficiency in the management of natural resources, and the promotion of training and education activities.

The third program illustrates the main changes of focus, subordinating the actions to this theme, which were previously part of the specific aim of the Strategic Plan, the "strengthening of democracy and good government." Initiatives of humanitarian assistance are also attached to this program. As Powell puts it,

> Given the rising number of collapsed states and internal conflicts in the post-Cold War period, some of which have become focal points of U.S. foreign policy, USAID will undertake a major new conflict prevention, management, and resolution initiative. This initiative will integrate the existing portfolio of USAID democracy programs with new approaches to anticipating crisis, conflict analysis, comprehensive assessment, and will provide new methodologies to assist conflicting parties resolve their issues peacefully.[38]

The arguments presented by the director of the USAID, Andrew Natsios, when justifying the funds requested for Latin America and the Caribbean, clearly synthesize the perception of the region in the country's foreign policy:

> Because the countries assisted by USAID in Latin America and the Caribbean are our neighbors, their economic, social, and political development have an extremely important impact on our own security and well-being. Americans

benefit directly when the economies of developing LAC countries expand and their markets open. Since 1990, the number of U.S. jobs supported by exports to the region has increased by 2.3 million. But when nations in this region face political instability and failing economies, the United States sees the consequences directly through increased illegal immigration and illegal narcotics. None of us should ignore the cross-border spread of communicable diseases such as TB and HIV/AIDS. Finally, environmental degradation and pollution can affect U.S. Border States directly and also aggravate regional instability and migration, as well as increase the risk of death and destruction from disasters in the region.[39]

Continuity and Change

Are there great innovations in George W. Bush's foreign policy as compared to his predecessor? The answer would be yes. If we compare the description of threats, the definition of objectives, and the goals of the strategic plans drafted by the State Department through Madeleine Albright and Colin Powell actions, we perceive more similarities than differences.

The document, *U.S. Department of State Strategic Plan*, released in 1999, defines and articulates national interests and strategic goals (table 4.1) seeking

Table 4.1   U.S. Department of State Strategic Plan (2000)

National interests	Strategic goals
National Security	• Prevent regional instabilities from threatening U.S. vital national interests. • Reduce the threat to the United States and its allies from weapons of mass destruction (WMD).
Economic prosperity	• Open foreign markets to increase trade and free the flow of goods, services, and capital. • Expand U.S. exports to $1.2 trillion by early twenty-first century. • Increase global economic growth and stability. • Promote broad-based growth in developing and transitional economies to raise standards of living, reduce poverty, and lessen disparities of wealth within and among countries.
American citizens and U.S. borders	• Protect the safety and security of American citizens who travel and live abroad. • Facilitate travel to the United States by foreign visitors, immigrants, and refugees, while deterring entry by those who abuse or threaten our system.
Law enforcement	• Minimize the impact of international crime on the United States and its citizens. • Reduce the entry of illegal drugs into the United States. • Reduce the incidence and severity of international terrorist attacks, particularly against American citizens and interests.
Democracy	• Open political systems and societies to democratic practices, the rule of law, good governance, and respect for human rights.

Continued

Table 4.1   Continued

National interests	Strategic goals
Humanitarian Response	• Prevent or minimize the human costs of conflict and natural disasters.
Global issues: Environment, health, and population	• Secure a sustainable global environment to protect the U.S. citizens and interests from the effects of international environmental degradation. • Achieve a healthy and sustainable world population. Strengthen international health capabilities.

Source: Fuente: Datos extraídos del U.S. Strategic Plan 2000 (USDS, 2002, pp. 11–12).

to respond to the transformations that have taken place as of 1990, outlining the surroundings of a new agenda that has as its main point the appraisal of the international development of the United States in a world marked by the growing dissolution of boundaries between domestic and international affairs.

Defined by reference to the past, the post–cold war era has as its most significant attribute the absence of any immediate, vital threat to national security. The demise of the Soviet Union has left the United States as the preeminent world power and invested it with unparalleled leadership responsibilities and opportunities. But the end of superpower competition has also eliminated the unifying strategy for U.S. foreign policy. Now, in addition to regional security issues, an array of threats—weapons proliferation, terrorism, ethnic and religious conflict, organized crime, drug trafficking, and environmental degradation—challenges U.S. interests and blurs the traditional dividing lines between domestic and foreign affairs.[40]

In August 2003, Colin Powell announced the strategic plan for 2004–2009, a document drafted jointly with USAID, which outlines objectives and goals (table 4.2) adjusted to the context prior to September 11, 2001. In keeping with the priorities attributed to the security and preventive combat of new threats, the document reaffirms the significance of the U.S. international leadership:

> We will strive to strengthen traditional alliances and build new relationships to achieve a peace that brings security, but when necessary, we will act alone to face the challenges, provide assistance, and seize the opportunities of this era. U.S. leadership is essential for promoting this vision, but others must share the responsibility. The history of American foreign policy suggests that we will increase our chances of success abroad by exerting principled leadership while seeking to work with others to achieve our goals.[41]

The comparison of tables 4.1 and 4.2 shows operational changes in the organization of strategic objectives and goals, searching for a greater focus on the theme of security to which development and governance are explicitly linked, including a specific item on the defense of the national territory. Out of those aspects, there was not verification of differences in the content that can indicate substantial drifting apart from the strategic visions. The main points outlined in the document of 2000 are also present in the 2004–2009 document with alterations that express responses to the scenario shaped by 9/11.

Table 4.2 State Department and USAID Strategic Plan (2004–2009)

Strategic objectives	Strategic and performance goals
Achieve peace and security	*Regional stability* • Close, strong, and effective U.S. ties with allies, friends, partners, and regional organizations. • Existing and emergent regional conflicts are contained or resolved. *Counterterrorism* • Coalition partners identify, deter, apprehend, and prosecute terrorists. • U.S. and foreign governments actively combat terrorist financing. • Coordinated international prevention and response to terrorism, including bioterrorism. • Stable political and economic conditions that prevent terrorism from flourishing in fragile or failing states. *Homeland security* • Denial of visas to foreign citizens who would abuse or threaten the United States, while facilitating entry of legitimate applicants. • Implemented international agreements stop the entry of goods that could harm the United States, while ensuring the transfer of bonafide materials. *Weapons of mass destruction* • Bilateral measures, including the promotion of new technologies, to combat the proliferation of WMD and reduce stockpiles. • Strengthened multilateral WMD agreements and nuclear energy cooperation under appropriate conditions. *American citizens* U.S. citizens have the consular information, services, and protection they need to reside, conduct business, or travel abroad.
Advance sustainable development and global interests	*Democracy and human rights* • Measures adopted to develop transparent and accountable democratic institutions, laws, and economic and political processes and practices. • Universal standards protect human rights, including the rights of women and ethnic minorities, religious freedom, worker rights, and the reduction of child labor. *Economic prosperity and security* • Institutions, laws, and policies foster private sector-led growth, macroeconomic stability, and poverty reduction. • Increased trade and investment achieved through market-opening, international agreements and further integration of developing countries into the trading system. • Secure and stable financial and energy markets. • Enhanced food security and agricultural development. *Social and environmental issues* • Improved global health, including child, maternal, and reproductive health, and the reduction of abortion and disease, especially HIV/AIDS, malaria, and tuberculosis. • Partnerships, initiatives, and implemented international treaties and agreements that protect the environment and promote efficient energy use and resource management. *Humanitarian response* • Effective protection, assistance, and durable solutions for refugees, internally displaced persons, and conflict victims.

Continued

Table 4.2   Continued

Strategic objectives	Strategic and performance goals
	• Improved capacity of host countries and the international community to reduce vulnerabilities to disasters and anticipate and respond to humanitarian emergencies.
Promote international understanding	Public diplomacy and public affairs • Public diplomacy influences global public opinion and decision-making consistent with U.S. national interests. • International exchanges increase mutual understanding and build trust between Americans and people and institutions around the world. • Basic human values embraced by Americans are respected and understood by global public and institutions.
Strengthen diplomatic and program capabilities	*Management and organizational excellence* • A high performing, well-trained, and diverse workforce aligned with mission requirements. • Modernized, secure, and high quality information technology management and infrastructure that meet critical business requirements. • Personnel are sage from physical harm and national security information is safe from compromise. • Secure, safe, and functional facilities serving domestic and overseas staff.

Source: Data extracted from the Strategic Plan 2004–2009 (USDS, 2003 Strategic Plan Fiscal Years 2004–2009, http://www.usaid.gov/policy/budget/state _usaid_strat_plan.pdf, pp. 42–4).

On the other hand, an important change of emphasis is verified in relation to the degree of danger in the new forms of conflict. Different from the Strategic Plan 2000, that underlines the absence of immediate and vital threats to national security, there is, on the part of the government of Bush, a growing overexcitement of terrorism as an existential enemy not only to the United States but more to the world order, expressed with satisfaction in a speech given at the National Endowment for Democracy in March 2005.

> First, these extremists want to end American and Western influence in the broader Middle East, because we stand for democracy and peace, and stand in the way of their ambitions. . . . Second, the militant network wants to use the vacuum created by an American retreat to gain control of a country, a base from which to launch attacks and conduct their war against non-radical Muslim governments. . . . Third, the militants believe that controlling one country will rally the Muslim masses, enabling them to overthrow all moderate governments in the region, and establish a radical Islamic empire that spans from Spain to Indonesia. With greater economic and military and political power, the terrorists would be able to advance their stated agenda: to develop weapons of mass destruction, to destroy Israel, to intimidate Europe, to assault the American people, and to blackmail our government into isolation.[42]

Table 4.3 Terrorist Attacks and Number (A–V)* of Victims per Region 1996–2003

Year	Africa A–V	Asia A–V	Eurasia A–V	Latin America A–V	Middle East A–V	North America A–V	Western Europe A–V
1996	11–80	11–1507	24–20	84–18	45–1097	0–0	121–503
1997	11–21	21–344	42–27	128–11	37–480	13–7	52–17
1998	21–5379	49–635	14–12	111–195	31–58	0–0	48–405
1999	53–185	72–690	35–8	122–9	26–31	2–0	85–16
2000	55–100	98–898	31–103	192–20	20–78	0–0	30–4
2001	33–150	68–651	3–0	194–6	29–513	4–4091	7–20
2002	5–12	99–1281	7–615	50–52	29–772	0–0	9–6
2003	6–14	80–1427	2–0	20–79	67–1823	0–0	33–928

Source: Drafted on the basis of information of the report on *Patterns of Global Terrorism 2003* (U.S.D.S., 2004).

Note: *A = Number of Attacks; V = Number of Victims.

The demarcation of the level of threat is an essential indicator for the definition of the present international posture of the United States. The perception of a growing insecure world will feed the national and global policies focussed on security. Nevertheless, if we take the data on terrorist incidents of the very State Department as reference, the conclusion is that there was an improvement in the years that followed the end of the cold war. The annual mean of attacks varied from 544,44 between 1982 and 1990 to 352,61 between 1991 and 2003.[43] Accordingly table 4.3 shows that in the period 1996–2003 the main alterations are not given by the number of attacks but by the number of fatalities.

Final Considerations

. . . Leaders and political thinkers such as Antonio Gramsci have long understood the power that emanates from defining the agenda and determining the framework of a debate. The ability to establish preferences tends to be related to intangible power resources such as culture, ideology and attractive institutions.[44]

Being hallucinated by progress, we believed that progress meant forgetting, leaving behind the manifestations of the best we have done, an extremely rich culture of a continent which is native-Indian, European, black, mixed-race and mulatto, whose creativity has not yet found its economical equivalence, whose continuity has not yet found a political correspondence.[45]

The documents analyzed in the previous sections show common ground in terms of defending the posture of international leadership in the Clinton and Bush administrations. Nevertheless, there is a shift in the emphasis from the Republican government regarding governance, in which the prevention and resolution of conflicts are given more prominence. Different from the emphatic speeches of the Clinton period, when democracy was exalted as the ultimate aim in the conquest of peace and prosperity, with Bush, the emphasis is in its operational significance, as one of the means to service of order.

Regarding the characterization of the countries, a conception based on proximity and attitude in relation to liberal democracy and capitalism is maintained. Representative democracy, free market, and the rule of law compose a common core, whose recognition, from the "rest" makes diversity negotiable.

In the view of the U.S. government, the instability factors engendered in the developing world make the increasing international involvement both necessary and inevitable. The defense of this posture does not stem from humanitarian priorities, but from national interests that link security to economic prosperity of the country, its businesses and citizens.

From this perspective, culture and interest are intertwined. The defense of values considered as universal is part of the objective of creating a free and safe world environment for the circulation of goods, services, and American citizens. Based on this conception, the foreign policy unfolds itself in three courses of action: the promotion of the opening of foreign markets; the aid to countries in transition and in development; military intervention in regions in process of collapse or that face aggression from terrorist groups or "rogue" states.

In relation to the first course of action, the two main mechanisms are negotiation of trade agreements and the strengthening of the regulatory power/ability of the multilateral economic institutions. The main targets of commercial liberalization are the transition countries, the biggest area of expansion of exports, which combine little familiarity with the market economy and a protectionist tradition of limited scope, generally aimed toward the support of traditional oligarchies. This situation strengthens the position of the United States, which is capable of presenting a wide and sophisticated agenda, linking the opening of markets with the establishment of regulatory mechanisms of the competing countries.[46] In addition, these mechanisms have their own legislation and that of multilateral organisms as references, in which their influence is notorious. Thus, spreading values such as free enterprise and the rule of law substantially contribute to the realization of the strategies of the Department of State related to expansion of investment, employment, and consumption in its own country.

Despite the success that has been achieved in carrying out these targets, the path is not free from obstacles. On the other side of the negotiating table, one can identify a group of heterogeneous countries that are equally incapable of formulating suitable agendas of international inclusion for these new times. In order to avoid or lessen catastrophic unfolding in this lack of strategic perspective, it becomes urgent to construct a new architecture that legalizes (in general agreement) parameters for this relationship, defining principles, values, and norms, as well as the instruments for vigilance and punishment. In the words of the United States in the OAS, Luis Lauredo, "the devil is in the details."

The expansion of markets and businesses may be made more difficult in different ways: through protectionist discrimination, through the growth of poverty and exclusion, through conflicts that isolate regions from the routes of global capital, and through a sense of insecurity derived from the increase of terrorism. The first is solved by wide-ranging liberalization agreements, invested resources, and expected returns. For the rest, the answers attempt to adequately combine local actions of preventive aid, surgical interventions to isolate and control chaotic situations, and attacks to targets situated in countries accused of supporting terrorism. As the experiences in Afghanistan and Iraq show, the breadth of the interventions may include war and destabilization of the existing order, followed by the imposition of trustworthy authorities.

In the case of Latin America and the Caribbean, knowingly far from the level of conflict observed in the Middle East, the priorities the Department of State programs are the "second generation" reforms. This option is based on four main presuppositions: (1) in the region, the ideological battle against the critics of liberalism is over; (2) the structural reforms are irreversible; (3) the business community, regardless of their country of origin, act based on global logic; (4) there are no significant national restrictions—capable of resisting any negotiation process—in relation to the free circulation of capitals and goods.

As a consequence, the emphasis of the discourse changes, from the unrestricted defense of the market, to the social and cultural barriers that affect development. The neoliberal offensive in favor of opening of markets and deregulation gives way to a strategy that aims to promote initiatives capable of spreading values and practices that strengthen, in the basis of society, the structural reforms implemented by the central power.

On the aid agenda, investments in programs of local action are prioritized, directing resources to the regions that face situations of conflict that are related to the security agenda. In this process, special attention is given to education, to the strengthening of the civil society—especially in the most sensitive areas of governance, related to the violation of legality, to exclusion and discrimination—as well as sustainable development. On a local level, municipal programs—with the consequent decentralization of decision-making processes—favor the adoption of approaches and work methods that transfer the responsibility for solving problems and facing challenges to the community.

Differently from the U.S. governments that clearly conceives its interests and objectives in the hemisphere, the Latin America and the Caribbean lack a perspective that articulates the whole region. The Summit Agreements that have been analyzed demonstrate that there is no questioning regarding the basic grounds of the initiatives proposed by Clinton and Bush. The definition of the agenda and the framework of the debate still remain with the United States.

At the Mar del Plata Summit the differences emerged stronger between MERCOSUR, Venezuela, and the other countries in the hemisphere in relation to the commercial liberation agenda. Argentina, Brazil, and

Venezuela were looking for an agreement to formulate a regional alternative. The main reference is the South American Community of Nations, created in December 2004, through which the three countries promote joint initiatives on fundamental themes such as communications, natural resources, and financing for regional development.[47]

Despite the difference of discourse in relation to the United States, a realistic perspective prevails. The countries that adopt state policies seek for greater autonomy in their international insertion, defining convergences, and differences with the Northern power. Although still restricted to South America, the initiatives of Argentina, Brazil, and Venezuela are aimed at a regional perspective of broader range, and its potential remains open. As Carlos Fuentes's quotation at the beginning of this section correctly synthesizes, Latin America faces the challenges that are characteristic of a region "whose creativity has not yet found its economical equivalence, whose continuity has not yet found a political correspondence."

Notes

1. Warren Christopher, Address and Q&A Session on "Investing in American Leadership," January 15, 1997 in Foreign Affairs of the United States on CD-Rom, 5(1). U.S. Department of State, Bureau of Public Affairs, Washington, DC.

2. Ibid.

3. The international affairs budget includes funds for the activities and programs developed by the Department of State and for the ones that involve foreign policy priorities in other governmental institutions. "What is the International Affairs Budget?" January 21, 2001, on www.state.gov/m/fmp/index.cfm?docid=2342. Accessed on April 30, 2006.

4. Christopher, "Investing."

5. Madeleine Albright, Press Briefing, December 20, 2000, Washington, DC, Office of the Spokesman, U.S. Department of State, on http:// secretary.state.gov/www/statements/2000/001220.html. Accessed on April 30, 2001.

6. U.S.D.S. (U.S. Department of State). Background on International Affairs Resources. Fact sheet released by the Bureau of Public Affairs, December 15, 1999 on www.state.gov/www/budget. Accessed on April 30, 2001.

7. Ibid.

8. Ibid.

9. Ibid

10. USAID, Congressional Presentation FY 2000, Overview of Latin America and the Caribbean, p. 22 on www.usaid.gov/pubs/cp2000/lac/. Accessed on April 30, 2001.

11. Ibid., p. 23.

12. The analysis is based on the USAID document, 2001, chapter 2.

13. USAID, Congressional Presentation FY 2000, Latin America and the Caribbean Presentation, on www.usaid.gov/pubs/cp2000/lac/. Accessed on April 30, 2001.

14. USAID, Congressional Presentation FY 2000, Overview of Latin America and the Caribbean, on www.usaid.gov/pubs/cp2000/lac/. Accessed on April 30, 2001.

15. USAID, Congressional Presentation FY 2000, Overview of Latin America and the Caribbean, on www.usaid.gov/pubs/cp2000/lac/. Accessed on April 30, 2001.

16. Ibid.

17. Luis Lauredo, "Remarks at the Conflict Prevention and Resolution Forum," Washington DC, September 12, 2000, on www.state.gov/p/wha/rt/soa/. Accessed on April 30, 2001.

18. Lauredo, "Toward the Quebec City Summit," Remarks to the Institute of the Americas 2000. Washington, DC, 29 de março em www.state.gov/p/wha/rt/soa/. Accessed on April 30, 2001.

19. Ibid.

20. Cuba is the exception, which was excluded by the United States, based on the argument that the establishment of democracy is a pre-requisite to participate in the summits. See Luis Ayerbe, 2003 O Ocidente e o "Resto": a América Latina e o Caribe na cultura do Império (Buenos Aires: CLACSO-ASDI).

21. Madeleine Albright, "The OAS and the Road to Santiago: Building a Hemispheric Community in the Americas," *Dispatch*, Washington, DC, March 1998, p. 1.

22. Robert Zoellick, "Free Trade and the Hemispheric Hope," Prepared Remarks. Washington, DC, p. 7–8 May, on www.ustr.gov. Accessed May 7, 2001.

23. Ibid., p. 5

24. Ibid.

25. Lino Gutiérrez, Remarks at the Miami Conference on the Caribbean and Latin America, Miami, December 8, 2000, on www.state.gov/www/policy_remarks/2000/001208_gutierrez_ccla.html.

26. Lauredo, Building Hemispheric Democracy. Address at Trinity College. Washington, DC, January 25, 2001, em www.state.gov/p/wha/rt/soa/. Accessed on April 30, 2001.

27. Zoellick, "Free Trade."

28. Madeleine Albright, Remarks to the Council of the Americas, May 4, 1999. Focus on the Issues: The Americas, March, United States Department of State, Bureau of Public Affairs, Washington, D.C., p. 9 on www.state.gov/www/focus_index.html.

29. Declaração de Nuevo Leon 2004 Cúpula Extraordinária de Chefes de Estado e de Governo das Américas http://www.sice.oas.org/FTAA/Nleon/Nleon_p.asp. Accessed on January 15, 2005.

30. Ibid.

31. Ministerial Declaration, 2003.

32. Among the main determinations of the Interamerican Convention against corruption, we can highlight the following: the possibility of criminally prosecuting civil servants that demand or receive benefits, as well as other people involved in this act of offering, promising or bribing in exchange for attitudes or omissions in the development of state officers' responsibilities; the penalties have the United States Foreign Corrupt Practices Act (FCPA) as a reference, which defines cooperation procedures, especially regarding issues such as extradition. (U.S.D.S., 2001b).

33. Albright, "Remarks to the Council of the Americas," May 4, 1999. Focus on the Issues: The Americas, March, United States Department of State, Bureau of Public Affairs, Washington, DC, pp. 9–10 on www.state.gov/www/focus_index.html. Accessed on April 30, 2001.

34. Colin Powell, Remarks at the Council of the Americas' 31st Washington Conference. Washington, DC, May 7, 2001, on www.state.gov /secretary/ rm/2001/. Accessed on July 15, 2001.

35. Roger Noriega, The Bush Administration's Western Hemisphere Policy, January 6, 2004, on http://www.state.gov/p/wha/rls/rm/27975.htm. Accessed on November 20, 2005.

36. Noriega, "The Summit of the Americas. Rescuing the Reform Agenda," American Enterprise Institute, p.1, 27 de outubro, em http: //www.aei.org / publications/pubID.23385,filter.all/pub_detail.asp. Accessed on November 20, 2005.

37. According to data presented by the Minister of Economy of Venezuela, Jose Sojo Reyes, the commercial exchange between the two countries went from 18.491 million dollars in 2002 to 28,922 millions in 2004 thus occupying position 16 among the biggest commercial partners of the United States in the World. (Reyes, 2005).

38. Powell, "Testimony to House Appropriations Subcommittee on Foreign Operations, Export Financing," Washington, DC, May 10, 2001, on www.state.gov/secretary/rm/2001/. Accessed on July 15, 2005.

39. Andrew Natsios, "Testimony before the Senate Appropriations Committee, Subcommittee on Foreign Operations," May 8, 2001, on www.usaid.gov / press/spe_test/testimony/2001/ty010508.html. Accessed on July 15, 2001.

40. U.S.D.S. Strategic Plan 2000, p. 13 on www.state.gov/www/budget/strat plan_index.html. Accessed on April 30, 2001.

41. U.S.D.S. 2003 Strategic Plan Fiscal Years 2004–2009, p. 1 on http://www.usaid.gov/policy/budget/state_usaid_strat_plan.pdf. Accessed on November 20, 2005.

42. Bush, George W. President Discusses War on Terror at National Endowment for Democracy, Washington, DC, October 6, 2005. http://www.white house.gov/news/releases/2005/10/20051006-3.html. Accessed on November 20, 2005.

43. U.S.D.S. 2004, *Patterns of Global Terrorism* Release by the Office of the Coordinator of Counterterrorism, p. 176, in http: //www.state.gov/ s/ct/rls/pgtrpt/2003/c12153.htm. Accessed on November 20 2005.

44. Joseph Nye, *O Paradoxo do Poder Americano* (São Paulo: Editora da Unesp, 2002), p. 37.

45. Arizpe, Lourdes "Cultura, creatividad y gobernabilidad," em Mato, Daniel. (Comp.) *Estudios Latinoamerianos sobre cultura y transformaciones sociales en tiempos de globalización*, (Buenos Aires: CLACSO-ASDI, 2001), p. 33.

46. Analyzing the diplomacy of presidential summits, Rojas Aravena (2000) detaches the difficulties of adaptation of the Latin American countries to follow the execution of the initiatives approved in each meeting. Adding the agreements and proposals approved between 1990 and 1999 in the Summits of the Americas (295), of the Latin American Summits (471), of the Group of Rio (347) and the APEC for the Cooperation in the Pacific Basin (84), it is arrived a total of 1.197 initiatives. In the case of the developed countries, that count on a permanent team of negotiators specialized in the diverse subjects of the agenda; the systematic accompaniment of the decision-making process is possible. In the case of the Latin American countries, the structure of the foreign policy ministries lacks this level of expertise, compromising the

elaboration of national strategies capable to tie to the macro objectives with the detailing of proposals in the scope of the techniques commissions that elaborate the initiatives to be argued in the presidential meetings.

47. The South American Community of Nations (CASA), founded at the third South American summit in Cuzco, places as one of its fundamental principles the "determination to develop an integrated South American space in political, social, economic, environmental and infrastructure, that fortifies the own identity of South America and contributes, from a subregional perspective and in joint with other experiences of regional integration, for the fortification of Latin America and the Caribbean and grants a greater gravitation and representation to them in the international forums" (Declaration of Cuzco). In March of 2005, the Presidents of Argentina, Brazil and Venezuela emit, in Montevideo, a joint declaration, in which they propose more systematic efforts for the advance in the agreements of CASA "relative to the fortification of the Telesur and the Petrosur, the creation of a not-reimbursable Fund to take care of Fund to take care of the problems acute than they originate themselves in the poverty, a South American Bank for the Development and others". Ministério das Relaãões Exteriores do Brasil, 2005.

Chapter 5

Plan Colombia—A Key Ingredient in the Bush Doctrine

German Rodas Chavez

Without addressing—even briefly—the reality of the Republic of Colombia of the twentieth century, no explanation about the present situation can be coherent. That is why it is necessary to recall some of the historic events. Often there is insistence on a justification for aspects of Plan Colombia, which purport that the roots of Colombian violence are a result of recent historical events and, centered in the diabolic behavior of radical and extremist groups that supposedly have emerged, including the victory of the Cuban Revolution. From this perspective, only when those revolutionary processes are severely and strongly confronted will a horizon of peace be opened for Colombia. Since Colombia's violent origins are derived from other factors, they are addressed below.

The economic crisis of 1929 affected Latin America as well as the United States, generating great dissatisfaction for the Colombian population. The Liberal Party took on this crisis, as was evident in their propaganda campaign, in which were included slogans such as *customs protectionism*, a subject that attracted the national bourgeoisie, alongside the proposal for social changes in favor of the middle and working classes. Such proposals resulted in the first ever Liberal victory in national elections in the year 1930. The first Liberal president then proposed the Vanguard Legislation to realize Liberal goals, such as the eight hour working day, a six day work week, and the setting of a minimum wage.

Thanks to the above-mentioned conditions, in 1934, the Liberal candidacy of the national bourgeoisie was handed to Pedro Alfonso Lopez Pumarejo. It was more broadly accepted when he incorporated in his platform, aspirations mostly felt by various parts of Colombian society. This opened the way to left wing liberalism, led by the charismatic leader Jorge Eliecer Gaitan, who gave his enthusiastic support for elections.

In this framework Lopez Pumarejo triumphed, who during his time in office obtained the support of the Communist Party of Colombia which resulting from those same elections, he interjected with his own candidacy. Once the Second Latin American Conference of Communist Parties was held in October 1934, however, according to the decisions of the meeting, he chose to support "the national bourgeoisies." This became evident in Colombia through his support for the then-president, Lopez.

Lopez Pumarejo set forth a series of measures for his term that he had named during his electoral campaign "The On-Going Revolution." This series included three basic reforms: fiscal, educational, and agricultural. Shortly after his inauguration, the Liberal president established a plan for his government agenda and imposed, taxes according to the wealth of tax payers, thus allowing him to have a better national budget. This reform facilitated the creation of teachers' training schools, the construction of schools, and the opening of secondary level educational centers that were free of charge and secular. At the same time the state assumed the functions of the only "deliverer" of bachelor's degrees and created the National University as a decentralized, autonomous institution.

The treatment of the agrarian issue was fundamental in Colombia at that time. Although 70 percent of the population lived in the countryside, property was distributed almost exclusively for the benefit of great planters and land owners, who at the same time were in the minority. On the one hand, they benefited from "leasing" their lands to 90 percent of landless farmers, though on several occasions they were owners of "idle land." In the face of this reality, the government submitted a bill stating the principle that land ownership would only be recognized after verification of the relationship with the Colombian productive system. The piece of land and lands not cultivated in the past 10 years would become government property to be redistributed among those who had no land.

This initiative received direct opposition in the Congress from conservatives, deeply linked to the large estates, and from "right" wing liberal groups, who at the end of Lopez Pumarejo's term, chose a candidate who would not interfere with land ownership and would forget the reformist ideals, and instead would give way to the manufacturing boom by substituting imports. This trend succeeded because of the outbreak of World War II and its effect upon the economies of countries like Colombia. The relative prosperity of the period that came afterward was used by the ruling liberal sector to promote a divide and conquer strategy inside the workers movement and to break away from the unitarian Trade Union Confederation of Colombia.

The above-mentioned circumstances upset the liberal left which was led by Gaitan. These forces supported Lopez Pumarejo's plan of returning the focus of government to his original agenda, which in 1942, after a nationalist campaign full of promises on immediate social changes allowed him to win in the election that year. However, the liberal right wing allied with the conservatives and attempted a military coup in July 1944. The popular mobilization prevented the attempted coup, but the regime was left fractured without the real conditions to establish a presidency and this ultimately led to the president's resignation in 1945.

In the elections held in 1946, Gaitan ran as a reformist presidential candidate with a social agenda, in which agrarian reform theme was one of his focal points. The liberal right then fielded another candidate thus facilitating the victory of conservatives, through division of votes. The victorious party brought into office the director of the National Federation of Coffee Growers, Mariano Ospina Pérez. In his first two years in power, he caused the assassination of no less than 15,000 people, in an unprecedented move also characterized by the 1948 assassination of Gaitan.

"The Bogotazo," as the attempt of popular upraisal after Gaitan's death was called, initially endangered the governance of conservatives. However, it failed because a vanguard was missing, capable of wisely leading the movement and it unleashed a rage from the conservative power structure resulting from their conviction that the time had come to bury their opponents. Due to these circumstances, repression and violence from the state were institutionalized broadly throughout Colombia.

In the face of such brutal conditions, agrarian self-defense groups emerged. These groups were nothing more than farmers led by local leaders of liberal orientation. Through this framework, the conflict expanded throughout the country. On more than one occasion, groups of farmers rose up with liberals, as the only way to ensure survival in the face of governmental violence and state terrorism that had been established as mechanisms to silence the voice of the popular sectors in Colombia.

In 1950, the conservative government intensified the policy of "blood and fire in the razed land" and the great owners of cattle farms financed the creation of "counter guerrilla forces." This resulted in confrontations of authentic savagery, devastating the Andean region. Furthermore, the agrarian self-defense groups, dubbed by the government as "gangs," were formed by the victims of government violence but dedicated themselves to steal and plunder.

In the midst of these conditions and, as a unique case in Latin America, the Colombian Communist Party chose to arm itself and struggle through a policy they called "self-defense of the masses." In this context they made every effort to persuade the "guerrillas" to abandon the local and sectarian vision of the struggle. From such a perspective, they also organized a broad mass front against repression and banditry and contributed to the creation of the National Guerilla Conference, held in Boyaca in September 1952. Representatives of the 13 major fronts attended this conference that issued a platform linking the armed struggle with agrarian reform and formation of popular governments in areas controlled by guerrillas. The most progressive groups of rebels fulfilled the agreements, but the rest maintained their local vision of the confrontation.

Subsequently, the progressive guerilla groups got together in a second Congress in June 1953 and chose Jose Guadalupe Salcedo as Supreme Commander of the Guerrilla Forces of the Plains, and drafted juridical rules and regulations that covered military, administrative, and organizational matters. This was done in the face of the ferocious repression of the conservative government. The guerrillas attempted to overcome this repression institutionally, through a military coup–d'etat on June 13, 1953, bringing to power General Gustavo Rojas Pinilla. He tried to pacify the conflict with slogans such as "peace, justice, and liberty for all."

Rojas Pinilla tried to prove that his task was outside of any partisanship, liberal or conservative, and as part of that image, he called for demobilization of the "rebels," 4,000 men who until then had fought in the self-defense units in the plains. Guadalupe Salcedo himself laid down the weapons but shortly after, was assassinated in a cowardly manner as many fighters had believed the pacifist speech of General Rojas Pinilla.

The guerilla group, encouraged by the communists in Tolima, was the only one that remained armed. In this area, the struggle became more intense when some of the liberal groups, who had fought together with the self-defense, joined the military forces to confront the guerilla. The struggle somehow became different. The deterioration of Rojas's power became evident as a result of the international situation. Moreover, there was his expressed attempt, an inappropriate attempt against the "order," to build a political grouping that would break the bipartite model that was being shaped by the liberal and conservative leadership to plunder the economy of Colombia to their benefit. This political reality took place in the middle of the coffee price fall, thus paralyzing the national economy and bringing about the urban workers' struggle that started to connect the rural groups who remained fighting.

With the possibility of an agreement between the organized workers and the sectors of farmers in arms, liberals and conservatives organized a way out in 1956. Alarmed by this possibility, leaders of both political parties began to oppose Rojas Pinilla. Led by Liberal politician (and former president) Alberto Heras Camargo, high level discussions between liberal and conservative party elites led to a series of agreements aimed at restoring bipartisan civilian government. Resistance to the military regime culminated in May 1957 when Rojas Pinilla was removed from power by a five-man military junta that was to serve as an interim government until bipartisan civilian rule was restored in 1958. For the next 16 years the agreement known as the National Front, institutionalized bipartisan rule in Colombia. This arrangement was civilian in character but not democratic. The Front ended the partisan violence of the prior decade but it did not address the fundamental inequalities in the country epitomized in poverty, marginality, and growing injustice for the great majority. In the process the National Front provided fertile ground for the development in the 1960s of armed guerrilla groups like the Revolutionary Armed Forces of Colombia (FARC) and the National Liberation Army (ELN), two groups that exist as armed Actors until present day and serve as targets of Plan Colombia, the primary focus for the remainder of the chapter.

Brief History of the Plan Colombia

Plan Colombia (CP) was named with the purpose of not only making it appear as though the designation of operations would involve and be implemented inside the Colombian territory, but also because "supposedly" it was the very initiative of Colombians, articulated by the government of the then president Pastrana. The first version of the Plan Colombia was developed in the last quarter of 1998 and was followed by amendments until August of 1999. Nevertheless, in September of the same year, substantial changes of content took place in the CP, clarifying who had actually worked on this geopolitical, military, and economic initiative.

In December 1998, President Pastrana submitted the Plan as "a set of alternative development projects that would channel the shared efforts of the government and multilateral institutions of the Colombian society." The Plan seemed to be the central theme for the articulation of a peace policy, since it considered the creation of economic and social conditions to propitiate the social coordination. Furthermore, in relation to the presence of illegal crops, the Plan submitted a nonmilitary initiative thus emphasizing preventive actions, and strengthening all the control initiatives.

A second version of the CP was submitted in June 1999, during the meeting of European, Latin American, and Caribbean heads of state that took place in Rio de Janeiro. In the new version, not very different from the previous one, the idea for the "promotion of environmental sustainability" was reinforced. The authors of the Plan attempted to make the European countries finance everything related to the substitution of illegal crops, but they did not succeed.

In any case, the two versions of the Plan, through which they attempted to involve the countries from the north, maintained the political, social, and economic strategies linked to negotiations and reform. Since the Plan did not interest all the northern countries, or once they had learned about what was occurring, they suggested their acceptance of the plans to the Colombians, who with the support of friendly countries close to the area of conflict, could not resolve their problems. As a result they decided to draft a third version, openly negotiated between American and Colombian officials.

The third version, of September 1999, underwent substantial modifications. The most important change centered its action on the antidrug struggle. The eradication of illegal crops with the participation of the guerillas took a back seat and the focal point was to destroy every link of drug traffickers with the armed groups, which would be possible through a military confrontation, although it was not expressed openly. This way, the Plan fully endorsed the North American antidrug policy and also shaped in the region, the perspectives required by the transnational financial capital for their development and expansion. The third version of the Plan enabled Pastrana to negotiate all possible support from the Clinton administration and its allies. In the framework of bilateral talks the Colombian president requested the world public $1.5 billion for the implementation of the coordinated "project" between the United States and Colombia.

A fourth version of Plan Colombia was circulated at the beginning of 2000, this time with the expressed audience being the Europeans and Japanese. It skillfully emphasized the theme of biodiversity, the environment, and ecological protection required in areas where drugs were produced "in complicity with the guerrilla." It brought about a situation that was in opposition to the European and Japanese interests and therefore prevented the care of an area that sooner than later could become an ecological area of strategic support for the central areas in the globalized economy. In brief, the fourth version was drafted so that Europe and Japan could assimilate the message that the Plan seeks to also defend their strategic environmental interests.

The existence of four versions of Plan Colombia had the purpose to cause the pertinent readings in the different arenas in which the Colombia conflict and its nearest regions were raised. On the one hand, it was a way to involve the most different sectors of the developed world in support of the U.S. policy in the Andean region. On the other hand it became a perverse information mechanism regarding a policy of accomplished events that had happened in the region. It has been estimated that under this initiative and thanks to the Colombian budget, $7 billion have been outlaid, with the support of the United States, to the bilateral agreements with Europe and other countries and to the resources coming from multilateral and international institutions. While the nature of the Plan Colombia was discussed, keeping in mind the potential allies and the North American levels of contribution, it was evident that through separate lines other tactical and strategic actions were developed that, with no doubt, were part of the Plan Colombia and that today are supplementary with the same geopolitical articulation.

However, for instance, the North American pressures on the old border conflict between Ecuador and Peru, from which the different governments, the local bourgeoisie, and the war businessmen have benefited, to be rapidly overcome through the signing of a peace agreement by presidents Mahuad and Fujimori in 1999. This was done in the middle of commitments and offers from the United States, totally unfulfilled to date, that the governments of Ecuador and Peru were to receive $3 million dollars to consolidate multiple development work in the border area.

Beyond the importance of overcoming territorial conflicts, the pressures to resolve the confrontation were based on the U.S. desire that the armed forces of Ecuador and Peru transfer their military and war activity to the new warlike confrontation foreseen in the Plan Colombia between the regional armed forces and the "drug-guerilla" forces.

Moreover, while the nature of the Plan was being negotiated in April 1999, and as a corollary to the contacts that began in January of the same year, the American Embassy and the Ecuadorian government presided over by Jamil Mahuad signed a "provisional agreement" to turn over the port and airport of the city of Manta to the U.S. Armed Forces to "control and fight" the alleged drug-traffic activities especially from Colombia. This way, the North Americans took action to substitute their military base in Panama. This was done because on the return of the Canal to its legitimate owner, they, (the North Americans) had lost the military base. This decision is now considered by some U.S. policy makers as a mistake, as one can understand from reading the document Santa Fe IV.

For all the above, Ecuador was the U.S. target, in relation to the military base, a position made more crucial when Venezuela refused to install it in their territory by the nationalist policy implemented in Caracas following the election of Chavez in 1998.

Later, in November 1999, the national government of Ecuador authorized its Minister of Foreign Affairs Benjamin Ortiz, obedient employee of North American interests, to sign the "Cooperation Agreement between the Government of the Republic of Ecuador and the Government of the United States of America, concerning the right to have access and use by the American Government the facilities of the base of the Ecuadorian Air Forces in the city of Manta, for anti-drug air activities."

The said agreement was not known or approved by the National Congress plenary, as is provided in the constitution of Ecuador. On the contrary, in an inappropriate and unconstitutional manner, it was ratified by the Congress Commission on International Affairs, presided over by Heiz Moeller, later Minister of Foreign Affairs of Ecuador.

This is how the North American military base started to operate according to the geopolitical vision of those who long ago had already defended the strategic role of the Plan Colombia. All this was implemented through a policy of "consultations" with other countries. Different versions of the Plan were submitted to confuse and deceive the different partners and possible allies.

In summary, a Plan was designed from the early 1990s, at the end of the so-called cold war, when the antidrug crusade was shaped, as a political tool and pressure mechanism for other matters of interest for the United States in the region, and as a new way for Washington to get involved in internal affairs of each of the Andean countries.

To follow up the strategic objectives of the United States, on May 16, 2001, the Andean Regional Initiative (ARI) was implemented, which should be considered as the second stage of the Plan Colombia. The commitment of the Andean countries is evident in this strategic frame, discreetly negotiated with the Clinton administration, to counteract the effects of the CP in the region.

The strategy of ARI has been improved upon by President George W. Bush in the framework of the globalizing project of neoliberalism meant to put in motion the Free Trade Agreement in the context of a series of actions tending to stop the social uneasiness in the Andean region caused by the Plan Colombia, and in opposition, propitiate the shape of a less overheated environment that would allow, at some point in time, the illumination of the next step: FTAA.

The Plan Colombia: A Geoeconomic Project

Throughout its history, Capitalism has maintained a characteristic that is inseparable from its development. The polarity generated by the existing contradictions in the economic relations, between the countries that have concentrated wealth and world power, and a periphery of underdeveloped countries, among which are the countries of the Andean Region, that constitute a larger portion of the world population, have had poverty as a common characteristic. The polarity and asymmetry of relations between the center and the periphery of countries have been coincident with the very existence of the capitalist system that has built up its framework on the basis of this reality and above all, through the adequate control of all possible means of the conflicts that could prevent strategic growth.

In the environment of polarization of the world system that has taken place in the middle of what is known as globalization, this phenomenon is nothing but the globalization of capital in a context that assumes the transition of national monopolistic capitalism to transnational monopolist capitalism. Today there is an increase in the asymmetry between the center and the periphery of countries owing to the investment of the center in the periphery and the extraction from it to the center with abundant exploitation. When this extraction becomes difficult, the globalizers of neoliberalism have decided to act immediately to prevent any imbalance in their project. This happens at present in the Andean region due to many reasons, among which is the presence of irregular military forces in arms, because of the presence of economic and political groups supported by the drug-trafficking or by the growing mobilization of social sectors opposite to the prevailing model.

This circumstance is fully expressed in the context of the Plan Colombia, an intention that, though it is in a military-geopolitical stage, has a geoeconomic background. What they are trying to impose is the Andean Regional Initiative, as a prelude to FTAA, to meet the final objective through bilateralism; in other words, Free Trade Agreements (FTA), the discussion of which is the tone of the U.S. relations agenda with many Latin American countries.

In the context of neoliberal globalization, the North American regime has great interest to empower its industrial and commercial activity to the maximum, with the purpose of not repeating the accumulation crisis experienced in the recent past. Also, part of their expectation is to handle the strategic reserves that exist in Andean biodiversity and hope to use them in due time whenever the inputs or raw materials are needed in their industrial activity. It is a two-way interest in which the strategic vision of the exploitation of Andean natural resources is more important than open areas of the markets, which, obviously, in no case can it be opposite to North American interests.

The above discussions affirm that there is a geoeconomic desire demanding the construction of commercial corridors of raw materials flowing in the Andean region to North American industrial production, and furthermore, to favor the transportation of industrial wastes from the United States to the Pacific Ocean, and above all, the placing of sweat-factory production in the region. These same corridors will take the rich Andean biodiversity to the industrial zone of North America.

The corridors located in the Andean region will be an extension of those with the same geoeconomic approach, irrespective of specific peculiarities. They are intended to be built in the Northern region of the continent through the Panama Puebla Plan (PPP) involving Mexico and Central America. With the Panama Puebla Plan and the Plan Colombia, the United States attempts to ensure the industrial operation of their country and strengthen their national economy.

Ecuador and Colombia: Communicating Vessels of a Military Policy

In June 2002, Alvaro Uribe Velez won the presidential elections in Colombia. In October of the same year, Colonel Lucio Gutierrez Borbua won the elections to be proclaimed as president in Ecuador. Uribe obtained the victory with a clear political proposal stressing the military character of the confrontation of the groups rising up in arms. Gutierrez obtained his victory after a process of institutional crises in Ecuador during which he played a great role. On January 21, 2000, he along with important social and political sectors defeated, former president Mahuad, head of the government, who dollarized the economy in Ecuador and allowed the greatest robbery of the banking system against the Ecuadorians.

Lucio Gutierrez, in his electoral campaign, was able to articulate a discourse that generated expectation, both internal and external. He was able to define political and social agreements that showed an apparent will to respond to the interest of the dispossessed, all of which made people assume, aside from his allies and voters, that they had before them, a leader with a commitment to the structural transformations, an anticolonial image, and a willingness to act on behalf of the national sovereignty.

Regarding the Plan Colombia, Gutierrez was critical, and tried to show its lack of focus on problems unrelated to the people of Ecuador. He stressed it more than once, specially in the first electoral campaign. In this respect, he even questioned, although in a weak manner, the installation and functioning of the Manta Military Base. As a presidential pre-candidate he received an essay from the author about the conflicts in Colombia and said the following: "It will serve me because I am dedicating myself to the study of this problem and to prevent them from using us in a matter out of our concern and only the North Americans are the ones who will benefit from it."

Nevertheless, despite the change of conduct and the proposals of Gutierrez between the first and second electoral round, it seemed as though Colombia and Ecuador would have presidents with different approaches on the Plan Colombia, an asymmetry of thoughts, which in the end seemed to favor the international policy of Ecuador.

This appraisal changed rapidly after concrete events. One of them took place when at the end of 2002 the "Capilla del Hombre" (Chapel of Man) was inaugurated in Quito (a work conceived by the Ecuadorian painter Guayasamin). Presidents Hugo Chavez and Fidel Castro were present at the inauguration. Gutierrez, then, literally escaped from the country so as not to meet them and made every effort to talk to Uribe, who had taken over his functions in August of that year.

If what has been mentioned is an anecdote, other considerations point out that Ecuador and Colombia progressively started to forge a concerted

attitude regarding the Plan Colombia most likely under the guidance of the
U.S. State Department. This reality became concrete from the moment
Gutierrez succeeded in the first electoral round and made efforts to show his
servility to the United States. This behavior increased after his first official
visit as president to the United States. The policy was fabricated after
Gutierrez started to abandon his principles before the United States, who
then reported this to the then minister of Foreign Affairs of Ecuador and the
indigenous leader Nina Pacari Vega, among other officials.

The change in Gutierrez's performance will always leave a question
unanswered: Did he give up his ideas to obtain supposed support from the
United States in favor of its government, or did the performance of the
regime in this and other matters disclose the convictions that, strategically,
they remained covered in a counterinsurgent plan fabricated to provoke
January 21, 2000 and the subsequent events?

With the government of Lucio Gutierrez devoted to the strategic interest
of the U.S. president, Uribe's military actions gained unexpected strength.
The communicating vessels of militarism in the Andean region had been built
to perfection. The tactic that the Ecuadorian Army should look after the
Northern border once the conflict in the border with Peru was over, was, in
Uribe's mind a decision that could not be postponed.

In this climate of events, the Armed Forces of Colombia outlined a strata-
gem which was to "sweep" insurgent focus from Colombia toward their border with Ecuador, and then wait for the Ecuadorian military to deal a final
blow. In this way, the dirty work would be in the hands of the Ecuadorian
military, who mobilized a huge contingent of men and their war arsenal to
the Northern border, and all this in the middle of serious concerns of
important Ecuadorian military officials.

To favor the Ecuadorian military work under strict surveillance from the
Manta U.S. military base, Gutierrez was expected to build three "supply"
posts in favor of the North American troops to supplement the activities of
the military base. This initiative was not fulfilled because of the general
opposition of the country when it was brought before the National Congress
with ridiculous justifications like the one affirmed by Minister Patricio
Zuquilanda, who said that the supply posts located in the Ecuadorian forest
would help control El Niño. As it is known, El Niño is a climatic risk factor
in the continent of specific causes with its origin in the Pacific Ocean that
surrounds the coasts of Ecuador.

The political crisis and the questionable arguments of the Minister of
Foreign Affairs forced the government to withdraw its initial proposal
regarding the so-called supply post, not without showing the differential
practice of the regime in relation to the tactical interest of the Plan Colombia
and its mentors. The skepticism of Ecuadorian officials about their projected
role on the Colombian border caused problems for both the United States
and Uribe.

In the face of this reality, the Colombians have looked for mechanisms to
de-legitimize the Ecuadorian Armed Forces. For instance, they magnified the

phenomenon of traffic of weapons as a formula of pressure aimed at changing their behavior and opinion regarding participation in the conflict with Colombia. Under this pretext a concerted and permanent blackmail against the government of President Gutierrez has been witnessed. Gutierrez has had to put up with the constant denunciations of alleged contributions to his electoral campaign of economic resources coming from persons linked to the drug-trade and of political groups from other countries. All this was done not precisely to enhance the performance of the government and the country, but rather to pressurize him to take up the duties originally assigned to Ecuador in Plan Colombia for this period.

What has been said above has its support, but there are serious suspicions that in Ecuador a policy of fait accompli is under operation that will favor the Colombian warlike interests and that under the protection of the Ecuadorian government, of some police and military officials and of the Minister of Foreign Affairs. They implement actions like when one of the most important political-military officials of the Revolutionary Armed Forces of Columbia (FARC) was made prisoner on January 2, 2004. In the City of Quito, the guerrilla fighter Simon Trinidad (detention that was perpetrated by Colombian agents), who was immediately deported to Colombia, in the middle of inadequate and irrelevant official explanations, opposite to the statements made by the American Ambassador in Ecuador, Kristie Kenney: "Ecuador must protect itself and protect Colombia." Such words seem to define the profile of the official policy of the regime of Gutierrez, subjected in this matter, as well as in economic management, to the formula of those who, since the Monroe Doctrine, control the region for their exclusive interests. This extent is demonstrated by the visits of the Chief of the U.S. Southern Command, James T. Hill, to meet with the military and police leaders to "receive information on the defense plans implemented by Ecuador in the Northern border."

What to Do?

This chapter concludes with some reflections for the region allowing the widest social and political sectors to assume the historic role that they are to play in Plan Colombia and its sequels. It also dwells on the region's response to neoliberal globalization, on the basis of the understanding that the economic, political, and social model is the real support of the Plan Colombia.

It is imperative to start a true process of regional unity with the widest sectors of the population. To meet this goal it is necessary, also, to find the proper mechanism to overcome the false contradictions between what is called the "politicized civil society" and the political parties with a struggling tradition for a new social, political, and economic order. The widest unit must overcome every reductionism and any sectarianism. At a time when a crisis oppresses the Andean region, it is not possible to exclude any sector that is victim of the neoliberal globalizing model and of the violence expressed in all its forms. At the same time, it supposes the articulation of an appeal of unity with a deep anti-imperialist content. As things are, one of the sectors that should be incorporated as an ally in the anti-neoliberal struggle is the productive one, led by the financial and banking sectors to the total crisis. Moreover, this sector in the Andean region has been deeply beaten in its development due to state violence and the military objectives of the Colombia Plan in such a way that it has made a wide range of men and women willing to confront the Plan violence and cruelty of the economic system that has divided them.

In the Andean world, given its multicultural and multinational variety, it is indispensable to establish, in this broad social unity, agreements that will incorporate the expectations of a mestizo world and of the Indian peoples in the same unity of action and in the same line of work under an integrating vision of national unity and respect for the widest diversity. This is fundamental because the racist deviations and the exacerbation of ethnocentric postures contribute to the desegregation of the social struggle and to the configuration of a superimposed world, in which the Indian peoples would seem to have objectives diametrically different from the rest of the regional collectivity. Therefore, in this field, the fracturing of national unity should be prevented, because it contributes to the game of neoliberal interests in their perspective to wipe out the construction of the national state—one of the fundamental strategic tasks of our region.

From the project of the Andean unity, they are to strengthen the links with Mercado Comun del Cono Sur (Southern Cone Common Market) (MERCOSUR) as a fundamental tool to lay the foundations for Latin American action, in the strategic vision to attain concerted common actions that will allow for an effective self-determination of the people, the full exercise of sovereignty and the development of economic and social policies that will contribute to the democratization of our countries, and of course, the quest for the solutions to structural problems, in the middle of which injustice should be defeated to build peace and equity.

The Defense of the State

According to the arguments discussed in the previous paragraph it is precise to advance ideas not only concerning the construction of the national state, but to empower every effort to prevent the qualitative rupture of the present states. Under the excuse of modernizing them, or to put it better, to sell them in the middle of privatization, they intend to provoke a situation of asset stripping the state. They favor the invasion of any financial superstructure that will prevent the elemental regulation of societies and that will respond to the decisions of the great transnational financial capital. Intervention is also expressed in the geopolitical and military field as it happens with Plan Colombia. These actions aim to destroy the environment and loot natural resources to benefit the Northern countries often done with the cover of opposing money laundering and drug trafficking.

The Defense of the National Sovereignty

The subjection of the state, its institutions, and society as a whole to the predominant purposes of the hegemonic countries and of neoliberal globalization leads to a growing process of denationalization and the loss of the national identity. In this environment, the ideological manipulation of certain institutions, like the armed forces, is an additional element with which work has been done to fracture any patriotic performance. More so, under the excuse of the existence of "common enemies," military corporative actions have been articulated to confront them, thus bringing about the perspective of a military confrontation and, therefore, the design of regional war scenarios.

In this respect, the idea of the indispensable support to counterinsurgent actions has also been encouraged to local armies by the military forces of the hegemonic country close to the region—and assumingly a natural ally in the struggle against the "evil forces," as is the United States of America. Looking at things as they are, as it happened in Ecuador, the risk of infecting the region with military bases is a growing reality in the face of which the defense of sovereignty becomes indispensable; more so, when the national sovereignty is affected not only from the concerted military occupation, but also through the presence of ideological superstructures that erode the social conscience and deform the culture of its peoples. Furthermore and due to the absorption of national economies, because of the expressed interference of the transnational financial capital that imposes all sorts of submission to their interests, the phenomenon of the growing loss of the national sovereignty is a circumstance that already wounds our dignity. It is for all this that the defense of national sovereignty has different connotations and some fronts of struggle, under the common denominator of the search for respect of national values, of the territory, of the culture of peoples, and the history of countries, among other things.

The Struggle for Power and Democracy

The control of ruling classes and of the prevailing systems over the institutionality of our countries to ensure the governance that will benefit them has displaced the horizon of some progressive sectors and the Left, as well as certain social groups for the possibility of articulating a project for power.

While we are already witnesses to growing signs of crisis and the decay of neoliberalism, it is also true that we have still not been able to articulate adequate answers before this circumstance. We are pursuing the wrong perspective of only attaining the economic balance, and leaving aside the political and social context. This is perhaps due to the influence of those concepts that put forward the idea that only "in a proletariat dictatorship" will it be possible to build the authentic democracy, under which formula, in the middle of the accumulation of forces and of the development of he struggle, there has been no work to consolidate the forms of ideological and political power nor have the substantial values of democracy been grasped. Still in some places there are discussions on the false dichotomy between the democratic and the revolutionary, when it is evident that the revolutionary goes through the defense of participatory democracy with high content of proposals, as it happened, for example, with the election of Luis Garzon as the mayor of Bogotá—electoral success that proved to all of the Colombian society that it is possible to build a peace proposal in front of a policy of state terrorism.

Support for the Search for Peace in Colombia on the Basis of Political Negotiation

The indispensable action that all the social sectors should take of opinion, of political leadership, and of a democratic exercise of power is the negotiated search for peace in Colombia. It is not possible to maintain the levels of indifference before the events that for decades have affected the Colombian people; more so, when at this point in time the levels of confrontation have been established under the indispensable pretext to maintain interfering policies in our countries by the United States.

The countries of the Andean region, as well as those of the MERCOSUR, are convened to contribute the necessary democratic mechanisms to strengthen peace, justice, and equity, which excluded the authentic explosives of the conflict that Colombia is living.

In this setting, it is imperative to promote, as a valid mechanism to promote the development of our peoples, the political negotiation of the parties in conflict in Colombia. More so, the attempts to spread militarist governmental policies to overcome the Colombian crisis will not but favor the predation of every integrationist desire and in the wrong way strengthen the consolidation of bilateral forms of relation of our countries with the central countries. These forms of relations are a frame that with the excuse of consolidating the political-military relations of Latin American countries with the United States will conclude promoting, in all spheres, the formula through which dependency and inequity will reach the highest expression, in comparison with the interest of building the great homeland dreamt by Miranda, Bolivar, Marti, and the men and women of our America who struggle to consolidate a united region capable of building its own historic destiny, apart from every tutelage.

Chapter 6

Amazonia, MERCOSUR, and the South American Regional Integration

Enrique Amayo

There is no need to prove it. Geography images themselves are highly suggestive
Da Cunha, "Primeira Parte"[1]

Introduction

Euclides da Cunha wrote the above words in one of his many books about the Amazon. This prolific writer and thinker whose ideas are key to understanding the process through which Brazil ceased to be a monarchy and became an independent republican country is known both in his home country (Brazil) and abroad rather as the celebrated author of *Os Sertões:*

> One of the main books in Brazil's history . . . it gave rise to over 10 thousand research projects, as professor Roberto Ventura said in his lecture in the 2002 event *Semana Euclidiana* [Euclides' Week]. Scholars researching the works by Euclides da Cunha came together for this annual meeting in São José do Rio Pardo, a city in São Paulo State. [In the 2002 Week] no more than two papers focused on the works Euclides da Cunha wrote about the Amazon region.[2]

In 2004, events were organized throughout Brazil to commemorate the hundredth anniversary of *Os Sertões's*[3] publication. However, his writings about the Amazon are not well known, even in Brazil. In 1903, he was a member of the team the Brazilian foreign minister, Baron of Rio Branco, appointed to define the borders between Brazil and Peru, thus ending the disputes between the two countries over a huge area in the Amazon. This is when da Cunha collected the valuable data about the Amazon included in his writings.[4] There was a point in time when these disputes almost created a bellicose situation. Euclides wrote these words, "There is no need to prove it. Geography images themselves are highly suggestive" to argue, from a military perspective (i.e., geopolitically and strategically) that should a war break out those disputed lands could benefit either his country, Brazil, in case troops came from East, or Peru, if troops came from West.[5]

In the early twentieth century, da Cunha studied the Amazon and pointed out several relevant issues to that date, including the main points in the current debate about regional integration.[6] In his view, large construction works were needed to prevent a war in the area. For example, he suggested that Brazil ought to build a railroad (*Transacreana*). Since the land under dispute could bring advantages to Peru, a railroad would make up for the loss from the Brazilian perspective. He discusses this problem in a 14-page work that concludes, "Furthermore it is vital to see this railroad as a great international road for an alliance that is pro-civilization, and pro-peace."[7] Today, his thoughts could be deemed as pro-integration, pro-peace, and against hegemonic stands.

Another issue da Cunha thought was relevant to Brazil's future was to have an access to the Pacific Ocean. He believed the United States' control of the Pacific coast had been vital for it to become a global power, and da Cunha wanted a similar situation for Brazil, therefore he was motivated to explore the problems related to this area.[8]

A few years ago, I wrote that:

> From our perspective, the Amazon will not remain apart from the Pacific Ocean. Sooner or later the links will be established, and the natural exit will be through Peru; we call it *natural because* it is the shortest distance, and the less difficult, between the Brazilian Amazon and the Pacific coast. You only need to look at maps to come to this conclusion.[9]

Unfortunately, at that time the author was not aware that da Cunha had produced some of the most interesting ideas about the Amazon. He studied almost the same lands and borders that interest me. Of course, there was a big difference: in addition to examining maps in libraries, he traveled to those places multiple times, and visited those borders, unfortunately the author could only accomplish the first part.

This chapter focuses on the integration of issues from the Brazilian perspective. Brazil, the largest country in South America[10] has a coastline on the Atlantic Ocean only. So how could Brazil access the Pacific Basin that is now the fastest growing economic region at global level?[11]. For the integration to become real, Brazil needs a connection to the South American countries with coasts on the Pacific, especially Peru. Brazil is the largest member of MERCOSUR (the Southern Market Treaty that includes Argentina, Paraguay, and Uruguay), and also has borders with member countries of the Andean Group—GRAN (also known as Andean Community-CAN). Since Brazil and GRAN countries share the Amazon Basin, this region should be able to give a basic contribution to the South American regional integration process. My analysis takes into account the current dynamics in the United States, and worldwide, that are largely driven by what the United States sees as their own strategic interests.

Amazon: A Shared South American Region
(ASSAR)

Eight independent countries, plus one colony, share the Amazon region.[12] It is hard to find accurate measures for this area.

> According to the criteria used to measure the area, it encompasses from 605 to 780 million hectares [6'050,000 to 7'800,000 Km^2]. Considering the first data, Brazil owns 64% of it, Peru 16%, Bolivia 12%. The remaining 8% are shared by Colombia, Ecuador and Venezuela, and to a very small extent, the Guyanas . . . when dealing with the Amazon . . . , it is very confusing [to determine the figures] when talking about it at the continental level.[13]

On July 3, 1978, in Brasilia, eight independent countries holding part of the Amazon (Bolivia, Brazil, Colombia, Ecuador, Guyana, Peru, Suriname, and Venezuela) signed the Amazon Cooperation Treaty (ACT).[14] Their purposes were mainly defensive since there had been attempts in the past by some rich countries to argue in favor of international management in this area. The latest attempt in favor of the international management by the president of a rich country was in 1989:

> Once more the Amazon internationalization haunts, this time coming from President François Mitterrand. At the Conference on the Environment, in The Hague, he proposed to create a Global Higher Authority for Environmental Issues with competence to do interventions, which could mean to limit the national sovereignty on spots seen as vital for humankind, such as the Amazon.[15]

On the other hand, the country trying the hardest to establish "indirect and permanent" control over the Amazon is the United States. This is key to understand current U.S. actions toward Colombia (such as supporting Plan Colombia with billions of dollars, logistics, and military advisers). These actions could spread to the borders of the other Amazon countries, except for Panama.[16] It could explain the United States' plans to have military bases in these countries, such as Manta Base in Ecuador, Iquitos, Peru, or even Alcantara, in Brazil. For this purpose, the United States needs free access to information collected by the massive Brazilian military project of surveillance, the SIVAM project (*Sistema de Vigilancia da Amazônia*—Watching System for the Amazon).[17] Besides the Brazilian Amazon, this project could watch the whole ASSAR. Cerqueira Leite, Brazilian physicist, says that SIVAM will allow to monitor "not only the Amazon but the whole northern part of South America including the Caribbean."[18]

The United States agreed to sell technology to build SIVAM, so long as it had free access to the information SIVAM would collect in Brazil. This required the authorization of a Brazilian Air Force General taking part in the negotiations on behalf of Brazil in order to be included in the agreement.[19]

The United States has a similar military plan for North America: NORTHCOM, the Unified Command Plan 2002, covering Alaska, part of the Caribbean, and areas near the Pacific and the Atlantic up to Panama. These countries' authorities support this regional U.S. project.[20] The southern governments support the United States as well, like in Plan Colombia and the military bases. These are attempts by the United States to impose their national interests worldwide, especially by controlling weaker countries. Here is the rationale for their plans involving South, Central and North America: "The limits between domestic and international affairs are increasingly blurred" when it comes to its national interests.[21] This is a valid explanation for the U.S. expansion and control of territories worldwide. Although the issue at hand here is ASSAR and MERCOSUR (Southern Market), we would say that U.S. national interests might as well require the control of resources and strategic spots anywhere in the world (from the Amazon to the Arctic, from Panama to South Korea).

The ACT emphasizes the importance of the Shared South American Region. French Guyana (a part of ASSAR) did not sign the ACT because of its colonial status. To include French Guyana would mean that France (its metropolis) would be accepted as an Amazonian country too. Then, through France, the European Union (EU) could demand the right to be acknowledged as having sovereignty over the Amazon. That Europe's value of the Amazon region can be seen from the fact that French Guyana (total size of 86,500 km^2, with the smallest part of ASSAR, less than 30,000 km^2) is a key element in some EU advanced technology projects. ASSAR's importance is not only due to tangible resources, since the nontangible are equally or even more important, like its strategic location stretching across the Equatorial Zone, which means an edge in terms of space exploration, mainly for launching skyrockets and satellites. Statistics in annex 6.1 and 6.2 help illustrate the distribution of territory corresponding to ASSAR, and its main features as well.[22]

Numbers show that when you add up the Amazon land owned by Brazil and GRAN countries (also known as Andean-Amazonic countries)[23] it amounts to nearly 98 percent of ASSAR. And if you add up both the Brazilian Amazon (the largest Amazon share) and the Peruvian Amazon (the second largest) it amounts to nearly 80 percent of the whole Amazon region. Numbers in annex 6.1 show that 1 percent of ASSAR is 66,350 km^2. So it is not surprising that when you add up even small Amazon shares (such as Guyana's and Suriname's that together amount to 80,000 km^2, or 1.23 percent of ASSAR) the total amount exceeds the size of the Netherlands (41,528 km^2) and Belgium (30,228 km^2) put together.[24] The massive Brazilian Amazon alone (named Legal Amazon, with 4,275,000 km^2) exceeds the sizes of India (3,166,414 km^2), Pakistan (796,095 km^2), Bangladesh (147,570 km^2), and Sri Lanka (65,610 km^2) together.[25] Compared to Europe, the Brazilian Amazon is about the size of Western Europe (3,769,861 km^2) plus Ukraine (603,700 km^2, in Eastern Europe). The Peruvian Amazon (968,000 km^2 of the Amazon Basin) is nearly half the size of Mexico (1,964,375 km^2), or, in terms of Europe, about the total size of Spain (506,000 km²), Portugal (92,365 km²), Great Britain (244,101 km²), Ireland (70,285 km²), the Netherlands, and Belgium combined.

The area occupied by ASSAR is huge, and Brazil and Peru share nearly 80 percent of it. This is one more reason to support the idea that Brazil's natural access to the Pacific Ocean is through Peru.[26] The road is yet to be built, although a natural way linking Peru to the Atlantic Ocean through Brazil already exists. Peru is a bi-ocean country with "direct" access to the Pacific and "indirect" access to the Atlantic Ocean.[27] The Peruvian shore on the Southern Pacific is 3,080 km long.[28] Its indirect access to the Atlantic is through the Amazon River (which originates in Peru) and its several tributaries flow into the Atlantic. Boats from countries that share international rivers have the right to freely navigate them under their own flags.[29] In this sense, all GRAN countries could have access to the Atlantic Ocean since the Amazon River flows from their territory into the Atlantic going across Brazil. The Andean Mountains (shared by all GRAN countries) are the starting point for most tributaries forming the Amazon Basin (more than 1,500 rivers).

The Andean-Amazonian countries could have access to the Atlantic coast, although not all of them are two-ocean-coast countries. Colombia is the only "directly" two-ocean-coast South American country; its shores are both on the Atlantic and on the Pacific. Bolivia has no direct access to the ocean (it is a land-locked country),[30] but could "indirectly" reach the Atlantic through its rivers. Venezuela's coast is on the Atlantic. Like Brazil, Venezuela has no access to the Pacific. Ecuador, a country on the Pacific Ocean, has no borders with Brazil. However, Ecuador could reach the Atlantic through its rivers coming from the Andes, going across the Peruvian and Colombian Amazon before entering Brazil.

Brazil has an Atlantic coast, and hence no access to the Pacific Ocean. But Brazilian vessels are entitled to free navigation on the Amazon Basin international rivers. However, none of those rivers reach the Pacific. The reciprocal rights to navigate on international rivers are limited to those river sections where navigation is feasible.[31] Boats under a Brazilian flag could go west, along the Amazon River and its tributaries, and reach the lower parts of the East Andean mountains where the rivers go abruptly up, making navigation impossible.[32] At this point, Brazilian boats would still be hundreds of kilometers away from the Pacific Ocean. Moreover, the boats would have to deal with the Andean Mountains lying between these two sites.

In terms of international communication and transport, the Brazilian Amazon has constraints that do not affect the Peruvian Amazon. Therefore, Brazil's quantitative edge (it owns the largest share of the Amazon) does not necessarily translate into qualitative edge. Peru, instead, has its coast on today's most significant ocean, the Pacific Ocean, and it could access the Atlantic (second most important) using the rivers in the Amazon. Nevertheless the Peruvian Amazon is 25 percent smaller than the share of the Amazon held by Brazil (see annex 6.1, column 06). Due to its location, the Brazilian Amazon could provide the access Brazil needs to reach the Pacific

Ocean. Da Cunha's writings on the Amazon point in this direction too. For that, Brazil would have to sign treaties with any of the South American Pacific countries. However, here we are focusing on the chances of an agreement being made by Brazil and GRAN (Andean-Amazon countries), not only because the Brazilian borders in the Amazon are the longest,[33] but also because the OACT is already in force between Brazil and the GRAN countries. These issues are vital since the countries involved share more than the Amazon, they share problems and interests connected to that region.[34] By applying these criteria to the GRAN countries on the Pacific Ocean, we can say that Brazil cannot reach the Pacific through Bolivia, a land-locked country, and in any case, an agreement between these two countries providing Brazil with an access to the Pacific would necessarily involve a third country, either Chile or Peru.

Like that of Colombia, the main problem in Brazil is political. The long-lasting undeclared civil war in Colombia explains, not only Plan Colombia, but SIVAM as well. Brazil's main security concern is the border with Colombia, a concealed source of conflict, where guerrillas and drug dealers go in and out across the Brazilian borderline. The entire 1,644 kilometer length of border between these two countries (835 km of land, and 809 km of rivers, lakes, and water channels) lies within the ASSAR, the largest tropical jungle on earth. It is very hard to monitor this borderline in the traditional way, that is, from land or water.[35] Political and security reasons severely limit Brazil's intentions to reach the Pacific through Colombia. The main problem for Ecuador is the absence of borders with Brazil. Any attempt to find a pass through Ecuador would necessarily involve Colombia and/or Peru.

Let us look at the Peruvian case. Since the guerilla movement Shining Path (*Sendero Luminoso*) was defeated in September of 1992, problems similar to Colombia's are almost nonexistent.[36] Peru is not a land-locked country like Bolivia, and it has almost 3,000 km-long borders with Brazil (nearly 2,000 km of them are rivers, lakes, and water channels, mostly navigable), entirely in the Amazon. Their borders are merely conventional in an area that is virtually integrated by the vast network provided by the rivers of the Amazon Basin. The Amazon River has its sources and tributaries (mostly navigable) in Peru.[37] Downstream navigation is possible in the Peruvian and the Brazilian Amazon (since they are connected) to finally reach the Atlantic Ocean. It is possible to navigate upstream from the Atlantic, specifically from the Marajo Island (where the Amazon flows into the Atlantic), going west, deep inside Peru, to reach spots located only a few hundred kilometers away from the Pacific coast. For example, about 4,500 km away from Marajo Island, you find Saramiriza, on the Marañón River, almost 400 km from the Pacific Ocean. There you could build a large river port for 700-ton vessels (equivalent to 25 trucks carrying 30-ton each).[38] Nevertheless the distance we just mentioned between Saramiza and the Pacific is measured in a straight imaginary line. The Andean Mountains lie between these two locations. However, in this area (Northern Peru), the mountains are relatively low; their peaks rarely reach 4,500 m. The lowest section of the Peruvian Andes

(Paso de Porculla, around 2,008 m high) is in that area.[39] Therefore from Saramiza (in the Peruvian lower Amazon, around 350 m above the sea level),[40] it is very hard to go straight west to finally reach the Pacific. Navigation up to Saramiza is no problem. The problem is after Saramiza, and the road you would drive to Paso de Porculla. From this point you can head west to the Pacific, up to the cape "Punta Pariñas" (part of it is known as Punta Balcones or the extreme west point in South America).[41] This is at a close distance from sea ports of Paita and Bayovar. You arrive at the Pacific at one of the most strategic South American locations. This westernmost point in South America[42] is relatively the closest point to the West Coast of the United States (a major area in terms of the US economy) and to Japan. Currently this is the economic axis in the Pacific including the U.S. West Coast, China, Asian Russia, and the Asian Tigers.[43]

Shorter distance means less expensive transport, mainly on large vessels. The Peruvian coast benefits from having the best position in South America to transport commodities to key spots in the Pacific. Peru has an additional advantage because the sea in that area has an immensely rich fish population.[44] Furthermore, the Bayovar Desert (part of the same area) has huge amounts of phosphates or sodium sulphate (Peru is a major producer of this valuable natural fertilizer). Last but not least, conditions there are exceptional for building a deep port. This is enough to show the great strategic significance of these territories for Peru and South America. The best points for Brazil to reach the Pacific Ocean lay in this area. Brazil is a major soy bean producer, and its largest soy crops are located closer to Peru than to the Atlantic coast. Brazil would certainly benefit from selling larger volumes to the insatiable Asian market, with more competitive transport costs. Peru would benefit mainly from the port construction, and corresponding revenues from a port that probably would be the largest in the Pacific coast of South America. Moreover, the volumes of Peruvian sales of fishery and phosphates to Brazil would increase.[45] With the easy access, Brazil could buy the natural fertilizer at lower prices, causing less damage to its environment. Therefore, both countries would benefit from a link between the Brazilian Amazon and the Pacific Ocean through northern Peru, a model to other partnerships in the subcontinent. However this project is not likely to become a reality.

The project the Brazilian and Peruvian governments agreed upon involves southern Peru. There have been negotiations involving an outlet into the Pacific for some time. For instance, in 1991, the two countries signed an agreement to build a highway.[46] Brazil had attempted similar moves with other South American countries, like the project under the Amazon Cooperation Treaty known as Corredores (Corridors). In the 1990s, the Treaty's Technical Committee analyzed 14 Corridors, 5 of which are connected with Brazil's aim to reach the Pacific: (1) Belem-Iquitos Corridor, northern Peru (basically our description above); (2) Interocean Corridor, from Belem through Manaus and the Putumayo River (the border between Colombia and Peru), across Ecuador (Quito), arriving to the Ecuadorian port of Esmeraldas; (3) Rio Negro Corridor linking Brazil, Colombia, and

Venezuela; (4) Caceres-Santa Cruz Corridor, connecting Mato Grosso (Brazil) to Bolivia; (5) Transocean Corridor from Rio Branco (State of Acre, Brazil) through Iñapari (Department of Madre de Dios, Peru), crossing the Andes, to arrive at a few southern Peruvian ports.[47]

The latest option is Brazil's choice, and is already under construction. Brazilian President Lula da Silva considers the strengthening of South and Latin American relations as the axis of its foreign policy.[48] Lula, along with other South American presidents, wants to connect the two independent integration projects—MERCOSUR and GRAN. This union would favor the creation of a regional consensus to deal with the Free Trade Area of the Americas (FTAA)—the hegemonic project sponsored by the United States.

These countries are aware that regional integration demands individual change in infrastructure: highways, bridges, ports, transport, energy, and telecommunications. Since September 2000, they have established the *Iniciativa para la Integración de la Infraestructura Regional Suramericana* (*IIRSA*)—Initiative for Integrating the South-American Regional Infrastructure.[49]

Peruvian president Alejandro Toledo, on a visit to Brazil, said during an interview

> VALOR: What do you expect from Brazil and Lula da Silva's administration?
> TOLEDO: We have talked for approximately one hour and he (Lula) offered, with a great deal of intelligence and audacity, a strategic alliance between Peru and Brazil.
> VALOR: What would this alliance be like?
> TOLEDO: The issues are: highway integration using foreign credit, so that the caps on IMF credits would not be a concern; the river integration, allowing Brazil to have an exit to the Pacific Ocean. We must turn and look straight at each other, before turning our eyes to some place else. We are so close and have so much in common, yet we stand side by side, each one looking at Miami. In bilateral terms, we have a lot to earn. Brazil now buys sodium sulphate from a far away country, Morocco, while we, the neighbor, can provide this product. We can export and buy each other's products. Strategically, it makes sense to look straight at each other, because of where we are located. I hope Brazil and Peru will enter into a bilateral agreement as soon as this year.[50]

The integration highway mentioned by Toledo is part of the Transocean Corridor Rio Branco-Iñapari, arriving at the southern Peruvian ports.[51] Right after Toledo's visit to Brazil, *National Geographic* published an article about that area.[52] On page 105, a map shows the exit to the Pacific through the southern Peruvian ports of (moving from south to north) Ilo, Matarani, San Juan, and Pisco. Ted Conover (the photographer is Maria Stenzel) wrote about the existing roads near the Peruvian/Brazilian border. In Peru, roads are too narrow and unpaved whereas in Brazil they are relatively good and wide, and they will soon be totally paved. Pictures on pages 104 and

105 show a very well-kept Amazonian environment. Beneath the pictures, the caption reads,

> Los Amigos River (above) winds through a protected Peruvian area containing a series of reservations of overwhelming biodiversity. In Brazil, they replaced the jungle with pastures along highways BR-364 and BR-317 in Acre (right, above). Three quarters of the tree cutting in the Brazilian Amazon took place on a 50-kilometer-wide stripe along paved roads.[53]

On page 108 it states that the Peruvian area Madre de Dios "has been the main concern of environmentalists." A survey by the Peruvian government shows that forests in higher areas, toward the west, have the largest biodiversity on earth. Huge parts of this jungle still remain untouched today. People wonder whether the road construction will indeed have a positive impact. Conover reminds us that Chico Mendes, the Brazilian protector of the Amazon, was against this highway construction, which he saw as causing damage to the area.

> On (highway) BR-17, the ways are paved through inner Acre to the Peruvian Amazon, even though in this region Chico Mendes and his followers fought against the proliferation of roads in the jungle. This rubber gatherers' leader deeply felt the consequences after highway BR-364 opened, in the 1970s. He was awarded several international prizes for organizing a peaceful resistance movement against the highway. In 1988, gunmen under the orders of two landowners murdered him. As a result of this struggle, the Workers' Party, governing Acre for several years, showed greater concern about the environment. Nevertheless new highways have been built. . . . the road starting in Rio Branco [Acre's capital city] is now almost totally paved up to Assis Brasil, at the border with Peru, and we can see the machinery and equipment poised to conclude its final section.[54]

According to *National Geographic,* having an exit to the Pacific Ocean became such a priority to Brazil that it offered to "assist with funds to the Peruvian Transocean road."[55] During the same time as Toledo's visit to Brazil, President Lula da Silva said

> It is important for us to have the courage to change the relationship between Brazil and Peru into strategic relations to defend our sovereignty, culture, economy, the Amazon . . . , and a model for sustainable development . . . The agreements we now sign are a great start. Actually, next year we will open the bridge from Assis Brasil to Iñapari. Brazil will certainly invest funds from its National Bank for Social and Economic Development (BNDES) to support the infrastructure projects, very important to the integration project, the dream Peruvians and Brazilians have dreamt for centuries.[56]

At the highest political levels in Brazil and Peru, the highway from the Brazilian Amazon to the southern Peruvian ports is tangible. Although there are a few roads off the Amazon borderline, there is no international bridge to link the Brazilian paved highway going from Assis Brasil (Acre) to Iñapari (Madre de Dios). From there it is possible to drive toward the ports in southern Peru, even if the road on the Peruvian side is not paved. Actually a new road will be needed.[57] We could say that this road is already an unavoidable reality.

In reality, the development of an intermodal system relying mostly on railroads would be destructive for the overall environment, especially major archeological, historical, and cultural sites.[58] Since the end of the nineteenth century, Peru has had *Ferrocarril del Sur del Peru* (Southern Peru Railway), starting at Mollendo Port (Department of Arequipa), and having lines branch to Cuzco, and Puno on the Titicaca Lake. The line to Cuzco goes to Quillabamba Province (on the Amazon, in the Department of Cuzco, with 72,104 kms^2), not too far from Madre de Dios (a department with 85,183 kms^2) and from the Brazilian border in Acre (extension of 152,522 kms^2). As we said before, Euclides da Cunha was acquainted with this area, where the railroad *Transacreano* should have been built, according to his plans. In his words, this railroad would be "the great international road for an alliance, pro-civilization and pro-peace."

The railroad option, which is much less destructive than the highway, could build off of the railroad that already exists. Euclides's vision, incorporated in it, would prove to be valid. He planned a railroad that, in our view, could be connected to the old Southern Peru Railway, thus linking the two countries. Obviously the Southern Peru Railway would need total remodeling and updating. The less destructive option would be to have a railroad linking Brazil (key country in MERCOSUR) to Peru (GRAN country on a key location in South American Pacific).

Amazon, MERCOSUR and GRAN

According to the *Encyclopedia Britannica*, 2003 Book of the Year, South America's size is 17,824,637 km^2. Brazil constitutes 47.78 percent of South America, almost half the subcontinent. The other half (9,310,590 km^2 or about 53 percent) is shared by 11 countries, 9 of which are Hispanic-American. By far Brazil is the largest country in South America.

From 1991, Brazil (8,514,047 km^2), Argentina (2,780,092 km^2), Paraguay (406,752 km^2), and Uruguay (176,215 km^2) engaged in the integration project MERCOSUR. Together these countries totaled 11,877,106 km^2, or 66.60 percent of South America: two-thirds of the subcontinent. Except for Paraguay (a mediterranean country), these countries have extensive shorelines: Argentina with 4,725 km shores,[59] Brazil, 7,367 km shores[60] and Uruguay, about 500 km.[61] Jointly, MERCOSUR countries have 12,292 kilometers in shores—undoubtedly a massive amount. Therefore MERCOSUR is the most important bloc in South America, judging from its surface and shore extension. Nevertheless these shores are entirely on the Atlantic Ocean, and they encompass the furthest eastern point in South America that amounts to a strategic edge toward Africa.[62]

GRAN started in 1969, and in its early times Chile was a member, but Venezuela was not. Chile pulled out of GRAN under Pinochet's dictatorship in the mid-1970s.[63] According to the same source mentioned above (part of this information does not match the data of annex 6.1, column 02) Bolivia has 1,098,582 km²; Colombia, 1,141,568 km²; Ecuador, 272,045 km², Peru, 1,285,216 km², and Venezuela, 916,445 km². This means GRAN's surface is 4,713, 855 km², or 26.50 percent of South America (less than half the size of MERCOSUR).

Four GRAN countries have shores: Colombia's shores are about 2,100 kms long,[64] half of them on the Atlantic Ocean, specifically on the Caribbean Sea, and the other half on the Pacific Ocean. Venezuela's shores are 2,183 kms long[65] only on the Atlantic side, nearly 80 percent of them on the Caribbean. Ecuador's shores on the Pacific are approximately 650 kms long[66]. And Peru's shores on the Pacific are 3,080 kms long.[67] Bolivia is a land-locked country. So GRAN countries' total shores equal approximately 8,213 kms (or 67 percent of shores in MERCOSUR countries) of which 4,880 kms are on the Pacific and 3,183 kms on the Atlantic. Although larger than GRAN's, the totality of the MERCOSUR countries shores are on the Atlantic. Moreover this part of the Atlantic is not a part of the Caribbean Sea.[68]

Although smaller, GRAN territories are better distributed than MERCOSUR's. In addition, GRAN, through Colombia, holds the northern-most point of South America. This translated into an advantage in terms of communication (trade etc.) with the Atlantic in Central America, Mexico, the Caribbean countries (Cuba, Dominican Republic, etc.), and the United States (from Texas to Florida).[69] Colombia borders Panama, a country in a privileged location since it holds what today possibly still amounts to the most significant area on earth in strategic terms (the Panama Canal Zone is the shortest distance between the largest oceans of all, the Atlantic and the Pacific).

Peru holds the westernmost point in South America, an important fact regarding connections with today's global economic axis in the Pacific Basin. The people who share this Basin (American, Asian, Oceanic, and Antarctic Continents) amount to nearly 60 percent of the world population, a giant market whose weight keeps growing, in absolute and relative sense, in relation to the rest of the planet. Strictly in economic terms, these countries now produce approximately 60 percent of the World Gross Product and their economic weight will continue to increase over time. They produce almost the same percentage of some of the most advanced technological goods as California's Silicon Valley, the richest U.S. state, Japan, Asian Tigers, Australia, and vital portions of China and Russia. Of the world's richest areas, Western Europe is the only one lacking direct access to the Pacific Basin.

GRAN has strategic advantages regarding MERCOSUR. However MERCOSUR has the most industrialized and urbanized areas of South America, Latin America, and maybe the whole developing world. On the South American Atlantic coast, there is a 300 km-wide strip of land stretching several thousand kilometers (a total surface of about 900,000 km²) between Buenos Aires (Argentina) and the city of Salvador (Bahia, Brazil), where you can find the following cities: São Paulo (the world's fourth largest with 17,800,000 inhabitants), Buenos Aires (Argentina's capital city, and the world's tenth largest with 12,600,000 inhabitants), and Rio de Janeiro (the world's eighteenth largest city with a population of 10,600,000).[70] On the same coast, we have: Montevideo (Uruguay's capital city, 1,378,707 inhabitants), and several cities in Brazil, like Porto Alegre (1,320,069), Curitiba (1,586,898), Belo Horizonte (2,229,697) and Salvador, and Bahia (2,439,881).[71] Adding those up we have a population of 49,954,515. We can also add other cities in the state of São Paulo (like Campinas, 951,824, Ribeirao Preto, 502,333, Santos, 415,543, etc),[72] plus the city of Rosario, Argentina, with around 1 million inhabitants.[73] We can then conclude that in this territory of around 900,000 kms. (a relatively small area, corresponding to nearly 8 percent of total MERCOSUR) there are 80 million inhabitants, which makes it one of the most populated and urbanized territories on earth.

The area is also highly industrialized. In 2001, the Brazilian Gross Industrial Product (GIP) ($223 billion) was the world's eighth largest, and Argentina's ($84 billion) GIP was the world's nineteenth largest.[74] In manufacture production Brazil ($177 billion) and Argentina ($55 billion) rank similarly. Brazilian car manufacturing exceeded 1 million units, and Argentina's almost 500,000 units. The Brazilian corporation EMBRAER, the only aircraft industry located in the Southern Hemisphere has a production volume that ranks among the top airplane manufacturers worldwide. From these numbers we can assert that MERCOSUR has economic advantages over GRAN.

We could do a similar analysis, involving the area from Arequipa (Peru) to Medellín (Colombia) in the Pacific GRAN countries. From south to north we have the city of Arequipa (718,103 inhabitants), Lima (7,400,000 inhabitants), Trujillo (630,000), Guayaquil (1,973,880), Quito (1,478,513), Cali (2,077,386), and Medellín (1,861,265).[75] Together they total 16,139,147 inhabitants, only a third of its Atlantic equivalent. Some other important urban centers in Peru are Ica (194,820 inhabitants), Puerto de Chimbote (298,800), Chiclayo (469,200), Piura (308,155), Sullana (170,000); in Ecuador Machala (197,350), Cuenca (255,028), Portoviejo (167,956), Puerto de Manta (156,981), Ambato (160,302), Ibarra (119,243), Puerto Esmeraldas (117,722). In Colombia, Pasto (332,396), Puerto de Buenaventura (224,336), Popayan (200,719), Neiva (300,052), Palmira (226,509), Armenia (281,422), Pereira (381,725), and Manizales (337,580).[76] The total population in this last group of cities amounts to 4,900,296 inhabitants. In these South American Pacific cities there are 22,392,537 inhabitants, or around 25 percent of its equivalent area on the Atlantic. Notice that Lima is the core city in the region under analysis[77]

These figures are useful to point out trends. So it is possible to say that MERCOSUR, compared with GRAN, contains the most crowded urban areas in South America and the most industrialized areas too. Venezuela's Gross Industrial Product ($28 billion) ranks thirty-eighth worldwide; Colombia ($25 billion) ranks fortieth, and Peru ($22 billion) ranks forty-fourth.[78] In manufacture production, Peru ($14 billion) ranks thirty-ninth and Colombia ($13 billion) ranks forty-second worldwide.[79] Clearly, at the industrial level, GRAN also plays a secondary role to MERCOSUR.

We can conclude that in South America, MERCOSUR has economic advantages, and GRAN has strategic advantages. Economic and strategic resources are, by their nature, complementary. Brazil and MERCOSUR's economic advantages would dramatically increase if joined with Peru and GRAN's strategic advantages, to the benefit of South America as a whole, leaving behind any hegemonic project of the United States.[80] Brazil and GRAN countries share approximately 98 percent of the Amazon and both are key members of the Amazonian Cooperation Treaty. Brazil is located between MERCOSUR and GRAN countries, a sort of huge bridge linking the most independent integration processes in South and Latin America. Therefore Brazil plays a key role in these integration processes. To develop direct links between Brazil and Peru, through their Amazon borders, also means developing direct links between MERCOSUR and GRAN. In other words, economy and strategy will be connected for their mutual benefit. More than that, it will also mean linking economy to history.

Conclusions

Brazil and MERCOSUR have the most powerful economies in South America, although Peru and, by extension, the GRAN countries are the most powerful in historical terms. Today's Peru corresponds to the core of the old Andean world, one of the few centers in the world where the Agricultural Revolution took place (another one in the American Continent is Mesoamerica). Its agricultural history is approximately 10,000 years old.[81] Here, almost 5,000 years ago, the oldest urban revolution in the Americas took place; one of the oldest in the whole world. Amidst the great archeological findings in the last 25 years in Peru, that are changing the predominant view on South American history is the City of Caral, the oldest city on the continent, at a relatively short distance from Lima and the sea. Its importance can be assessed from the following:

> In the American continent, the ancient civilizations history may be partly rewritten as a result of research evidencing the most ancient urban life in America. The remains of a great city, object of digging operations in the archaeological site of Caral, 200 kilometers north of Lima, may be over four thousand years old. "These findings challenge every concept we have had about the development of the ancient Andean civilizations," wrote John Haas on *Science* journal. The city constructions made out of rocks date from 2,600 to 2,000 B.C., according to the new data based on carbon, done at the Field Museum of Chicago. Moreover, they show a developed civilization, with two-story houses and irrigation channels.[82]

Brazil, MERCOSUR, Peru, and GRAN would benefit if the economic, strategic, and historical advantages are aggregated. For that, at least two things are needed:

First: Brazil's President Lula must put his nonhegemonic speeches into action to make things change. For instance, Brazil should change the hegemonic view embedded in SIVAM. It has the ability to control ASSAR, the northern part of South America and the Caribbean (sharing with the United States, free of charge, all collected information). As a Brazilian newspaper published:

> Amazon: Sivam's Radar Can Watch Colombia. Delivery of data to the neighbor country depends on an agreement; the information could help the war against drug traffic.[83]

In the beginning of this report journalist Katia Brasil [sic] writes,

> With no need to cross over the Brazilian border, SIVAM's surveillance aircraft R-99A long range radars detect the movement of planes at a distance of about 200 km within the Colombian territory.[84]

Undoubtedly, SIVAM is able to survey other countries' territories, therefore it violates their sovereignty. The formerly mentioned Leite's interview published by VEJA magazine,[85] and the study by Isabel Rossi, show that a few top institutions in Brazil (like the Brazilian Society for the Advance of Science—SBPC) and activists from the Workers Party (before it gained power) have protested against the lack of transparency with which SIVAM was carried out, under the total control of the military. Now we see that this project also violates other countries' interests, mainly the Amazon countries. It could be a source of future unrest to the extent of impairing the South American integration process, and it would benefit nothing but the U.S.-based projects for Latin America. SIVAM should be democratized and become a transparent project, with the Brazilian civil society and other Amazon countries taking part in its management. The other countries should contribute with proportional funds to run SIVAM, and have unlimited access to information related to their territories. This common task could be coordinated by OACT, which then would gain strength while sending the message that nonhegemonic and horizontal integration schemes are possible.

Second, it is unacceptable, and we must protest against it, that a highway is the choice to connect Brazil and Peru, despite the hard work done by cultural heroes of Brazil, such as Euclides da Cunha, who devised the railroad links serving peaceful purposes. It is unacceptable that the existing Southern Peru Railway is not even being considered. This railway or an intermodal system (a mixture of waterway, railway, and highway, less destructive to the rainforests in the Amazon) would certainly be the best link between the two countries. Sadly, we realize that the highway was chosen at a time when the Brazilian minister of environment was Ms. Marina da Silva, a close collaborator of Chico Mendes.

Finally, my suggestion for the name of the international railway (that unfortunately may not be built) is, Ferrocarril Transoceánico Tahuantinsuyo—Euclides da Cunha (*Transocean Railway Tahuantinsuyo—Euclides da Cunha*), to honor the ancient Inca territory's core (in Quechua, the Inca language—Tahuantinsuyo means the Society of the Four Regions) beside the great Brazilian writer. It would also be a sound way to join the economy and history.

Annex 6.1 The Amazon: A Shared South American Region—Extension and Population

(01)	(02)	(03)	(04)	(05)	(06)	(07)[a]	(08)	(09)
Bolivia	1099	724	10.91	65.87	16.94	172.00	18.37	0.24
Brazil	8500	4275	64.45	50.30	100.00	213.00	22.75	0.05
Colombia	1140	399	6.02	35.00	9.33	70.00	7.48	0.17
Ecuador	284	133	2.05	46.83	3.11	95.00	10.15	0.71
Peru	1290	968	14.60	75.00	22.65	300.00	32.00	0.31
Guyana	215	45	0.70	20.93	1.05	40.00	4.28	0.89
Suriname	164	35	0.53	21.34	0.82	7.50	0.80	0.20
Venezuela	912	56	0.86	6.14	1.31	39.00	4.16	0.70
Total	13604	6635	100.00			936.50	100.00	

Ecuador and Venezuela correspond to *Hydrographic Amazon*,[b] from Brazil *Legal Amazon*,[c] from Peru *Amazon Basin*[d] and from Guyana and Suriname, the author's deductions[e].

Sources:

[a] Amazon Cooperation Treaty. *Amazonía sin Mitos.* TCA-Interamerican Development Bank, Washington DC, 1992, p. 28.

[b] "Amazon Cooperation Treaty," *Diagnóstico de los Recursos Hidrobiológicos de la Amazonía*, SPT-TCA, Lima, No. 32, October 1994, p. 3.

[c] Comissão Interministerial para a Preparação da Conferência das Nações Unidas sobre Meio Ambiente e Desenvolvimento (CNUMAD). Subsídios Técnicos para a Elaboração do Relatório Nacional do Brasil para o CNUMAD. Draft. Brasília, 1991. Legal Amazon—LA—is a definition used in Brazil with the purpose of extending to other territories outside the Amazon area, the same policies designed to the Amazon. So the Brazilian Legal Amazon is larger than the Brazilian portion of the Amazon Basin.

[d] Dourojeanni, p. 25. In Peru, politically, the Amazon is defined as Jungle, and the size they attribute to the Jungle is smaller than the part corresponding to Peru in the Amazon Basin. "Basin" is a geographical concept, therefore it is more accurate, and its persistent use would allow for better comparison, which is not the case.

[e] These are logical inferences given the numerous difficulties to obtain geographical data on these countries.

Notes:

Legends: 01—Name: Country; **02**—Area; Thousands of km²; **03**—National Amaz.: Thousands of km²; **04**—Nat. Amaz./Total Amaz; **05**—03/02; **06**—Nat.Amaz./Braz. Amaz; **07**—Indigenous Pop. Amaz. Thousands of km²; **08**—Ind. Pop.Nat.Amaz./Pop. Indig. Amaz Total; **09**—07/03.

Note: It is nearly impossible to have the same definitions and units for the ASSAR, since each country uses what they consider as the most convenient (in the political sense) data making it difficult to compare the eight Amazonian regions. Although common parameters were not found, I tried to establish comparisons as accurate as possible, and the annex above was designed as follows: Column 03 data from Bolivia, Colombia, Ecuador and Venezuela correspond to *Hydrographic Amazon* (Amazon Cooperation Treaty. *Diagnóstico de los Recursos Hidrobiológicos de la Amazonía.* SPT-TCA, Lima, No. 32, October 1994, p. 3), from Brazil *Legal Amazon* (Comissão Interministerial para a Preparação da Conferência das Nações Unidas sobre Meio Ambiente e Desenvolvimento (CNUMAD). *Subsídios Técnicos para a Elaboração do Relatório Nacional do Brasil para o CNUMAD.* Draft. Brasília, 1991. From Peru, *Amazon Basin* (Dourojeanni, *Amazonía. Que Hacer* p. 25). From Guyana and Suriname, the author's deductions.

Annex 6.2 Brazil: Borders and Limits (Foreign Office)

Country	Total (km)	Dry border line (km)	Rivers, lakes, & water channels (km)	Landmarks N°
1. French Guyana	730	303	427	10
2. Suriname	593	593	–	60
3. Guyana	1.606	908	698	134
4. Venezuela	2.199	2.199	–	2.682
5. Colombia	1.644	835	809	128
6. Peru	2.995	992	2.003	86
7. Bolívia	3.423	751	2.672	438
8. Paraguay	1.366	437	929	910
9. Argentina	1.261	25	1.236	310
10. Uruguay	1.069	320	749	1.174
Total	16.886	7.363	9.523	5.932

Source: E-mail: wrmkkk@omega.incc.br Update on May 16, 2002. *Ocean Coast: 7.367 km.*

Notes

1. Da Cunha, E. "Primeira Parte. Terra sem História (Amazônia)," in *À Margem da História*, Martins Fontes, (São Paulo, 1999), p. 84.
2. V. Magalhães Ramon, note 23, p. 6. This book by Da Cunha was the inspiration and source of information for the widely known novel *La Guerra del Fin del Mundo* (The War of the End of the World) by Peruvian writer Mario Vargas Llosa.
3. As an example, the excellent *Cadernos de Literatura Brasileira* dedicated to Euclides, and *Cadernos de Fotografia Brasileira*, recreating Canudos, the city where Antonio Conselheiro lived, that was swept away from the map. In 1891, in Canudos, the actions by Conselheiro and his followers, described in his opus magna "*Os Sertões*," took place.
4. Da Cunha, E. "Relatório da Comissão Mista Brasileiro-Peruana de Reconhecimento do Alto Purus—O Rio Purus," in *Obra Completa* vol. I, pp. 681–734. (This report was firstly published in 1906 by the Brazilian National Print.) The way they settle the permanent borders between the two countries, in my opinion, favored Brazil, and this happened to a large extent as a result of Euclides's excellent qualifications.
5. Euclides da Cunha, military engineer, left the Army because he disagreed with the policies adopted by the Brazilian Empire (1822–1889). When Brazil became a Republic, he was offered the right to rejoin the Army, which he declined.
6. As an example see the Master Thesis by Magalhães Ramon, I. V. "A Amazônia e a integração ao Pacífico. Euclides da Cunha: no Centro da História?" University of the State of São Paulo-UNESP, Brazil, May 2004.
7. "A Transacreana," in *À margem da História*, p. 84.
8. For instance, in his work "O Primado do Pacífico," in *À Margem da História*, pp. 123–132.
9. Amayo, E. "Da Amazônia ao Pacífico cruzando os Andes—Interesses envolvidos na construção de uma estrada, especialmente dos EUA e Japão." *Estudos Avançados* 1993, 17, p. 119.

10. Brazil (8,514,047 km^{-2}) is the largest country in the South American sub-continent, and in Latin America. It is the third largest country in the American Continent, and the fifth largest in the world. See *Encyclopaedia Britannica*, 2003 Book of the Year. From now on this will be the source for the statistics we used, unless expressly stated otherwise.

11. "Da Amazônia ao Pacífico cruzando os Andes—Interesses envolvidos na construção de uma estrada, especialmente dos EUA e Japão," Estudos Avançados 17, 1993.

12. For this reason, from now on, I refer to it by the acronym ASSAR (Amazon a Shared South American Region).

13. Dourojennni, M. J., *Amazonía. Que Hacer?* (Iquitos, Perú: Centro de Estudios Teológicos de la Amazonía, 1990), p. 25.

14. Since November 2002 the ACT has its permanent office in Brasilia. ACT members met in Caracas (14.12.1998) and changed its name to Organization of the Amazonian Cooperation Treaty—OACT.

15. Amayo, E. "Da Amazônia ao Pacífico cruzando os Andes—Interesses envolvidos na construção de uma estrada, especialmente dos EUA e Japão," *Estudos Avançados*, 1993, 17: 129.

16. It is important to research those implications that are relevant for the future of Colombia, and other bordering countries; from the point of view of Brazil, see for instance Borges, Fabio: *Os possíveis impactos do "Plano Colômbia" no Brasil. Aspectos econômicos, estruturais e diplomáticos.* Colombia has its borders with, clockwise, Panama, Atlantic Ocean (Caribbean Sea), Venezuela, Brazil, Peru, Ecuador, and the Pacific Ocean.

17. See the Master level thesis by Rossi, Isabel Cristina, *SIVAM: um caso de dependência tecnológica, 1990–1996.* She discusses the project huge costs, and corresponding loans from the United States of around $1.7 billion. At the end, including interests and guaranties, Brazil will pay back over $5 billion.

18. Interview. "Rogério de Cerqueira Leite . . ." (see VEJA in the Further Reading Section).

19. With a denouncing tone, the newspaper *Folha de S. Paulo—FSP* published a series of reports based on U.S. official papers with the information just mentioned, when SIVAM was opened by former president Fernando Henrique Cardoso, on July 25, 2002. As far as we know, Brazil did not officially deny the critics. Examples: "Exclusive—Intelligence Made Sure SIVAM Went to US Company," *FSP*, July 23, 2002, p. 1; "SIVAM meant a geopolitical victory to the USA. Air Force denies American company was favored during bidding for Amazon surveillance project," "US considers SIVAM as geopolitical victory. Papers reveal that, to USA, presence of American company 'boosts their interests'," "American lobby wanted to 'energize' Brazilian officials, *FSP*," July 24, 2002, p.1 and A8; "[Journalist] Janio de Freitas—No answer [*official answer to denouncement by Folha de S. Paulo*]," FSP, July 25, 2002, p. A5; "Military official denies favoring," " 'Bidding is from 1994', says FHC," " 'With time, skin turns into leather' says the President while defending SIVAM," FSP, July 26, 2002, p. 3.

20. See paper by Loza Vasques, Marta Guadalupe, *El refuerzo hegemónico de los EEUU en América Latina: la complementación geopolítica de los Planes Colombia y Puebla—Panamá y el inicio del 'Comando Norte'*, The Northern exception, specifically the Caribbean, is the Cuban government.

21. Ayerbe, L. F. *O Ocidente e o 'Resto'. A América Latina e O Caribe na Cultura do Império*, CLACSO–Conselho Latino-Americano de Ciências Sociais, Buenos Aires, 2003, p. 61.

22. The section of ASSAR owned by each of the eight mentioned countries corresponds to their respective national Amazon region. We will refer to the Bolivian Amazon with the letters BOA, to Brazil's as BRA, Colombia's, COA, Ecuador's, ECA, Peru's, PEA, Suriname's, SUA, Venezuela's, VEA.

23. The Andean-Amazon countries are also known as Bolivarian (this concept should include Panama) since all of them were marked, to different extents, by the campaign for independence led by Simon Bolivar.

24. To better understand the significance of Amazon dimensions, see my paper, "Why to study the historical formation and main current problems of Amazonia?. The indigenous question, democracy, diversities and bio—piracy," (see Further Reading section)

25. These territories formed The British India, a colony of the British Empire at its apex (Victorian Age, 1837–1901) so important that it was known as The Pearl of the British Crown. In 1948, the independence, and the violent fights between Hindus and Muslims (culminating with the murder of Mahatma Gandhi, the father of the independence movement), undid the agreement.

26. For further information, see my writings of 1993 and 1995 (See the Further Reading section).

27. For more detail, see: Arróspide M. R., "La Bioceanidad del Perú—Vía transcontinental peruana," Lima, Instituto de Estudios Histórico Marítimos del Perú, 1990.

28. Perú. Instituto Nacional de Planificación—INP. Atlas Histórico Geográfico y de Paisajes Peruanos. Presidencia de la República—INP—Asesoría Geográfica, Lima, 1969, p. 22.

29. In 1867, Brazil acknowledged this right and opened the Amazon River to international navigation; V. Burns "The Decree Opening the Amazon to International Traffic." In *A Documentary History of Brazil*, pp. 246–247.

30. Bolivia lost to Chile its Pacific coast of approximately 300 km, and became a Mediterranean country. It was one of the outcomes from the War of the Pacific (1879–83) that started when Chile, in February 14, 1879, invaded the Bolivian coast in Antofagasta (an area rich in nitrates, gold, copper, sea products etc) For details see my book, "*La Política Británica en la Guerra del Pacífico.*"

31. Free access in nonnavigable sections would mean the same as free access by land. If the free transit is mutually accepted in the navigable and nonnavigable (by land) sections, they would be accepting some limit on their rights of sovereignty over their territories. This right so far is an essential element in the concept of National State, since the French Revolution in 1789.

32. The navigable Lower Amazon—LA—is around 80 percent of ASSAR; a part of the Andean-Amazon countries and Brazil. For instance, the Amazon River becomes navigable in Peru at an altitude of approximately 300 m above the sea level; then it goes for around 700 km in the PEA, 150 km of which are borders between PEA and COA; it goes other 3,500 km in the BRA to finally reach the AO in front of Marajó Island. Notice that, along 4000 km, the altitude decreases only around 300 m (a few centimeters per kilometer, what makes it a singular river, with its calm waters moving very slowly). The Andean-Amazon countries include the Higher Amazon—HA -(where most

CA rivers start) and the LA. Brazil is number one as to its Amazon region size, although entirely located in the LA. Peru, on the other hand, is number one regarding territories in the HA, and second one, in the LA.

33. Brazil's longest borders are with the GRAN countries, instead of MERCOSUR countries. See Annex 6.2: borders with Bolivia: 3,423 km; with Colombia: 1,644 km; Peru: 2,995 km; Venezuela: 2,199 km; it means that 10.261 kms are shared with GRAN countries (except Ecuador). Borders with Argentina: 1,261 km; with Paraguay: 1,366; Uruguay: 1,069; total area shared with the MERCOSUR countries: 3,696 km. In relation to the total Brazilian borders (16,886 km, excluding the sea borders of 7,367 km), Brazil's borders with GRAN are 61 percent of its total borders, and borders with MERCOSUR are 22 percent of Brazil's total borders. Therefore its borders with GRAN are almost 3 times longer than its borders with MERCOSUR. The Brazilian borders with GRAN are almost entirely in the Amazon (that explains why 5,484 km of these borders are rivers, lakes and water channels, of which 2,672 km are shared with Bolivia, 809 km with Colombia, 2,003 with Peru; between Venezuela and Brazil all borders are dry).

34. These reasons, when applied to Chile (the South American Pacific country with the longest coast), explain why we virtually kept it out from this analysis. Chile is not an Amazon country, and it has no borders with Brazil. An exit to the Pacific going through Chile would involve a third country, namely Argentina, Bolivia, or Peru. Maybe the geographic reasons help to explain the consistent policies adopted by Chile for more than 25 years: they put little effort to support the independent South American integration processes like MERCOSUR and GRAN, and much more energy to reach bilateral agreements with global powers as the United States. Chile has been negotiating with MERCOSUR for several years, maintaining only its partial membership. In relation to GRAN, Chile was one of its founders, and an active one, in 1969, during the Salvador Allende administration. (November 1970 to September 1973). However, in 1976, dictator Pinochet withdrew his country expecting to weaken GRAN. On the other hand, on May 2003, Chile signed a bilateral agreement with the United States, after negotiating for 12 years. Chile is the only South American country to have this status. Today, especially after the war against Iraq, United States is widely perceived around the globe as a power having global imperial projects. The United States would be hardly interested in seeing projects such as MERCOSUR and GRAN to become successful in our continent, let alone that those countries unite in a South American Community (established in Cusco, during the meeting of South American Presidents and Heads of State, in December 9, 2004). Based on its logics of power, the United States appeals to bilateral agreements, and grants to countries accepting them a few leftovers in order to reach its strategic goal which is to divide and win. Several South American countries are now following Chile's steps, and Colombia, Ecuador and Peru are holding meetings in an attempt to sign a free trade treaty with the United States. It is not the first time in U.S. history that a project of Empire, with its tactics and strategies, shows up. The U.S. controlled Cuba and the Philippines during many years; it started controlling Puerto Rico, Virgin Islands, Marianne Islands, etc at the end of the 19th century, and the beginning of 20th century, after the 1898 war against Spain whose reason was Cuba. Nevertheless this imperial project was defeated to a great extent since the U.S. civil society protested against it

under the leadership of intellectuals like Mark Twain. The book *Mark Twain contra a Guerra* (Mark Twain against the War) is a collection of anti-imperialist articles written by this great American writer, organized by the Brazilian professor María Silvia Betti (See in Further Reading section Betti and O Estado de S. Paulo 02/03/03).

35. See details in Borges, "Os possíveis impactos do Plano Colômbia," on *Brasil. Aspectos econômicos, estruturais e diplomáticos*, and Rossi, "SIVAM: Um caso de dependência tecnológica," 1990–1996.

36. More detail on the troubles that guerrilla movements like Shining Path (SP) and Revolutionary Movement, *Túpac Amaru*, might cause the projects to link Brazil to the Pacific coast, see my works from 1993 and 1995, as well as *La Ciudad de Lima: de Perla del Pacífico a 'Calcuta de América Latina'*, (see Further Reading section). If the guerrilla movements revive, especially Shining Path, I would update what I said then: the war policy adopted by the SP, destroying the infrastructure, would make it impossible for Brazil to have access to the Peruvian Pacific. If this were the case, what applies to Colombia would then apply to Peru as well.

37. "*National Geographic Society. South America*," October 1972, map (see Further Reading section). My geographic references here were mostly taken from the NGS map, unless clearly stated otherwise. International geography acknowledges that the Amazon River originates in Peru with the same name—as the map clearly shows the two rivers forming the Amazon in Peru: River Marañon and River Ucayali. Nevertheless, geographers in Brazil do not acknowledge this fact. For example, in the Project Radambrasil map (see Further Reading section: Brazil) the river is called "Marañón" before it enters Brazil; already in the Brazilian territory, it becomes "Solimões" up to the point where it joins Rio Negro (whose origin is in Colombia/Venezuela border) near Manaus. Only from that point in space, its name becomes Amazon River. However, it is internationally acknowledged that since 1541, the Amazon River became part of the western, and global, history. Its name was given during a "discovery" enterprise ordered by the first European governor in Peru, the *conquistador* Francisco Pizarro. Why is it that Brazil does not accept what is acknowledged by geography and history worldwide? I have discussed the subject, and have a hypothesis: for geopolitical reasons and cyclic hegemonic trends in Brazil; more detail in my works of 1993 and 1995.

38. More detail in: "Brasil—Perú: un gran proyecto de integración. Entrevista con el Embajador del Brasil," *Quehacer*, no. 71, pp. 62–66 and "De Brasil a Japón pasando por el Perú. Una entrevista con Enrique Amayo," *Quehacer*, no. 70, pp. 72–80.

39. Perú. Instituto Nacional de Planificación—INP, "*Atlas Histórico Geográfico y de Paisajes Peruanos*," Presidencia de la República—INP—Asesoría geográfica, Lima, 1969, p. 22.

40. V. Arrospide M., R. "Via Interoceánica Peruana," *Revista del Instituto de Estudios Histórico Marítimos del Peru*, Lima, no.13, July–December 1994, p. 81.

41. Perú. Instituto Nacional de Planificación—INP. "*Atlas Histórico Geográfico y de Paisajes Peruanos*, p. 22.

42. For instance, based on this road from Saramiriza to Paita, the approximate distance would be 726 kms.; See. Arrospide M., R., "*Via Interoceanica Peruana*," p. 76.

43. Applying the same criteria to other parts of the South American continental mass, we would have the following results. The furthest Northern point is in Colombia, so this country has an advantage in relation to the Caribbean and the U.S. Western coast. Brazil has the furthest Eastern portion, what gives it an edge in relation to Africa's Western coast. And Chile owns the furthest Southern lands, having advantages in relation to the Antarctic Continent. Information based on the map mentioned, and others such as in *"Encyclopaedia Britannica do Brasil. Geopédia,"* vol II (see Further Reading section).

44. More detail: see my works of 1993 and 1995, and the mentioned *Quehacer* interviews.

45. This territory is in Piura Department (equivalent to State, in Peru). Off this Department, on the Pacific Ocean, towards West, the two largest ocean streams on earth meet: the Peruvian Stream (cold, comes from the South) and the Equatorial Stream (warm, comes from the North). This circumstance turns this region an exceptional case in terms of sea life.

46. The Brazilian ambassador in Peru raised these possibilities during the mentioned interview.

47. V. Perú—Cámara de Diputados.

48. V. Acuerdo de Cartagena . . . In terms of political division, a State is equivalent to a Department, in Peru.

49. Lula, the Workers' Party leader (PT) was elected President of Brazil on October 3, 2002. On January 1, 2003, he said in his inauguration speech, "Our great priority in foreign policy is to build a politically stable, prosperous, united South America, based on democratic ideals and social justice we will support the institutional agreements needed to create a true identity between MERCOSUR and South America. We will show the same dedication to cooperate materially and to have significant conversations with the Latin American countries . . ." See Folha de S. Paulo, *"Discurso do Presidente Lula."*

50. "In September 2000 [Brazilian President Fernando Enrique Cardoso], the twelve South American presidents met in Brasilia . . . and decided to provide the regional integration with a new drive, which was considered an essential element of their development strategy. They undertook to design and apply an Action Plan for the South American Physical Integration, on a 10-year term. They requested technical and financial support from the Bank for Interamerican Development (BID), the Corporación Andina de Fomento (CAF), and the Fondo Financiero para el Desarrollo de la Cuenca del Plata (Fonplata)." V. www.iirsa.org, Accessed on October 19, 2005.

51. See in Valor, "Declaração do Senhor Presidente da República, Luiz Inácio Lula da Silva, à Imprensa, durante visita de trabalho do Presidente do Peru, Alejandro Toledo," *Palácio Itamaraty*, April 11, 2003, p. A-14.

52. IIRSA has 10 projects (going across South America, from North to South, and from East to West) named "Integration and Development Axis" corresponding to the mentioned Corridors. Here, Toledo is referring to a part of the Integration and Development Axis Peru-Brasil-Bolivia. V. www.iirsa.org, Accessed on October 19, 2005.

53. "Peru: uma estrada do Brasil ao Pacifico," V. *National Geographic—Brasil*. Two subtitles in the Brazilian edition of NG read: "The hard way. Peruvians confront an odyssey to travel between the Amazon jungle and the Andean cities. Nevertheless they ask themselves: is it worthy to pave the Transocean

roadway, the dreamed way between the Brazilian border and the Pacific?" and "To the sea, for Peru. Way of riches or ruins?"

54. Ibid.
55. Ibid., p. 115. The 1970s, the "Economic Miracle" decade, were the toughest period under the military dictatorship in Brazil from 1964 to 1985. Chico Mendes's killers, a father and his son, escaped prison and even though they were recaptured, they have not received the deserved punishment. The murder happened during the José Sarney administration, the first administration by civilians, after the "Democratic Opening" in Brazil. Chico Mendes was a member of the Workers' Party.
56. Ibid., p. 116. It also says that the state of Acre's Secretary for Science, Technology and Environment, Carlos Edegard de Deus, thinks that the goal for this roadway would be "to export forest goods, soy beans and, later on, manufacture goods to Asia."
57. See *Brasil,* "Declaração do Senhor Presidente da República, Luiz Inácio Lula da Silva, à Imprensa, durante visita de trabalho do Presidente do Peru, Alejandro Toledo." Also from September, 2005, "the Interocean Roadway connecting Brazil to Peruvian ports of Ilo, Maratani and San Juan, on the Pacific Ocean, starts to materialize today when we lay the keystone in Puerto Maldonado (Peru), and effectively start the works. . . . With the participation of presidents of Brazil, Luiz Inácio Lula da Silva; Peru, Alejandro Toledo; and Bolívia, Eduardo Rodríguez . . . The road is 2,600 kilometers long, of which 1,100 inside Peru . . .," V. O Estado de S. Paulo, "Construction of Interocean Rodway starts."
58. Bridge and roadway are already under construction: "PROINVERSION [*Peru's Investment Promotion Agency*] bids the construction works for an inter-ocean corridor Peru-Brazil. Investments needed are $892 million . . ." V. Newsletter electronic newspaper *Alert@ Económica,* January 19, 2005.
59. In the papers I say that this road would go across the land in Southern Peru where are the origins of a few most important civilizations in America before the European invasion, namely Tiahuanaco, Wari, Incas, etc. These sites are key to understand civilization and cultures in the American continent, as well as in the world. It would take extra care to build a roadway on these lands.
60. Source: www.areasprotegidas.org/argentinageografiafisica.php. Accessed on July 8, 2005.
61. Source: *Brasil—Ministério de Relaciones Exteriores* (See. Annex 6.2.)
62. Source: *The New Encyclopedia Britannica,* vol. 29, p. 459. Results from rough estimates based on our source (map) with the help of a rule and the map scale.
63. This is obvious, and during the World War II this land was used. The United Stated, in alliance with Brazil, built military bases to use against the Axis countries in the Northern Africa campaign.
64. This needs an explanation. Pinochet withdrew Chile because the remaining governments, by request of the Peruvian administration of Velazco Alvarado, wanted to put a cap on the money remittance from foreign investments in their countries. Pinochet was against it, and his position became clearer later on when he became an advocate for neoliberalism. After Chile's withdrawal, this country became a main partner for the international capital, and accomplished its geopolitical goal, to weaken GRAN. The latter did not occur in its entirety, though, since Venezuela joined GRAN almost at the same time.

65. Source: *The New Enciclopaedia Britannica*, vol. 16, p. 572; see explanations in note 62.

66. Source: www.areasprotegidas.org/venezuelageografiafisica.php. Accessed on July 8, 2005.

67. Source: *The New Encyclopedia Britannica*, vol. 17, p. 1038; note 62.

68. See note 29.

69. This sea is a key region in terms of world history because in here a very important stage in the process of incorporating the New World into the western and World History was played, from the moment Colombo arrived, in 1492. More recently, it was also vital for the United States to project itself at continental and world levels. Mainly after 1898, when the United States (as part of its imperialist policies) took Cuba and Puerto Rico. In 1903, it helped "to free" Panama from Colombia. Later on, the Canal Zone was cut out from Panama and the Panama Canal was built (it opened in 1914, when the First World War started—a mere coincidence?) and became a fundamental tool to control the international trade for decades. The Canal Zone, ruled by a governor who reported directly to the president of the United States, returned under Panama's formal authority on the last day of 20th Century.

70. These Colombian territories are very important to transport goods of all kinds, including illegal drugs.

71. Source: *The Economist—Pocket.—World in Figures*, 2001 edition, p. 17.

72. Source: *Encyclopedia Britannica*, 2003 Book of the Year, pp. 785–793..

73. Ibid. p. 785. The size of the state of São Paulo is 248,177 km^2 and its population, 36,966,527 (Ibid., p. 565). It is 11 times smaller than Argentina, although its population is slightly larger than Argentina's. São Paulo is one of the most densely populated and urbanized areas in the west, with many roadways connecting important cities, and forming one massive urban complex. Argentina has 36,223,092 inhabitants (Ibid., p. 545).

74. Ibid., p. 784.

75. Source: *The Economist—Pocket.—World in Figures*, 2001 edition, p. 40; these figures probably refer to the year 2000. Although an update is needed, my intention was to point out to trends. The list only ranks the 50 top countries in the world, that is why you don't see Uruguay or Paraguay (members of MERCOSUR).

76. Source: *Encyclopedia Britannica, 2003 Book of the Year*, pp. 786, 787–790. The information on Lima is from *The Economist—Pocket.—World in Figures*, 001 edition, p. 17. Among the 30 largest cities in the world, Lima ranks 26. We used the same source for São Paulo, Buenos Aires and Rio de Janeiro.

77. Source: *Encyclopedia Britannica. 2003 Book of the Year*, pp. 786, 787–790.

78. Not only for its population. This is the only South American capital city on the coast, and the largest Latin American city on the Pacific, and it has a millenary history. From 1535, the *conquistadores* built Lima on top of ancient pre-Colombian urban areas (destroying them), and turned it into the capital of the Spanish empire in South America. In Lima, they opened the University Nacional Mayor de San Marcos (founded in May 1551, the oldest in the Americas, in charge of starting several other higher education institutes in Latin America since the end of sixteenth-century). Lima had the first printing press in South America (books started to be printed in 1584). The city played a key role when the West began to exploit the South Pacific after Alvaro de Mendaña's voyage (he left the port of El Callao in 1567, following some

complex routes established by the pre-Incas high cultures on the seacoast). Lima also played a unique role in South American Independence since it was the residence for the most important *Libertadores* (Túpac Amaru, San Martín, Bolívar, Sucre, O'Higgins, etc.). This helps to explain why GRAN's permanent offices are located in Lima. Finally, in 1990, UNESCO stated that Lima is a Cultural Patrimony of Humanity (for further information see my 1999 and 2002 articles).

79. *The Economist—Pocket.—World in Figures*, 2001 edition, p. 40; this list only includes the first 50, therefore Bolivia and Ecuador (both in GRAN) were excluded.

80. Ibid., p. 41; the list included 42 cases, Venezuela was excluded.

81. The United States became a continental, and worldwide, power after the railway connection between the Atlantic coast (New York) to the Pacific coast (San Francisco) in the 1860s. This railway materialized the prospective agricultural richness of the U.S. inland (the famous "Prairies") and gave way to the largest national market in the world. After this, in less than four decades, the United States became the first economic world power. Euclides da Cunha did pay attention to these relevant facts, as we see in his work "*El Primado del Pacífico.*"

82. See: Brack, E., A. "Peru: ten thousand years of domestication," *Legado*, No. 3, Año 2.

83. "Caral may be the oldest city of all in the Americas. This site in Peru indicates that the local civilization is older than thought." *O Estado de S. Paulo*, April 30, 2001. And still: "Forget the Egyptians. Archaeologists from Peru and United States were able to obtain dates showing that as early as in 2,627 B.C. the ancient inhabitants of the central coast in Peru were living in cities, and built pyramids, one century before the construction in Egypt of the famous Gizé monuments. Researchers, led by Ruth Shady Solís, from University Nacional Mayor de San Marcos.believe that Caral. is the oldest city in the Continent . . . Jonathan Haas, from Chicago's Field Museum . . . and his wife, Winifred Creamer, are co-authors of the study about Caral's age, published by Ruth Shady . . . in the U.S. journal *Science*." See "In Peru, the oldest city in the Americas. Dates reveal that Caral, on the Peruvian central coast, is older than the great pyramids in Egypt." Folha de S Paulo, April 27, 2001, p. A14.

84. *Folha de S. Paulo*, "Amazon: Sivam's Radar May Watch Colombia. Passing information on to the neighbor country depends on agreements; it may help fight drug dealers," March 24, 2003, p. A7.

85. Ibid., "With no need to cross the Brazilian borderline, the long range radar in Sivam surveillance aircraft R—99A is able to detect aircrafts flying at a distance of around 200 km inside the Colombian territory."

Chapter 7

Latin America vis-à-vis the FTAA: Between Relaunching and Alternatives

Jorge Mario Sánchez-Egozcue and
Lourdes Regueiro Bello

This chapter attempts to identify the main integration dynamic in the Latin American and Caribbean region within the framework of two events: on the one hand, the political changes taking place in South America after the electoral triumph of Lula in Brazil, Kirchner in Argentina, Tabaré Vázquez in Uruguay, and Hugo Chávez in Venezuela and on the other, the stagnation of negotiations for the Free Trade Area of the Americas (FTAA) from the 2002 ministerial meeting held in Quito and the attempts to save it in Miami at the end of 2003 to the recent presidential summit held in Mar del Plata. Likewise, the chapter includes some considerations on the current restrictions faced by integration processes in Latin America, emphasizing the structural factors supporting the different reactions to this topic.

The Mar del Plata Summit: the Stagnation of FTAA Negotiations is Reaffirmed

In November 2005, the Mar del Plata Summit was to be a convenient occasion for the relaunching of hemispheric negotiations. Although a change was perceived since the first preparatory meetings, in contrast to previous meetings, none of the analyses could anticipate what happened in the end. Disagreement that was so marked that the existing homogeneous agreement on the final declaration was broken, thus confirming divergence as one of the results of the meeting and not as part of the preparatory negotiations. This was in contrast to the previous summits and ministerial meetings in which despite no progress being made, there was explicit support for the project, except for the reservations stated by Venezuela.

The speech delivered by President Kirchner left no doubts and it demonstrated the contrast between the stand of Mexico, the Central American, and Andean countries together with the United States against Brazil, Argentina, and Venezuela. The FTAA could not progress in a substantial way in the continent, as long as the U.S. stand on agricultural subsidies did not recognize the existing commercial asymmetry and provide acceptable options for conflicting parties, a step that nowadays seems unlikely from the U.S. domestic perspective. The main topic derived from this outcome will be the end of the Latin American and Caribbean integration plans.

It is important to bear in mind that what happened in Mar del Plata had a precedent, namely:

- The stagnation of negotiations due to the persistent—and unresolved—contradictions between the United States and Brazil on agricultural subsidies.
- The bilateral nature of the negotiation process having the FTAs as an expression of the U.S. ability to generate options to allow progress on the agenda in a comprehensive way and in more reduced spaces.
- The FTAs progressed in those countries and subregions with less resistance to the progress on the U.S. commercial agenda where fewer "special" concessions were required.
- The structure of the process implied the temporary exclusion of negotiations with CARICOM, MERCOSUR, and Venezuela.[1]

From the inter-American perspective, two strategic processes were identified that constitute the basis for the evolution of other treaties in the hemisphere. The most important one, despite obstacles, is still the FTAA project proposed by the United States since it shapes the rest of the continental discussions, thus promoting a North-South integration with a Pan-American content and a global scope. On the other hand, the South-South model promoting a "reactive coexistence" vis-à-vis this project and represented by MERCOSUR is structured on a scheme of subregional reinforcement and represents a relative political independence from Washington and, more recently, the Bolivian Alternative (ALBA) that, unlike the FTAA and MERCOSUR does not have a normative character but a set of agreements not embracing all economic relations and with a different philosophy.

The structural factors conditioning the different positions against liberalization in general, and the FTAA in particular, are: the economic dependence on the U.S. market, the size of the economies, the role played by the subregion in the strategies set forth by transnational corporations in the United States, the reaction capacity against liberalization processes, and the costs and benefits associated with them. The combination of all these factors resulted in different degrees of convergence and resistance. Bearing in mind these elements, three positions with different levels of resistance against the project proposed by the United States can be identified:

- Convergent: Central America and the Caribbean;
- Intermediate: countries from the Andean community who, in a general sense are convergent, but since they do not have diversified and larger economies than the Central American ones, have developed a more prolonged and complex FTA negotiation with the United States; and finally

- An integration strategy more independent from Washington: the MERCOSUR and Venezuela who are not willing to sign the agreement based on the conditions set forth.

These different responses have forced the United States to modify the original concept of the "single" proposal after the launching of the FTAA at the Summit of the Americas in 1994 in Miami, thus progressively adapting it to a "flexible selective liberalization" strategy. The strategy includes different and simultaneous negotiating modalities, both bilateral and subregional, with a common strategic objective: to achieve the implementation of the more sensitive elements before the holding of the WTO Ministerial meeting in Hong Kong as well as to readapt their strategy to the scenario set after Mar del Plata.

Against the several economic and commercial synergies, the United States has developed the competitive liberalization strategy as a pillar of its trade policy, namely: "The prevailing trade policy doctrine of 'competitive liberalization' contends that since multilateral liberalization is difficult, preferential deals should be adopted as a second best route to achieve broader liberalization. Thus, the objective is to use these bilateral PTAs (in conjunction with global and regional negotiations) to create momentum for trade policy."[2]

The activism deployed by the United States Trade Representative (USTR) in trade agreements with different scopes under the Bush administration is significant.

Agreement	Status
Multilateral Agreements	
GATT	Contracting Party—January 1, 1948
WTO	Member—January 1,1995
FTAA	Negotiations began is 1994 but are currently stalled
Free Trade Agreements in the Western Hemisphere	
NAFTA	Entry into force—1994
United States—Chile	Entry into force—2004
CAFTA-DR	Date of signature—August 5, 2004. Expected to enter into force in January 2006*
U.S.-Andean FTA	Negotiations began in May 2004 but have not been concluded
U.S.-Panama FTA	Negotiations began in April 2004 but have not been concluded
Other Agreements	
United States—Israel FTA	Entry into force—1985
United States—Jordan FTA	Entry into force—2001
United States—Singapore FTA	Entry into force—2004
United States—Morocco FTA	Signed, not yet in force
United States—Australia FTA	Date of signature—May 18, 2004, not yet in force
United States—Bahrain FTA	Date of signature—September 14, 2004, not yet in force

Sources: Organization of American States (OAS), Foreign Trade Information System (SICE); Inter-American Development Bank, *Beyond Borders*, p. 26.

* CAFTA-DR has been ratified by Dominican Republic, El Salvador, Honduras, Guatemala, and United States. Costa Rica has not yet ratified the agreement.

Tomado de: Villarreal, M Angeles: "*Trade Integration in the Americas*," CRS Report for Congress, RL 33162, November 22, 2005 from Internet: http://fpc.state.gov/documents/organization/57510.pdf, p. 14.

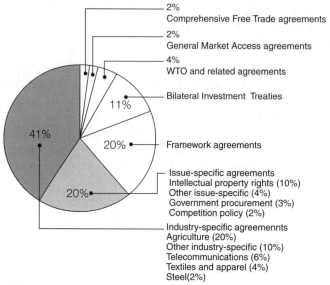

2% Comprehensive Free Trade agreements

2% General Market Access agreements

4% WTO and related agreements

Bilateral Investment Treaties

11%

41%

20% Framework agreements

20%

Issue-specific agreements
Intellectual property rights (10%)
Other issue-specific (4%)
Government procurement (3%)
Competition policy (2%)

Industry-specific agreemennts
Agriculture (20%)
Other industry-specific (10%)
Telecommunications (6%)
Textiles and apparel (4%)
Steel(2%)

Sources: GAO analysis of Agriculture, Commerce, and USTR data

Note: Subtotals for issue - and industry-specific agreements do not add up to category totals because of rounding.

This strategy supposes the promotion of agreements of different kinds and scope depending on the region and the American interests in them, as can be seen in the figure above.

The FTAs do not have a significant weight; nevertheless, to the Latin American region this is the typical way of negotiation. Bearing in mind that these are more comprehensive agreements both in extension and depth in the trade agenda of the United States, we can assume that Latin America is the region where the implementation of this U.S. global trade agenda will be more comprehensive.

The Latin American Perspective and the United States Perspective

The history of integrationist processes in Latin America clearly reflects the outcome of a conflict, whose effects are broader and deeper than those associated with the adaptation of their economies to international changes. The creation of attitudes and opinions on topics affecting hemispheric relations has always been a question of expanding ramifications where external pressures and obstacles to achieve a consensus between domestic political and economic factors converge.

As intellectuals, politicians, and personalities from different positions have pointed out, the true challenge for Latin Americans is the definition of their own project, a viable one against hegemonic pressures and the American cultural influence. Such a definition cannot be homogeneous; neither can the conditions and resources in these countries. However, it implies the articulation of the individual interests of each country at three levels that do not always coincide: the global, hemispheric, and subregional levels.

In the economic sphere, the main challenges of the region, as identified by the Economic Commission for Latin America and the Caribbean (ECLAC) include: (1) the global economic risks, (2) dependence on exports of raw materials with low value added, (3) adoption of reforms aimed at promoting efficiency, and (4) problems of income and inequality.[3]

In the Latin American case, the incidence of tensions and opportunities generated by the international context are translated into a conciliatory Latin American fear of rejection by the United States. Generally, trade relations outside the hemisphere play a more limited role as a result of their geographic proximity to the United States, and/or their economic small size, that is, "the size of the market and the geopolitical sensitivity play an important role."

Likewise, negotiations with the United States cannot be the same for food exporting countries like Brazil and Argentina, as for the net food importers. This explains the considerable intransigence of the exporting countries against the U.S. persistence to keep agricultural subsidies. In summary, the structural differences result in differential resistance and negotiating capacities for Latin American countries whose main objective in the negotiation is to gain access to the U.S. market. That is why the global trade activism developed by the current U.S. government, materialized in a great number of agreements signed or under negotiation, acts as an additional pressure upon Latin American countries to negotiate with the United States due to its fear to enter late into that market.

In the case of United States an excessively active extracontinental presence close to its frontiers with Canada, Mexico, and the Caribbean results in a stronger response to the idea of sharing markets located further toward the south. The experience of the 1990s is more illustrative with the new entrance of textile producers from Asia into the Central American and Caribbean region. This caused a strong disagreement in the U.S. Congress among lobbyists from the domestic producers on the threats this might pose. However, due to the magnitude of commercial flows, the challenge represented merely a portion of the exchange with any region that led to the approval of the United States Trade and Development Law for the Caribbean Basin (TDA 2000–CBTPA), which better clarified conditions for the countries with access to the American market in exchange for the obligation to import textile fibers to their producers.

From the economic and commercial point of view, the United States was interested in these agreements for the implementation of the rules and standards that could give them facilities and security to U.S. capital, as well as to promote the liberalization of services, investments, and preferential access to strategic resources.

Bearing in mind the motivations, interests, and conditions of the United States and Latin America, it is valid to state, in the first place, the admissible margin of tolerance and separation from the concept of American national security for each region and, in the second place, whether an extrahemispheric commercial relation could become an alternative or counterweight of Latin American countries to the United States. Likewise, it would be legitimate to evaluate whether the on-going functional readaptation in interregional relations could reduce the weight and significance of a relationship with the United States.

The Extra-Hemispheric Actors

In Latin America, the bloc that has developed strong extrahemispheric relations both in the North-South axis and the South-South axis has been the MERCOSUR that has signed "Fixed Tariff Preferential Zone" (FTPZ) agreements with India, considered as the first step in laying the foundations for a trade liberalization agreement. Two members, Argentina and Brazil, together with Chile, embarked on an intense commercial offensive with China and have taken some initial steps to approach the Middle East. MERCOSUR also persists in negotiations aimed at the creation of a free trade area with the European Union (EU).

Nevertheless, the importance of these agreements is relatively limited. In the Latin American perspective, two main pillars standout due to their strategic importance: the European Union and China, each with its own peculiarities due to their character but with some common elements serving as a contrast to the American integration model and the subregional grouping dynamic.

The European Union

The main characteristics of transatlantic commercial relations between Latin America and the European Union can be summarized as "highly concentrated" and, save a few exceptions, "with a tendency to decline," giving way to new intrahemispheric agreements. The Latin American participation in total trade with the 15 European Union countries in 1994 to 2003[4] declined from 5.8 percent to 4.6 percent. The 5.9 percent European exports (EU-15) to Latin America dropped to 4.6 percent and imports from 5.7 percent to 4.7 percent.

The European Union capacity to maintain or expand its involvement in Latin American markets is strongly oriented to two subregions: MERCOSUR (representing 44 percent of the Latin American total trade with the EU-15)[5] and the Andean Community of Nations (with a much more reduced weight, 12.8 percent). At the individual level, there are three outstanding countries: Brazil (33.9 percent), Mexico (25.3 percent), and Chile (8.9 percent). The rest are not so significant both from the subregional—MCCA (Central American Common Market) (4 percent), CARICOM (2.9 percent), and national point of view.

Though Mexico is the largest market in purchasing volume for European exports to Latin America (it absorbs 40 percent of the total exports surpassing even purchases by MERCOSUR), in relative terms, Brazil, Argentina, and Chile are the countries with the highest levels of European imports in their economies. The main exporter in the subcontinent to the European Union is Brazil by a broad margin. Recently, the levels of trade increase are more active in small countries, as was already mentioned, since the year 2001, this trend has been slow, with a constant reduction in trade relations, save Mexico, which has been reporting a slight increase.

The most important political instruments to promote trade between the European Union and Latin America are based on a differentiated approach introduced in the mid-1990s in a Policy Document of the European Commission entitled "The European Union and Latin America: Current Situation and Perspectives for a Closer Association 1996–2000" defining the guidelines to promote a reciprocal trade liberalization.

Unlike the U.S. strategy that is discussed later, the premises of the European Union-Latin American trade relations are defined according to the WTO rules and the Generalized System of guarantees and Preferences (GSP) of the European Union which include gradual deregulation mechanisms differentiating receiving countries from specific conditions. Another important instrument in the European Union trade policy is the Lome Convention that gives preferences to ACP (Asia-Caribbean-Pacific) member countries, thus eliminating tariffs from almost every Caribbean export. The basis of the last generation of agreements of advanced cooperation between both parties can be found in) progressive and reciprocal institutionalization of trade which when that, compared with the previous ones, deepen and extend instruments in key areas (intellectual property, science, technology, telecommunications, and information technology). These objectives have a broader scope than commercial concerns and are introduced as part of an approach to support sustainable development, macroeconomic stability, measures to reduce poverty, and consolidation of governance and democracy, thus turning them into a "leverage" in negotiations and allowing the introduction of extra-economic conditions by combining the political objectives with strictly commercial issues.

In practice, they constitute a "common reference framework" that materializes through the implementation of specific free trade agreements with Mexico, Chile and the MERCOSUR. In the case of Central America and the Andean Community, the December 2003 agreements are considered an intermediate stage to further liberalization. In the case of the Kotonou Agreement the Caribbean countries go through a 12-year transition period in tariffs and special treatment regimes until the year 2008.

The main challenge faced by trade integration between the European Union and Latin America has two components. The first one is the erosion generated by the new agreements signed during the last decade between individual countries and regions in Latin America and between those countries and the United States. This erosion represents progressive deviations from the financial and trade flows both to the United States and among member countries in subregional agreements. The second challenge is the distractive effects generated by the European Union enlargement.

The most important difference between the EU and the FTAA integration model lies in the recognition of asymmetries and the need for a differential treatment in the reciprocal liberalization processes from the WTO multilateral standards, as well as the inclusion of parallel financing programs to facilitate the transition process from the current trade regime to the liberalization process. Nevertheless, this factor is only important for the smaller Caribbean economies and has a secondary character for the overwhelming majority of important partners basing their negotiations on components that are more active than liberalization itself.

It has also been stated that one of the most visible political failures between the European Union and Latin America has been associated with the expressed inefficacy of the Ibero-American Summits as a negotiation forum to implement effective additional mechanisms to support the expansion of trade and financial links between both parties. There is a lack of institutional structure and financial support that might promote a follow-up process and concrete responses to objectives stated in other meetings on this issue. In the fifteenth summit held in Salamanca, the recent creation of a General Secretariat to unify the political criteria in agencies like the United Nations constitutes an important step to break previous inertia. However, as the newly appointed Secretary, Enrique Iglesias has pointed out, the reduced margin for a political maneuvering imposed by an agreement on the different powers does not predict great outcomes in the near future.

In summary, save MERCOSUR and some "large" countries (Brazil, Argentina, Chile, and Mexico) the commercial integration role between the European Union and Latin America in the creation of alternatives for hemispheric integration processes does not constitute an element strong enough to challenge the prevalence of the U.S. agenda or to become a feasible short-term alternative for the rest of the "small" countries.

In turn, the European Union must take dynamic initiatives to put an end to the eroding tendencies in trade with Latin America. These efforts must be channeled from within the existing institutional frameworks since the promotion of new institutions demands long and complex negotiation processes with standards soon to become effective after the expansion of the European Union. Consequently, the most probable course of action for the next two to four years suggests a deepening strategy "within" the existing agreements in order to achieve a more effective use of the already approved agreements and financial support programs so as to generate incentives and consolidate current exchange spaces.

Asia—China

The most important challenge of Latin American and Asian relations, seems to be associated with the recent Chinese strategic offensive to capture raw material markets on the continent in order to support its future economic growth.[6]

After fruitless years of attempts by Latin American countries to receive the attention of China and other countries of the region, there has now been a favorable shift. The turning point was marked by the official visit by the president of China, Hu Jintao in 2005, to four key Latin American countries: Brazil, its greatest trading partner in Latin America, Argentina, Chile, and Cuba. As a prelude to his visit, important changes took place that anticipated a future expansion.[7] The country-wise evolution has been as follows.

Brazil: There has been an annual average growth of 61 percent in exports to China in the last four years. In the year 2003, China was the third largest importer of products from Brazil as well as the main buyer of Brazilian soy and the second largest importer of steel with an explosive 500 percent growth. Aside from these raw material purchases there is the possibility for Chinese companies to invest around $8.5 billion dollars in the coming years.[8]

Argentina: Sale of Argentinean products (mainly grains and soy oil) to China increased 112.6 percent in 2003 and surpassed the threshold of $12 billion, thus becoming the fourth larger destination of Argentinean exports after Brazil, the United States, and Chile.[9]

Chile: From this country Chinese companies buy mainly copper (China is the main world consumer of copper—with global annual imports close to 3.5 million tons), cellulose, and fishmeal, while Chile imports from China's emerging power textile and electronic products. In the year 2003, trade exchange between the two countries reached $3.2 billion, making China into the third largest trading partner of Chile behind the United States and Argentina and ahead of Japan, Brazil, the European Union countries, and MERCOSUR. Equally important is the fact that Chile is also a "partner" of the first Free Trade Agreement signed by China in the area since it joined the WTO three years ago, a step that represents a significant advance for the economic giant.

Cuba: The case of Cuba is different when compared with the previous ones. Its market is not so important; nevertheless, the presence of China has generated a considerable shift in the economic performance of the island, besides promoting important benefits for the Caribbean region. China is the third largest trading partner of the island after Venezuela and Spain. In the year 2003, Chinese exports to Cuba accounted for $236 million (electronic manufactures, machinery, and telephone terminals) and imports $121 million (tobacco, chemical products, high-tech medical equipment, vaccines, and seafood). Equally important were investment projects in nickel (Cuba has the second largest reserve of this mineral ore in the world), which will double the current exporting capacity and with joint investments with Venezuela in areas such as infrastructures for oil pipeline transport (pipelines inside the country and a base for large oil tankers that could be vital for the Caribbean Basin) as well as the generation of electricity.[10]

In recent years the trade dynamic has shifted toward Asia. According to current growth rates, organizations like the IMF and the World Bank state that in less than five years China will become the second largest world economy, after the United States, and it is expected that in the Asian region, other nations will also experience a strong growth. These countries do not yet have enough resources and are important importers of raw materials in mining and fuel, energy, oil, steel ore, natural resources, processed food, and so on, so in practice the needs for Asian growth is complemented with Latin American exports. The demand projections surpass current capacity to meet them so a marked encouragement of investment in those sectors is also expected—a future guarantee to support the economic growth in coming years and to facilitate technological modernization.

Chinese imports now account for $300 billion per year, and those of MERCOSUR currently represent less than 2 percent of those imports. However, due to the effect of the market size, the guarantee of a slight increase in the percentage will mean considerable volumes of expansion. The benefits of the Asian alternative would be strongly oriented to specific countries (the large economies in the south) and will not involve the subregional blocks in a direct way,[11] at least not as collective institutional agreements of trade liberalization, though it is probable that they might generate some synergies favorable to the interior of the MERCOSUR as a consequence of demand for exports (and profits generated) and the corresponding increase of needs in infrastructure, equipment, and intermediate goods.

Among the aspects that might generate other important developments is the bold step taken by the Brazilian President Lula when recognizing that China was a "market economy,"[12] something that will presumably guarantee that China will favor Brazil vis a vis other local competitors, while posing some risks for national businessmen since such status implied limitations to sanctions that could be imposed in case of dumping and antidumping, thus reducing the protection of the industrial sector in the region. Regarding the risks, there is a possibility of China flooding the South American market as an exporter of low-cost manufactured goods as it has been doing in other regions, especially in the textile and footwear sectors resulting in the displacement of domestic producers.

Unlike the European option, the Asian variable has barely begun dealing with the integration models of reciprocal liberalization after signing an agreement with Chile that represents an extremely important precedent to determine the way in which future relations between Latin America and the Chinese giant will consolidate. Another element contrasting with the European model is the lower vulnerability of commercial flows of Latin American raw materials against price variations in international markets due to the inertia associated with the deep growth rates in the Chinese economy, an inertia that is believed to provide a relative stability to export demands.

The trade relations with both the European Union and China have common elements such as the attention paid to larger economies in the southern cone. Therefore, the countervailing effect in both forms of international integration vis-à-vis the American integration has less importance when Latin American countries are geographically closer to the United States and if their economies are "smaller." In none of these cases the access policy to these markets, the treatment of foreign investment, and so on surpass the WTO multilateral regulatory framework. Finally, in both forms of integration the "trickle down" effect aimed at the interior areas of the subregions or the south-south agreements is relatively weak since there are no significant synergies so far.

The Hemispheric Factors of Integration

The Main Power Lines

Globalization is concretely expressed toward the interior of the American continent as a conflict between two basic projections of internal character: one, the U.S. project attempts to create a continental free trade area from the political and strategic "vision" mainly generated "to and from" the north and, on the other hand, the option of "reactive coexistence" or "strategic regionalism" represented by the MERCOSUR bloc led by Brazil and the set of initiatives led by Venezuela under the umbrella of the Bolivarian Alternative for the Americas (ALBA). These projections mark the dynamic of what is occurring in the hemisphere in the integration sphere. The differentiating elements between them could be established through the difference in proposals and/or priorities of insertion; the differentiation found in the main allies serving its projection, and the nature of the proposal.

For Central America, the Caribbean, and the Andean countries (except Venezuela) the insertion compass indicates the search for a free trade agreement with the United States, for the MERCOSUR, though taking into account the importance and weight of that relation, is not the same. In the negotiations with the United States for the FTAA creation, asymmetries are evident, not only in the level of development but also in the nature of the demands; while the MERCOSUR demands refer to instruments of commercial policy hindering access to markets; those introduced by the United States are aimed at changing policies and reducing the regulatory and involvement capacity of the state. Despite the fact that agricultural subsidies pose an obstacle for negotiations with the European Union, there are differences since European demands are specific and concrete in services, investment, and government procurement, while in the case of the United States differences are more conceptual and could imply subordination to their interests.

Within this context, the response given by MERCOSUR has been the prioritization of negotiations within the WTO framework and consolidation of the bloc against negotiations in the FTAA and the European Union. This defined as a policy is a clear sign of a change in priorities thus explaining the attention paid to other areas. Recent agreements signed by Brazil and Argentina with China constitute an opportunity to alleviate the pressure of having to complete the negotiation with the United States, though it could mean the consolidation of the South American international insertion pattern based on a dependence on basic resources with low value added.

However, the political will of current governments does not necessarily reflect a consensus within the business sector concerning an insertion not giving priority to negotiations with the United States and the European Union.

The expansion in relations aimed at other areas is an achievement of the bloc policy which can allow it to increase its negotiating power. However, the expansion could also be a weakness if it does not have an institutional structure supporting it; or if it does not develop the capacity to relocate the productive resources in the interior of the network itself. From the commercial point of view, the institutionalized agreements with India and the South African Customs Union (SACU) are favored by the importance of manufactured goods that lessens the effect of negotiations with the European Union, the FTAA, and China itself.

The political will to reinforce the bloc clashes with an agenda of different needs and priorities of the four countries. For Argentina, the bloc priorities should be concentrated on the creation of a common currency to solve the trade imbalances generated by the competitiveness of the different exchange rates; the creation of the MERCOSUR parliament and the coordination of tax and fiscal policies. Paraguay focuses on treating asymmetries while Uruguay defends a greater flexibility so as not to discard the possibility of a bilateral negotiation with the United States. In turn, Brazil concentrates its efforts on strengthening the customs union whose common external rate responds to the interest of protecting the Brazilian economy.[13]

So far, the MERCOSUR image is more consolidated due to its advances in the external agenda and its capacity to articulate both positions and alliances in the multilateral and bilateral agenda with countries outside the region, instead of domestic advances. This could lay the foundation for a two track MERCOSUR and the risk of having an investment in priorities that in the long run could turn today's strength into a weakness.

The MERCOSUR, propelled by Brazil, is nowadays one of the global pillars of a new South-South cooperation model that is not attempting to become an alternative to relations with the North, but to complement and to increase its negotiating capacity. However, this strengthened external projection is running risks: the emergence of the South American Community of Nations has led some members of this bloc to favor the creation of a single agency representing South American countries in order to prevent an overlapping in integration structures. Such a projection could have two interpretations: a positive one aimed at enlargement and, in parallel, deepening and turning South American countries into an important international partner; the other one has as its main purpose the dilution of imaginary processes so as to lower the ceiling of deeper integration proposals.

Venezuelan proposals and positions are generating a redefinition of significant elements in Latin American cooperation among sectors, and integration in different spaces (CARICOM, the Andean Community of Nations, and MERCOSUR) as well as in topics on energy integration and the governmental role. It should be mentioned that unlike other agreements with a marked normative character, the ALBA has progressed more in agreements responding to concrete critical situations and turned energy integration into a pillar in alternative relations stemming from the political will aimed at structural change. Its identity, as an alternative proposal, stems from the relativity of market mechanisms, without ignoring them: social centrality; development of an economic complement; the strengthening of productive activity, above the speculative one; the priority of the state sector for strategic projects; the search for options devoted to lessen both the mechanisms for the transfer of South resources to the North, as well as dependence relations; the use of countervailed trade in goods and services to finance the intraregional exchange,[14] and the financial support and granting of facilities to job-generating economic activities.

So far, its proposals and initiatives seek the recovery of productive activities whose economic fate is the regional internal market and the creation of income sources. As a project it is taking its first steps and in the short run it is not expected to modify the prevailing economic structures, nor displace the FTAA proposal as a whole. Rather, it constitutes an expression of resistance to the neoliberal model. It does not substitute the model as a whole, but competes with its structures thus prioritizing the political negotiating framework instead of the strictly technical issues.

The key factor in the relations between the MERCOSUR and Venezuela is the energy integration that Venezuela can provide in the context of high oil prices. The incorporation of Venezuela in the MERCOSUR as a full member could become a positive factor for the MERCOSUR in reducing the internal conflict between its two leading members, Argentina and Brazil. During the twenty-ninth MERCOSUR Summit, President Chavez stressed the need to give priority to create economic complements and to recognize asymmetries among member countries.

Venezuela has played a role in the softening of financial pressures on Argentina by the purchasing assets of its debt, thus favoring a climate for a better understanding and enlargement of joint projects between both countries.[15] Although Venezuelan initiatives have been supplemental and functional for the MERCOSUR, Chavez does not limit himself to reforms. During the twenty-eighth MERCOSUR summit, President Chavez made three proposals that obviously go beyond the ideological projections and current practices of the MERCOSUR agreements. These initiatives were inclusion of the socialism-capitalism debate in that space; the creation of a MERCOSUR Truth Commission to expose the actions by the United States against integration; and the creation of the South American Bank to repatriate the part of the Latin American reserves in banks located in the North in order to use them in the consolidation of the MERCOSUR projects.

Likewise, there are important differences in the political relation with the United States. Venezuela is now in the cross-hairs of Washington; especially because, unlike Cuba, it has the real financial capacity to carry out those initiatives that, in the eyes of the North represent contempt for their traditional hegemony. On the contrary, Brazil is considered a more moderate and acceptable partner, whereas Argentina seems to be more concentrated in issues on its domestic agenda. However after the 2003 elections it has been inclined to the consolidation and enlargement of projects with Venezuela, including the construction of an oil pipeline, the pillar of the South American energy ring. Also, Argentina does not have the importance and recognition of Brazil in international fora. It must be added that communication among the leaders in the subregion has not always flowed in favor of regional projections.

The Venezuela Agreement of Energy Cooperation with CARICOM should be mentioned for its importance in the South-South cooperation. Its objective is to contribute to energy security, social and economic development, and integration of Caribbean countries by the sovereign use of energy resources based on the general principles of ALBA. Unlike the trend observed in current FTAA and CAFTA trade negotiations that tend to dilute preferential treatment, the Petrocaribe agreement includes special and differential treatment for the relatively less developed countries in the region. This initiative makes its contribution to social and economic development of countries in this area through a fund devoted to financing social and economic programs with contributions from financial and nonfinancial instruments, even contributions to be made from the financed portion of the oil bill and savings obtained from direct trade. These funds are called ALBA-Caribbean and Venezuela made an initial contribution of $50 million dollars.

The Petrocaribe agreement also states that freight charges shall be charged at cost and PDV Caribe, the PDVSA subsidiary, will guarantee a direct supply, without any intermediary resulting in additional savings for importers in the area. In order to have an idea of what this could represent to Jamaica—a country meeting 90 percent of its energy needs with imports—according to P.J. Patterson, Jamaica's former prime minister, during the last 10 years the energy bill grew considerably, and taking the year 1987 as a reference the GDP increased 20 percent while energy consumption grew 112 percent. The cost of imported oil doubled during 2001–2004 (from $420 million to $800 million). For the year 2004, Jamaica devoted 60 percent of its export income to the purchase of fuel.[16]

Another important element in the concept of Petrocaribe is the financial mechanism. This agreement offers payment plans and establishes differential rates according to the increase in oil prices. It constitutes a substantial advantage compared with that established by Venezuela 17 years ago when the price was below $40 a barrel. Under the new terms the payment period has been extended to 25 years including two grace years and the reduction of interest to 1 percent. Besides, the agreement establishes an extension of the short-term payment from 30 to 90 days. Perhaps the most significant element from the economic point of view is the Venezuelan willingness to receive one part of the differed payment in goods and services. Cuba pays for its oil in significant measure by providing Venezuela with contract workers in health, education, and technical assistance.

However, this cooperation still has some difficulties. According to the rules established in the 1973 agreement that gave birth to this integration project, the CARICOM Secretariat must certify that the agreement does not place any member country in disadvantage. Barbados and Trinidad and Tobago state that the Petrocaribe agreement places them in disadvantage since it harms the interests of Trinidad and Tobago who provides 50,000 barrels a day to countries in the area and suggests that Petrocaribe should be amended to allow Trinidad and Tobago to process the Venezuelan crude oil. Barbados has suggested that even though no country in the community has taken advantage of the Venezuelan proposal, if Barbados does it would violate the CARICOM rules, since the Secretariat has not yet adopted it. CARICOM must then determine whether Trinidad and Tobago has been affected by crude oil purchases outside the region.

In the case of the Andean Community of Nations, the problem is much more complex since it has to do with the feasibility of the agreement on two fronts simultaneously. On the one hand there is the alternative to consolidate links with MERCOSUR and the Andean Community of Nations and on the other the imminent negotiation of a free trade agreement with the United States. If the free trade agreement with the United States is approved, the Andean Community of Nations will be forced to reform the Andean policy that is incompatible with aspects demanded by the United States. These changes would demand Venezuelan agreement at a time when Venezuela assumes the presidency of the Andean Community but with opposition to the Andean–U.S. Agreement. For the time being, the conflict has not yet exploded, but it would not come as a surprise to see a silent rupture where the rest of the members of the agreement choose to give priority to the liberalization agreement with the United States in a virtual "emptying" of the agreement content. The completion of the agreement with the United States may well turn on the results of 2006 presidential elections in Peru and Ecuador.

For now, the ALBA proposals focus on: (1) political relations among Latin American countries as an integration project against the United States; (2) the facilitation of trade and financial services with priority criteria paying attention to deficit areas instead of the conventional market mechanisms, including cooperation in basic education, culture, science, technology, and social infrastructure.

In contrast, the FTAA is a project based on two elements—the political and commercial relations between the United States and Latin America, and its functionality in the most complex scenario of multilateral negotiations in the WTO Doha Round. This variant promotes the readaptation, more or less intensely negotiated through the dissolution or the absorption of many free trade agreements already existing and its main characteristic is the marked asymmetry of economic power and the negotiating capacity of the United States vis-à-vis the rest of the continent.

The third approach, the "strategic regionalism," or the creation of a South American Free Trade Agreement (SAFTA), differs in the conception of the hemispheric integration architecture since it does not propose the dissolution of the previous agreements into a new one but their consolidation as a way to increase the negotiating capacity against the United States. Therefore, it has a mixed content, it accepts only some of the aspects included in the FTAA project considered as convenient for the South American countries, together with the reinforcement of subregional integration and the removal of the more aggressive elements in the FTAA thus leaving aside more complex and sensitive issues to be solved within the WTO framework. Unlike the first one, it does not have a hemispheric projection or a global strategic scope.

The differences between these two positions are clearly expressed when defining the issues to be included in the negotiating agenda and the maneuvering margin of every bloc or country. This is known as the "floor versus ceiling"[17] problem. For many Latin American countries, the maximum concessions they are willing to negotiate (identified as ceiling) constitute the minimum requirements or starting point (identified as floor) of the U.S. position, as in the case of labor and environmental standards. This is due to the fact that the U.S. negotiating strategy stems from the implicit position of inducing the "transfer" of the NAFTA rules, which in many areas surpass the commitments established in the WTO multilateral sphere especially those associated with the intellectual property, treatment of foreign investment, and government procurement.

Though there are no formal rules established to evaluate countries that want to negotiate trade agreements with the United States, literature suggests some factors:"[18]

- Cooperation with the United States on foreign and security policies.
- Support to the United States position on the FTAA and the WTO.
- Capacity of trade agreements to promote political and economic reforms in countries and in the region.
- Capacity for a FTA to counteract disadvantages caused by American firms in other countries and blocs.
- The existence of an opposition or interest in a FTA in Congress.
- Support among businesspeople.
- Capacity of a country to expand a trade agreement and promote regional integration.
- The willingness of a country to negotiate broad agreements covering all economic sectors.

Paradoxically, on the one hand, after what happened in Mar del Plata, any attempt by the United States to impose the FTAA without any concession to the Brazilian demands could provoke the adverse effect of strengthening the relations between Argentina, Brazil, and Venezuela. On the other, evaluations made by American executives on the functionality of the FTAA and the FTAs for the nation's interests do not totally coincide with the interests of different economic sectors that feel threatened by the Latin American competition. As a result, the protectionist trends strengthen in the United States and make use of their political capital to prevent the adoption of these agreements or to obtain significant compensations. This was the experience of CAFTA, considered the most controversial trade agreement ever voted by the U.S. Congress since 1993 when the NAFTA was adopted. There were two influencing factors. First, the disagreement over the adoption of an agreement that did not meet the necessary labor demands for the adoption of a trade agreement by the United States and two, the resistance carried out by the textile and sugar sectors against the acceptance of the additional opening that CAFTA would represent for those countries into the U.S. market. In order to guarantee the votes for its adoption, the Bush administration had to make concessions to U.S. industries that resulted in an amendment to the agreement as it was negotiated by Central American governments. Some of these changes have resulted in delays in the implementation of CAFTA due to last minute resistance in Central America, especially Costa Rica. The implications of this negotiation are acknowledged in a document submitted to the Congress.

> To gain support for the agreement, the Bush Administration made some commitments that, on balance, will reduce the commercial benefits of the agreement to CAFTA countries as originally negotiated. Some analysis believes that this action may send a very negative signal to future negotiating partners about U.S. willingness to negotiate reciprocal trade concessions. An underlying problem for the administration may be that the partisan divide in Congress over trade issues, particularly labor standards, provides defenders of protected industries with greater power than in previous eras.[19]

It should be expected that similar debates would be reopened during the negotiations with countries and regions representing a danger for the interests of certain U.S. economic sectors. This has not happened in the U.S. agreements signed with Jordan, Morocco, Bahrain, and Oman since these are countries that in commercial terms do not constitute a threat to American producers and workers. However, the adoption of the Andean FTA could be very complex in the U.S. Congress.

As can be seen, the spectrum of positions from every Latin American country goes from one extreme to another depending on the specific conditions in every region, due to factors such as the degree of trade dependence with the United States, the flexibility in the reaction against trade liberalization, the size of the economy, the effective negotiating capacity, and the costs and benefits associated with the entry into force of a liberalization agreement.

The Sources of Differentiation

Trade Dependence

Within the framework of previous definitions we can identify three types of Latin American actors[20] (1) pro-FTAA countries, the most vulnerable countries from the economic viewpoint or depending on the United States from the political and commercial viewpoint (CARICOM countries and the Andean Community of Nations),[21] (2) nations with an intermediate position in the

ALCA: Mercados de destino de las exportaciones de bienes, según esquemas de integración, 1990,1996 y 2003 (*En porcentajes*)

País Informante	Mercosur (4)			C. Andina (5)			MCCA (5)			CARICOM (15)			TLCAN (3)			ALCA (34)			Mundo[a]		
	1990	1996	2003	1990	1996	2003	1990	1996	2003	1990	1996	2003	1990	1996	2003	1990	1996	2003	1990	1996	2003
1 Argentina	14.8	33.3	19.1	4.1	4.9	3.9	0.3	0.3	05	0.2	0.1	0.1	17.0	9.8	14.1	40.5	56.2	50.2	12,352	23,810	29,455
2 Brasil	4.2	15.5	7.8	2.8	4.0	3.5	0.4	0.3	0.8	0.5	0.3	1.0	27.9	21.8	28.0	37.6	44.6	44.3	31,397	47,164	72,757
3 Paraguay	39.6	63.2	59.2	1.6	2.9	4.0	0.1	0.0	0.2	4.2	0.0	0.0	4.5	4.4	4.2	56.7	73.7	68.6	959	1,043	1,241
4 Uruguay	35.1	51.3	30.9	1.5	2.8	1.4	0.1	0.1	0.5	0.1	0.1	0.1	12.2	7.6	19.7	50.0	66.9	56.7	1,696	2,391	2,178
Mercosur	**8.9**	**23.0**	**12.0**	3.1	4.2	3.6	0.3	0.3	0.7	0.5	0.2	0.7	23.9	17.2	23.6	39.2	49.4	46.5	46,403	74,407	105,631
5 Bolivia	34.5	17.6	35.3	6.5	24.3	27.0	0.0	0.0	0.1	0.0	0.0	0.0	20.1	23.7	16.5	64.8	70.7	81.7	923	1,087	1,579
6 Cotombia	1.1	1.7	0.9	5.5	17.7	15.2	0.9	1.8	2.9	0.8	1.5	1.5	46.1	41.8	49.8	61.6	68.4	76.3	6,765	10,443	12,500
7 Ecuador	0.6	3.1	0.9	6.9	9.0	17.9	1.8	2.4	2.2	0.0	0.0	1.2	53.7	40.2	42.8	70.9	63.9	69.8	2,713	4,762	5,873
8 Peru	3.6	5.4	3.9	6.5	7.9	8.2	0.7	0.6	0.8	0.3	0.0	0.3	24.9	26.1	32.1	38.3	42.9	54.0	3,313	5,226	6,728
9 Venezuela	2.0	3.7	1.1	2.7	7.6	4.4	2.0	1.8	2.0	1.4	1.3	2.1	55.2	62.6	47.1	66.2	80.5	58.2	18,037	23,029	24,934
Andean Community	2.8	3.7	2.4	**4.2**	**10.5**	**9.7**	1.6	1.7	2.0	1.0	1.1	1.6	49.0	50.1	44.4	62.7	71.2	64.1	31,751	44,547	51,614
10 Costa Rica	0.2	0.5	0.3	0.6	1.9	1.2	9.5	13.8	13.2	0.9	0.8	1.2	50.0	40.7	49.8	65.6	62.4	70.0	1,456	2,780	5,791
11 El Salvador	0.3	0.0	0.1	0.1	1.2	0.4	31.0	44.5	59.5	1.2	0.4	1.3	35.9	20.9	22.9	70.8	70.4	89.7	409	1,023	1,255
12 Guatemala	0.0	0.2	0.0	1.6	2.6	0.5	24.8	28.5	41.3	2.0	1.2	1.4	44.2	42.6	35.5	75.8	79.3	84.1	1,163	2,031	2,635
13 Honduras	0.0	0.1	0.3	0.5	0.4	1.1	4.4	10.6	26.4	0.8	0.3	3.4	52.5	54.9	43.1	58.9	67.7	75.5	554	1,313	956
14 Nicaragua	1.4	0.0	0.0	0.3	0.8	0.3	14.4	15.5	40.5	0.1	0.2	0.2	30.7	46.7	39.2	47.2	65.1	82.1	326	653	550
Central American Common Market (MCCA)	0.2	0.2	0.2	0.8	1.7	0.9	**16.0**	**21.2**	**27.5**	1.2	0.7	1.4	45.6	41.5	42.3	66.7	68.9	76.6	3,907	7,800	11,186
15 Barbados	0.0	0.1	0.1	0.3	11.3	0.1	0.0	00	0.0	31.2	39.3	50.4	16.1	19.9	20.8	47.6	72.0	73.7	213	213	165

16 Belice	0.0	0.0	0.0	0.0	0.0	0.1	00	0.3	8.0	3.0	9.2	56.4	45.2	57.6	64.5	48.3	67.1	105	154	191
17 Dominica	0.0	0.0	0.0	0.0	0.0	0.0	0.0	0.0	25.8	47.6	64.1	8.5	7.0	5.8	33.9	54.6	71.0	53	50	38
18 Granada	2.4	3.5	2.1	1.0	0.0	0.0	0.0	0.0	28.1	27.8	37.5	9.5	24.6	21.4	40.0	57.3	61.8	21	18	25
19 Jamaica[b]	1.1	0.0	0.0	0.2	0.2	0.0	0.0	0.2	6.4	3.7	4.1	41.1	49.1	43.3	49.1	53.7	59.6	1108	1347	1084
20 Santa Lucía	0.0	0.0	0.3	0.2	0.2	0.0	0.0	0.0	16.9	13.0	43.0	19.4	14.7	12.1	36.0	27.7	55.2	120	77	39
21 Suriname[b]	4.8	1.2	0.0	0.0	0.1	0.0	0.0	0.0	1.5	4.8	6.7	11.2	25.5	25.3	17.5	32.2	32.2	473	502	423
22 Trinidad y Tabago	0.2	1.6	2.5	3.3	1.6	0.2	0.8	2.7	12.9	22.1	18.0	58.5	52.1	58.3	77.6	85.6	85.5	2080	2456	5118
CARICOM (8 Countries)	1.0	1.0	0.6	1.2	1.5	0.1	0.4	2.5	11.1	15.5	19.2	44.3	45.6	56.4	59.4	68.0	84.1	4174	4817	5575
23 Canada	0.4	0.6	0.3	0.4	0.2	0.1	0.1	0.1	0.2	0.1	0.1	76.2	80.3	86.5	77.4	81.8	87.3	125 058	199 760	270 066
24 Estados Unidos	1.7	3.1	2.0	1.8	1.4	0.8	1.1	1.6	0.7	0.6	0.7	28.3	30.1	35.8	34.5	38.6	42.8	371 466	575 477	646 507
25 México	1.6	1.7	0.5	1.4	0.7	1.6	0.9	0.9	0.5	0.2	0.1	71.3	85.7	90.6	77.3	91.4	93.4	26 247	95 402	165 234
NAFTA	1.4	2.3	1.3	1.4	1.0	0.6	0.8	1.1	0.6	0.5	0.5	41.9	47.7	56.8	46.9	54.3	61.7	522 772	870 638	1081 607
26 Chile	7.9	11.8	6.2	6.7	6.4	0.4	0.3	1.4	0.0	0.1	0.1	17.6	16.8	24.3	29.9	36.1	39.1	8 292	14 979	19 794
27 Panamá	0.1	0.1	0.0	2.9	1.9	13.3	13.7	11.8	0.1	0.6	0.8	48.8	51.8	54.1	65.5	70.9	70.0	337	558	796
FTAA Countries	2.1	4.0	2.3	1.7	1.7	0.8	1.0	1.4	0.7	0.5	0.6	40.6	45.1	52.9	47.2	54.6	60.4	617 636	1 017 748	1 276 403

Source: From official Statistics.

a/ In millions of dollars.
b/ Without information for 2003. The value in the 2003 column corresponds to 2002 data.
Fuente: CEPAL: "PANORAMA DE LA INSERCIÓN INTERNACIONAL DE AMÉRICA LATINA Y EL CARIBE 2004: TENDENCIAS PARA EL 2005", Cuadro anexo 2.

trade exchange with the United States (Central American Common Market countries(MCCA), and (3) countries with a low trade level with the United States (20 percent or less) and, especially, a strong reciprocal complementarity in their exports at subregional level (MERCOSUR). This initial characterization identifies the FTAA motivations. Countries whose economic activity has a high or moderate component of trade with the United States have strong motivations to act in a convergent way within this project and their negotiating strategies are aimed at the optimization of short-term benefits through individual performance as a first option (Mexico, Chile) or in the second instance in a concerted way (CARICOM, Andean Community of Nations, Central American Common Market (MCCA)) whichever is more convenient.[22]

Trade dependence is not the only way to identify economic vulnerabilities, and the analysis should not be limited to the conventional premises used in the "developed country versus underdeveloped country" framework. A poorly examined aspect has to do with the causes, which, to a certain extent, can be considered new. With the implementation of an increasing number of integration agreements, and as economies become more interdependent, there are other factors that increase the exposure to new risks. When subregional integration agreements are signed among less developed economies, there is a lack of coordination of macroeconomic policies and exchange regimes. This becomes a destabilizing factor that affects both the commitments made and the economic stability of members. Likewise, the agreement on parallel commitments, beside the original agreements, could also exert pressures on the macroeconomic stability.

In some cases this is a problem faced by using a previous agreement as a model and then partially "transferring" its provisions to new agreements in an attempt to achieve a relative homogenization (as in the case of Mexico that has "dragged" the NAFTA provisions to other agreements it has signed). Other countries prefer to resort to a "segmentation" strategy thus creating specific procedures by exchange areas and trade partners (Chile).

Flexibility: Fast and Weak Integrators, Adaptability of Subregions

Trade dependence by itself cannot explain the different Latin American sentiments against the FTAA. Because of this, countries and regions have been defined by their short and mid-term reactions[23] vis-à-vis the trade liberalization agreement.

This classification demonstrates that there are two basic types: the fast and weak integrators.[24] The first type includes those countries or subregions with a short-term trade expansion where favorable effects overcompensate adjustment costs, either because the previous tariff regimes, exchange policies, and general macroeconomic conditions favored this expansion or because the profile of their exports results in immediate benefits for better conditions in access to the market, or because the complementary effects among member

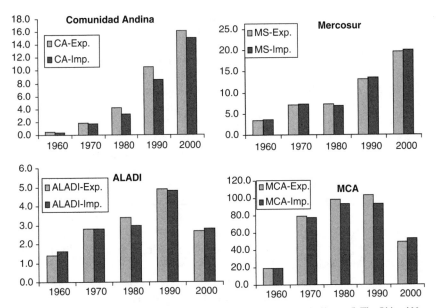

Source: Table 5.4 pages 158–159. IMF data. Direction of Trade Statistics, 2003. Chapter 5. The Old and New Regionalism: Benefits, Costs and Implications for the FTAA, Robert Devlin and Paolo Giordano. In "Integrating the Americas, FTAA and Beyond," Antoni Estevadeordal, Dani Rodnik, Alan M. Taylor and Andres Velasco, DRCLAS Harvard University Press, 2004.

Note: MCCA—Central American Common Market; CAN—Andean Community of Nations; MERCOSUR—South American Common Market; ALADI—Latin American Integration Association.
Latin America, Trade intensity of the regional integration agreements, 1960–2000

countries in the agreement are reinforced. In contrast, the weak integrators are those where there is a clear evidence of the prevalence of costs associated with internal adjustments induced by the agreement and the response is more difficult and slower.

The evolution of intraregional trade intensity shown in the following examples clearly express how these important modifications took place in the subregional behavior patterns since the 1990s in what is known as "new regionalism." As the environment changed as a result of the new trends toward liberalization, it is evident how they induced an acceleration of intraregional trade for members of both the Andean Community of Nations and the MERCOSUR agreement. In contrast, there is a significant retraction in the ALADI (Latin American Integration Association) and the Central American Common Market intraregional trade, which suggests that member countries in these agreements were facing a situation in which they were more exposed to the brunt of a loss of stability in subregional markets resulting in the active search for a redefinition of their trade strategies, as eventually happened.

Market Size and Economic Structure: Large and Small Countries

A nation's adaptation and negotiating capacity not only affects the efficient response to opening markets, but also the clear differentiation in terms of the vulnerability associated with other factors such as the economic size and structure, as in the case of the Caribbean countries.

The existence of a poorly diversified productive structure, and a concentrated exporting pattern in a few low-value commodities and services, together with the reduced size of markets and the insufficient domestic savings to guarantee investment and technological renewal with their own resources,[25] puts countries with these characteristics in a vulnerable position and gives them higher external exposure to the hemispheric mean. Such characteristics create a dependence on foreign financial flows and high tariffs that are more income sources than security. These characteristics of small economies explain their greater sensitivity to changes and effects in case of losing trade preferences and sudden fluctuations in commodity prices.

International recognition of the vulnerabilities of small countries is consensual. However, compensation is limited to the convenience of longer transition periods to facilitate their insertion into new types of integration agreements. Some proposals suggest supporting programs that increase risk-management capacity, make international obligations more flexible, and create funds for the training of negotiators and other transitional support structures. In practice however, there is a concrete fact: concessions are the result of negotiating capacity and this, in turn, is associated with the political "sensitivity" of a region or the economic "weight" it has. The Caribbean countries face a complex situation of high trade dependence on the U.S. market and the loss of the strategic importance they had during the 1980s acknowledged in the Caribbean Basin Initiative (CBI) through which they received tariff preferences and market access. At the time, these guarantees were justified with the purpose of overthrowing the revolutionary government in Cuba.

The current scenario is quite different. Its adverse factors include the substantial erosion of former preferences inherited from the CBI era due to the incorporation of Mexico into NAFTA, a process that caused strong deviations in trade and investment flows and the loss of the regional political sensitivity during the 1980s. As a response, early on, countries in the region resorted to a strategy of demanding equal treatment from United States (level playing field) in access to markets in relation to Mexico. Due to the lack of positive results, there was a further readjustment in two directions: the first was to reinforce liberalization among countries in the region[26] in order to create conditions that would approach the requirements defined by the United States. The other one was to strengthen the Association of Caribbean States (not recognized by the United States since it includes Cuba). Finally, in the year 2000, there was an updating of the CBI as the Caribbean Basin Trade Partnership Act (CBTPA), which improved access to the U.S. market of products that did not exist previously, as in the case of textiles. Until recently the lack of U.S. attention to the Caribbean and the poor results achieved from the regional point of view were generating a relative impasse compared to the activism carried out by the rest of the continent—especially contrasting with the Central American dynamism in Washington to receive the approval for CAFTA. If realized, MERCOSUR's plan for the Caribbean along with the materialization of the Petrocaribe proposal and ALBA Caribe funds could mean the salvaging of a regional perspective. However, we should bear in mind the possibilities and limitations of this cooperation.

Limitations of the Intra-Latin American Convergence

Limitations to the Caribbean-South American Approach

It is unlikely for the Caribbean countries to assume integration positions far from the "magnetic pole" represented by the United States[27] since their priority is to prevent a major marginalization from the FTAA, should it come into existence. Experience has demonstrated that there are still options to diversify, to a certain extent, the collateral costs of the lack of an U.S. attention, but at the same time, it also confirmed that without the intervention of external actors[28] the CARICOM countries have a more limited margin of action than the South American countries to promote relatively autonomous integration policies against the United States. In the best scenario, an active and prosperous cooperation between the Caribbean and South America would not modify in the short term the structural dependence of the subregion on U.S. investment and trade and, at the same time, they still have to face the difficult task of balancing the very important reciprocal asymmetries. It is unlikely that the private sector in both regions could react with great enthusiasm to an approach that is new, risky, and distant for it.

The Large Countries

In turn, the largest economies on the continent[29] have economic structures that are generally not so open where trade share is less concentrated on a single pole and have better capabilities to expand links to the interior of subregions. The Andean Community of Nations and, to a greater extent, MERCOSUR have a more sound and diversified base for trade among their members due to the complementarity in mutual demands, not found in insular economies where the similarity in exports (sugar, bananas, tobacco, etc.) do not provide a broad margin for reciprocal exchange. Likewise, they have a stronger industrial base. Brazil, for example, has an important strategic position in sectors such as electronic manufactures, aviation industry, chemicals, and other industrial products and would not be willing to give in to American transnationals, while Argentina and Chile have specialized in exports of raw materials and foodstuffs.

These differences among small economies with a poor reciprocal integration and high dependence on the American market, against larger economies having a completely different profile, constitute an "objective" differentiation element among Latin American nations and subregions. Aside from the views they might have on integration, it is indispensable to accept the role played by these intra-and interregional asymmetries and, consequently, the reality that the nature and content of the several subregional integration forms have conflicting elements not only in relation to the North but also among themselves. Though the compatible elements prevail over these differences the issue is not strictly economic but a political one. It has a lot to do with the "political climate" in the hemisphere and the outcomes accumulated during a whole decade of neoliberal reforms that constitute the backdrop for these processes.

The significance of these differences became evident shortly after the launching of the FTAA proposal during the 1994 summit in Miami. Soon after the first steps were taken during the preparatory meetings, there was a tacit recognition that the feasibility of the project lay in not forcing the practical limits of every subregion. Since then there has been a "differentiated flexibility" process of the model that evolved towards a number of negotiating strategies where priorities, means, and timetables were subordinated to the relative negotiating capacity of partners. Between the Miami Summit and the Cartagena Ministerial meeting, four negotiating alternatives were proposed: (1) the convergence of previous bilateral and subregional agreements, (2) the enlargement of a single agreement for the hemisphere as a whole, (3) the establishment of a new hemispheric free trade agreement preserving the existing agreements, and (4) the establishment of a strategy with several tracks where the core countries would assume all FTAA commitments and the peripheral countries would gradually join it. The United States position has managed to impose a simultaneous negotiating system including all issues.

Costs and Benefits

An example of how these perceptions have changed is the way in which the different negotiating scenarios are technically evaluated. Initially, there was the assumption that the fear of being marginalized from the process was quite a powerful incentive for Latin American governments to be involved and, and to take national level steps to prepare themselves for expected FTAA integration.[30] However, today we can reaffirm that a number of perspectives have emerged ranging from the estimation of static effects (creation and deviation of trade) and dynamic effects (effects on sectorial productivity and growth) on liberalization by using gravitational models, of both general and partial balance, as well as interactions between investment policies, growth, regional institutions, equity, and economic policy of reforms.

The main elements of the U.S. integration strategy can be identified as follows:

1. To accept that the FTAA can coexist with bilateral and subregional agreements though acknowledging its prevalence and without exceeding the content of commitments made, thus guaranteeing the FTAA supersede the institutional framework of all other agreements.

2. To use regional integration agreements as a geopolitical tool to strengthen the Unites States' international negotiating capacity and searching, to the extent possible, for the introduction of commitments (particularly with issues such as the opening of services and governmental purchases, investment, and intellectual property standards) go beyond the minimum requirements agreed by the WTO. This is done in order to have this factor as a tool for further negotiations during the Doha Round, as NAFTA did during the Uruguay Round.

All these negotiating pressures and strategies confirm that the interest in negotiations and the restriction of concessions to be granted substantially vary, due to the above-mentioned factors. Not only because each party attempts to maximize their own objectives and reduce costs and concessions potentially demanded, but also because the way in which countries and regions integrate, there is an essential conflict between the need for an active insertion in international trade and the support of "economic nationalism."

In the last instance, the true international actors are the transnational corporations whose objectives frequently tend to set aside the local employment, environmental, and poverty elimination needs, just to mention the most urgent ones. A competitive liberalization means the balance of those two objectives: It is no wonder the resistance of MERCOSUR to the "FTAA-style" liberalization that is so different from their attitude toward other forms of integration with Asia and Europe.

Therefore, the evaluations that minimize the integration problem in Latin America to the optimization of the negotiating scenario with the United States can be dangerously simplifying. The integration process' feasibility will depend, sooner or later, on its political and social outcomes. Trade cannot become an end in itself if it is not accompanied by benefits in the balance of trade and payment that translate into favorable changes for an important part of the population. The last 10–year experience with neoliberal reforms in the continent has clearly shown the importance of this statement.

On the other hand, it is also true that if the FTAA, the implementation of liberalization agreements, are not considered there will be an erosion of the subregional preference systems previously established and, similarly, it is logical to see an ambiguous attitude in many cases among countries involved concerning liberalization in any of its versions (the greater the depth of the trickle-down effects on the erosion of preferences the greater the resistance as happened with the MERCOSUR countries and, especially, Brazil).

The negotiating process to reduce FTAA tariffs is carried out mainly on the basis of products classified in different categories according to the liberalization horizon (instantaneous, 5 and 10 years) and the separated list of products considered as especially sensitive. U.S. supplies tend to be constituted by "positive" and "negative" lists (inclusion—exclusion) that vary according to the partner, thus in practice the negotiating system generates differences in treatment resulting not only from the exchange content in terms of commercial goods, services, or investment treatment, but also from the political "sensitivity" and the negotiating capacity of the partner involved.

Among the voices more unrestrictively supporting the partnership with the United States there is also the liberalization inside the FTAA and its role as macroeconomic "stability insurance" during uncertain times. This is because its structure includes transitional countervailing mechanisms and regional financial support funds for occasional adverse shocks in a volatile context such as sudden adjustments in the rate of exchange. Besides, the perspective of a guaranteed access to the U.S. market under these circumstances is considered as an important advantage since it implicitly protects from the negative effects and, in a certain way, assumes that the reciprocal obligations stated in the agreement could induce a greater economic discipline imposed from abroad.

The problem of this assumption lies in the fact that the main content of Latin American exports to the United States includes agricultural goods, in the most protected and subsidized sectors in the U.S. market and, in case of difficulties, it will be illusory to expect that these countervailing tools would be used to consolidate and protect areas in which the view of American producers pose a threat. It is of little wonder that this is one of the issues left aside in the FTAA discussions.

Geopolitics and Development: Integration is More than Access to Markets

Most Latin American integration schemes have shown a poor capacity to generate an intra-Latin American convergence at a crucial time in negotiations with the United States. It has been evident that in these subregions where there is an integration strategy in global chains of production by transnational corporations, the tendency is to jointly negotiate in favor of the U.S. agenda, even though this could mean a risk for domestic sectors. This is the case with Central America and could become the behavioral pattern in the Caribbean, after acknowledging the need for a special and differential treatment for insular and small economies. The same tendency is observed in those subgroups of countries that are recipients of unilateral and temporary initiatives by the United States, whose main objective in negotiations is to maintain the preferences it enjoys in those agreements, as is happening with countries negotiating the Andean FTA.

The performance of extrahemispheric powers in the economic dynamics of different subregions does not seem to alter substantially the hegemonic picture favoring the United States. For the European Union, Latin America is not a priority. In spite of its explicit support for multilateral negotiations, and not with individual countries, it has signed free trade agreements only with Mexico and Chile. Its main interest is concentrated in the most autonomous subregion from American policy, MERCOSUR. However, there are serious divergences in the negotiating process, whose solution is foreseen after the poor outcomes achieved by the WTO in Hong Kong, which postpone expectations to reach an interregional agreement.

In turn, Chinese economic needs represent a dynamic element only for the Brazilian and Argentinean economies. For the rest, it poses a net threat to local industry. From the financial point of view, it seems that investments from China are only significant to Argentina, Brazil, Peru, Chile, and Cuba. Therefore, the booming growth in Asia will not be a counterweight at the regional level. Only in the MERCOSUR case, relations with China, combined with those with India and other markets, could offer a space with more autonomy as compared with the U.S. one. This subregional option is possible with the size and diversification of the market (both in products and as destination). Nevertheless, it should be mentioned that there is the risk of consolidating a partnership based on products with a low processing level.

Regarding the possible creation of a more autonomous Latin American region, facts indicate that under current conditions only the enlarged MERCOSUR with the incorporation of Venezuela can achieve it. Its strength lies in energy integration as an economic pillar of the process for which the subregion has a true comparative advantage as well as a competitive one if current oil prices are considered. However, the pillars for that South American project are more based on the political will of the current governments rather than in economic structures, since so far they do not have the institutional and legal framework to provide them with the momentum that might lead them beyond the political will they have now.

This new integration scenario, mainly in South America, forces the broadening of perspectives from which reflections on this issue are made. Although an important part of the literature on the hemispheric trade liberalization issue is mainly concentrated on access to markets, the institutional difficulties, the coordination of policies and financial instruments, in a more coherent perspective, there is a deeper analysis at a broader level. There are implications for hemispheric political relations, the harmonization of a steady economic growth with policies aimed at reducing poverty, the conciliation of labor standards, the regulation of the environment, and long-term sustainability resulting from this opening.

The dynamics of interdependence in the social, strategic, structural, human, institutional, environmental, economic, and financial aspects lies where they have been increasingly displaced, the debates in international organizations[31] and, to a certain extent, the regional political practice acknowledging the importance of establishing a criterion and comprehensive framework for these problems. This does not mean that there will be an immediate complementary movement to current ways and forms of negotiating hemispheric integration agreements, but it clearly suggests a consciousness at the international level of the challenges this represents. As a result of this process the core of debate is displaced to the completion of agreements themselves, the negative impacts they pose and their social costs on the one hand and the change in regulations.

In the Latin American case, there is still a long way to go before these criteria materialize in development goals incorporated into integration agreements. At the most, they are conceived as countervailing measures to lessen the negative effects caused by the opening of trade especially in relation to agricultural performance, effects on small and medium urban enterprises, and programs aimed at alleviating poverty and containing emigration from the countryside to the city in order to channel the future stages without creating excessive tensions to the governance and stability of institutions.

In practice, the recent trade increases associated with the trade liberalization have been accompanied by an increase in poverty and exclusion figures,[32] translated into a greater social and political polarization. When commitments made initially by these neoliberal structural reform programs were not met, the credibility to continue dropped and the social basis of traditional political parties and the general democratic stability of the continent were eroded. The response to this process has been the tendency to find major problems with the previous model. This seems to be the main cause of the new wave of Latin American leaders (Venezuela, Argentina, Brazil, Ecuador, Bolivia) expressing the obsolescence of the liberal-democratic model and looking for their own approach against external pressures to impose neoliberalization.

The most important aspect of the FTAA integration project is the functionality it has for U.S. policy in Latin America. In this regard, the FTAA does not constitute a separate element, but one of several components of a strategy that consolidates the political bonds at the hemispheric level, thus reducing the possibility of conflicts and guaranteeing the economic and political dominance of the United States. The three elements of this strategic view are: (1) market access, (2) consolidation of neoliberal-inspired macroeconomic structural reforms, and (3) a greater institutional commitment between the United States and the region in order to protect the current architecture of hemispheric political and strategic relations.

Tensions between this project and MERCOSUR, the ALBA, the extra-hemispheric actors and other agreements are associated with a general process of reconfiguration of economic and political interdependences in the hemisphere that will not be exclusively solved within the framework of trade liberalization, but at the level of hemispheric political alliances that, in the last instance, respond to the projections and needs of every nation.

In fact, the deep interconnectivity with which they shape current international relations represents a redefinition of the contents of national sovereignty and implications, the different forms of association when defining and carrying out economic development and growth goals. To acknowledge the interdependence among all these elements in a broader and comprehensive approach does not mean the homogenization of methods and solutions, but the acknowledgment of diversity.

Notes

1. Though Bolivia has not formally initiated negotiations, this country attended as an observer the negotiating process of the so-called Andean FTA. We must clarify that the temporary exclusion does not mean a homogenous position of this group of countries on the agreement.

2. Andriamananjara, Soamiely: "Competitive Liberalization or Competitive diversion? Preferential Trade Agreements and the Multilateral Trading System", USITC, U.S. International Trade Commission, May 7, 2003. http:/www/usaid.gov/location/latin_america_caribbean/trade/index.html Accessed on January 6, 2005.
   * CAFTA-DR has been ratified by Dominican Republic, El Salvador, Honduras, Guatemala, and United States. Costa Rica has not yet ratified the agreement. Villarreal, M Angeles, "Trade Integration in the Americas," *CRS Report for Congress*, RI. 33162. November 22, 2005 on Internet: http://fpc.state.gov /documents/organization/57510pdf. p. 14.
3. José Luis Machinea, ECLAC Executive Secretary, cited in: http://www.usaid.gov/locations/latin america caribbean/trade/index.html.
4. Interamerican Development Bank—IDB Integration and Trade in The Americas. III EU-LAC. Summit: Special Issue on Latin American and Caribbean Economic Relations with the EU, May 2004. United Nations data—COMTRADE. Table 3. "European Union Trade with Selected Regions 1994–2003," p. 62.
5. IDB, Ibid, table 5, p. 66.
6. Other countries like South Korea and Vietnam have been also showing signs of interest during the last summit of the APEC, Asia-Pacific Economic Cooperation Forum in Chile but their influence will not be so important.
7. "¿Qué busca China en A, Latina? Mariana Martínez," BBC. Mundo, November 14, 2004.
8. BBC.Mundo.com "¿Qué busca China en América Latina?", November 14, 2004.
9. Ibid.
10. BBC.Mundo.com, "Chávez estrecha alianza con Castro," April 28, 2005.
11. It should be mentioned that there are two important characteristics in trade relations with China, one is the trade balance deficit and the consolidation of the traditional insertion based on commodity exports.
12. This had a reciprocal political gesture by China when assuming it will support the Brazilian request to have a seat in the United Nations Security Council.
13. Janina Onuki, "MERCOSUR, para além de uma agenda externa," in *Meridiano* 47, no. 47, June 2004 on Internet: http://www.ibri.rbpi.org.br.
14. This instrument will allow the payment of one part of the oil bill to some MERCOSUR and Caribbean countries which will mean an increase of demand for agricultural products facing restrictions of access to markets in industrialized countries, as for example bananas and sugar from the Caribbean and other sensitive products in the negotiations with the United States.
15. It should be mentioned that the reactivation of the Rio Santiago shipyard for the repair and construction of ships for PDVSA, the Venezuelan cooperation in the financing of the "Manos a la Obra" project to improve income, etc.
16. PJ Patterson, Statement to Parliament, July 13, 2005.
17. Maurice Wolf, "Americas Choice, The show Path to Global Trade Cooperation" in *El futuro del libre comercio en el continente americano. Análisis y perspectivas*. Sergio López Alyllon, ed. UNAM, Mexico, 1997, p. 87.
18. Fergusson, Ian F. and Sek, Lenore M, "Trade Negotiations During 109th Congress," *CRS Issue Brief for Congress*, Borrador, pp. 2–3.
19. Ahearn, Raymond J, "Trade Liberalization Challenges Post-CAFTA," *CRS Report for Congress*, RS 22339, November 30, 2005; on Internet: http://fpc.state.gov/documents/organization/57798.pdf.

20. This definition corresponds to Bulmer-Thomas and is supported by Briceño Ruiz with factors such as the favorable or adverse incentives. From the practical point of view, it is efficient for a preliminary approach. However, it should be noted that it makes no distinction to the interior of the three groups of differences resulting from the "type" or quality of the commercial insertion distinguishing some countries from others. Briceño Ruiz, José, "El MERCO-SUR, Mexico y el Caribe frente al Area de Libre Comercio de las Américas," *Foreign Trade* vol. 51, No. 5, Mexico, May, 2001. Bulmer-Thomas, Victor, "El Area de Libre Comercio de las Américas," *ECLA Magazine*, Special No. October 1998.

21. One significant part of the commercial dependence is explained by the weight of the oil bill.

22. Both the Andean Community of Nations and the MCCA have handled or left open the option of leaving their acurrent group to give priority to an individual agreement due to the delay in the conclusion of regional agreements, such is the case of Peru who stated its willingness to conclude negotiations with the United States before the end of the year 2005, even when it had to postpone collective negotiations with the Andean Community of Nations and finally signed in December 2005 due to the postponement of collective negotiations by Ecuador, and Colombia. Likewise, Costa Rica tried to do it in a similar way during the initial stages of negotiations with the MCCA (CAFTA).

23. There are estimations made with different techniques (models of general and partial balance, gravitational models) in order to evaluate potential impacts (losses) associated with trade liberalization, though these simulations provide a tentative evaluation of the main results to be obtained if the original goals proposed are met during the negotiations, in general terms they are criticized for the impossibility to distinguish the impacts caused by factors such as the gradual nature of negotiations and the crossed effects among countries.

24. This kind of taxonomy has been proposed by James Wolfenson, President of the World Bank, when analysing the relationship between international trade and development and is especially enlightening since it rescues the importance of *inequality* among competitors against neoclassic conventionalism. Cfr. "*Sistema de comercio mundial y la agenda de desarrollo*," EAS:4/00-103:2.

25. Using the conventional opening concept: Exports plus imports in relation to the GDP.

26. The similarities in the economic structure and the content of exports do not allow important increases in the intraregional trade of goods, and due to the same reason it is foreseen that the most important results will be in the infrastructure of transport and communication, environmental cooperation, common rules, and standards and macroeconomic coordination, which seem more difficult to achieve due to the important disagreements in terms of monetary policies, character of economic cycles and conflict of interests.

27. This in no way means that there could be a passive position or a subordination position prevailing in the area. Note that the Caribbean countries have a stronger position in the Latin American agreements on the need to incorporate Cuba against the exclusion pressures exerted by the United States.

28. Here we are not discussing in depth the implications of Caribbean economic links with the European Union since its influence for the region is a collateral one representing barely 13 percent of the total trade in the area in 2003 while the United States and Canada absorb 53 percent.

29. Mexico, a NAFTA member, is excluded here since it deserves another analysis.
30. See the well-known work made by the International Institute of Economy on "readiness" or accessibility indicators.
31. As an illustration, see the statement by James Wolfensohn, President of the World Bank, in "*El comercio y la reducción de la pobreza,*" EAS 4/00-103.2. Intervention at the tenth meeting of the United Nations Conference on Trade and Development (UNCTAD), Bangkok, Thailand, February 26, 2000.
32. According to UNCTAD the price fluctuation of raw materials jeopardizes developing countries "one of the issues under debate at the United Nations Conference on Trade and Development (UNCTAD) held in Brazil (June 2004) was the claim stating that with these free trade agreements and the market opening, the poor countries have not been able to escape from poverty and/or reduce unemployment." Saturday, June 19, 2004. TLC. Países pobres se defienden. Mariana Martínez, correspondent, BBC.Mundo http: // news.bbc.co.uk/bi/spanish/news/.

Chapter 8

Free Trade Agreements, CAFTA, and FTAA: Key Pieces in the Accumulation of Transnational Capital

Raúl Moreno

One of the main characteristics of the international scenario is the prevalence of a "unipolar political order" that has been consolidating its militarist nature as well as the unilateral emphasis in international relations. The invasion of Iraq has reaffirmed the turn experienced by corporate-neoliberal globalization toward a war neoliberalism. In this context, we see not only the increasing significance of the military industry[1] and the strong dependence of the world economic reactivation on weaponry production, but also the unilateral decision-making process resulting in the termination of multilateral agreements signed by the community of nations that constitute the foundation for understanding and peaceful coexistence of the peoples.

The links between the war neoliberalism and "free trade" become evident in the U.S. National Security document of 2002, according to which the "free market and free trade are key priorities for our national security strategy."[2] Hence negotiations at the World Trade Organization (WTO), the creation of a Free Trade Area of the Americas (FTAA), other free trade agreements,[3] and bilateral investment agreements are very important for the United States.

Former U.S. secretary of state Colin Powell stated that his "objective was to guarantee American control of a territory extending from the Arctic to the Antarctic with free access and without any limitation or obstacle to our products, services, technology, and capital across the hemisphere."[4] In the Americas, the "free trade" wave is expressed not only in the WTO agreements, but also in the FTAA project and the signing of bilateral agreements on trade and investment, whose content goes beyond the scope of the WTO agreements. Undoubtedly, these complementary instruments to neoliberal economic policies reproduce the logic of maximizing profits and have already been tested as the ideal instruments to facilitate the accumulation of international capital.

The capital deregulation process has been promoted by the agreements that constitute the foundation of the WTO and the broad range of regional and bilateral agreements on trade and investment. Based on that purpose, the earlier Bush administration promoted the project aimed at creating the Free Trade Area of the Americas and launched at the Summit of Presidents held in Miami in 1994, the year in which the NAFTA (North American Free Trade Agreement) became effective. NAFTA's principles and content markedly coincided with that of FTAA, prompting some specialists to call it the NAFTA+.[5]

WTO: The New Framework for the Accumulation of Transnational Capital

International financial organizations, such as the World Bank (WB) and the International Monetary Fund (IMF), have played an important role in creating the conditions to guarantee the opening and deregulation of economies, the key elements in the international accumulation of capital. Since 1994, in an open complementary action to the WB and the IMF, and to contribute to capital deregulation, a new actor emerged, namely, the World Trade Organization,[6] which constitutes a multilateral organization in charge of establishing the standards governing trade among countries[7] and representing the legal and institutional basis for the multilateral trade system.

The WTO higher body is the Conference of Ministers, with biannual meetings, and, within this conference, the General Council, which is the most important body. For every agreement there are consultation and decision-making bodies, also known as Councils of Goods, Trade of Services and Trading Aspects of Intellectual Property.[8] The main source of power of the World Trade Organization is the body in charge of solving differences with legal and executive powers to decree sanctions that can only be obviated if all members, including the demanding party, agree on not implementing them.[9]

The WTO has a set of agreements in the trade of goods, the first being the General Agreement on Tariffs and Trade (GATT), existing since 1947 and reformed in 1994. In this context there are other agreements on agriculture, health and phytosanitary measures, textiles, technical barriers to trade, measures on trade-related investment, antidumping, customs evaluation, pre-loading inspections, rules of origin, import licenses, subsidies, and safeguards.

The General Agreement on Trade of Services (GATS) is aimed at the liberalization of services, in general, and public utilities, in particular. It covers more than 170 sectors and subsectors, namely, education, health, and the environment. Likewise, there are other agreements like the Agreement on Trade-Related Intellectual Property (TRIPS), the Revision Mechanisms for Trade Policy, the Rules on Resolution of Differences, and the Plurilateral Sectorial Agreements (civil aviation, government procurement, dairy products, and bovine meat).

The WTO is made up of more than 135 countries, of which 101 are underdeveloped and, though they represent the majority, in practice, they have little or no capacity to influence the resolutions passed because the WTO has been characterized by an important lack of democracy. It would seem that according to the rules of procedure "the one who cannot pay, cannot play." The poorest countries have to face not only the limitation of having to keep their offices at the headquarters of negotiations in Geneva, but also the problem of having to establish ideal teams to allow them to take a position according to their national interests.

The WTO objectives are aimed at attaining "the liberalization of most sectors"; "the elimination of trade tariffs and nontariff barriers to trade." In case of any disagreement on interests in commercial relations they would promote "the resolution of differences through fair procedures" and with the apparent purpose of eliminating obstacles to trade, "the harmonization of a standard regulating aspects to protect consumers, public health and environment" by agreements on technical barriers to trade, health, and phytosanitary measures.

The main WTO principles are associated with the trade system and enshrine a nondiscriminatory, obstacle-free, foreseeable, competitive, and a more advantageous system for less-developed countries. However, in reality, this is a highly discriminatory and unfavorable system for small economies. The national treatment principle, demanding governments to give foreign investment a treatment identical to that given to national enterprises, aside from the huge technological, productive, competitive asymmetries places them in a disadvantaged position against transnational enterprises.

However, in spite of the so-called advantageous system for small economies that should give advantages to less developed countries, in practice this system is governed by a "double standard" that demands the opening and deregulation of southern countries while the northern countries keep their protectionist schemes with tariff and nontariff practices. This allows them to protect their strategic industries and/or the more uncompetitive sectors. Experience has shown that besides the above-mentioned principles, it would not be realistic to believe that economic powers will unilaterally eliminate barriers to trade and, much less, discourage their "unfair" practices as subsidies to domestic production and exports.

The WTO covers not only trade of goods and services but also the "trade of ideas" or intellectual property and its main functions include management and implementation of multilateral trade agreements inside the WTO, to act as a forum to hold multilateral trade negotiations, to solve trade differences, to monitor national commercial policies, and to cooperate with other international institutions participating in the adoption of world economic policies.[10]

The scope of the WTO goes beyond the trade liberalization context since through the numerous additional agreements it deals with issues such as agricultural trade, education, health, environment, intellectual property rights, and investment. In this regard, we refer to a multilateral level setting the pace in the accumulation process of transnational corporations. The existing regulations of WTO on investment, established in GATS and TRIPS, are aimed at eliminating regulations and liberalization. A similar situation can be found in the Agreement on Trade-Related Investment Measures (TRIMS) by virtue of which governmental regulations affecting investor benefits are limited.

After the WTO Round in Doha, Qatar, participants stated the need to make progress in four issues known as Singapore New Issues: investment, competition policies, transparency in government procurement, and trade facilitations that were dealt with during the WTO Round in September 2003 in Cancun, Mexico, and at subsequent WTO meetings, including the meeting in December 2005 in Hong Kong. The WTO is trying to become a forum to debate a wide range of issues beyond the strictly commercial framework and its competence. Besides, the multilateral treatment they are attempting to give to investment will result in important negative implications to small economies.[11]

The FTAA: A Strategic Bet for American Corporations

The main objective of the FTAA project, built from and for American corporations, is to consolidate a hemispheric bloc made up of 34 countries of the Americas[12] in order to allow the United States to act as a better balancing pole against the economic blocs of the European Union and the Southeast Asian economies.

The FTAA reaffirms and deepens the contents already in effect in the existing free trade agreements: free access of transnational corporations to governmental contracts and biddings,[13] prohibition to national states to impose requirements to foreign investment, solution of differences by international arbitrators, the possibility for an enterprise to put a state into trial with the imminent risk of paying compensation for losses to the "affected" enterprise by established regulations, and consolidation of protection of intellectual property rights of trademarks and patents.

After several presidential meetings and FTAA teams,[14] the course of negotiations made evident the imminent difficulty for this project to come into effect in 2005 as planned. The open opposition to the FTAA by the Bolivarian Republic of Venezuela, the critical stance adopted by Brazil on agriculture, government procurement, and intellectual property rights, as well as the position adopted by the MERCOSUR governments, in 2003 resulted in a confrontation and lack of agreement with the U.S. administration on the main FTAA issues. Thus, there was an urgent need to modify the negotiating tactics so as to provide the eighth Ministerial Round in Miami a way out with the purpose of preventing a rupture and continuing the process led by the United States.

It was evident that the initial American proposal for a "deep FTAA"[15] was unsustainable and would not eliminate the opposition expressed by some South American countries, with which the FTAA process would be doomed to failure. Thus, the U.S. tactic, supported by Brazil, was to find an emergency exit so as to elude and postpone debates and agreements on key and controversial issues within the FTAA, a situation that modifies, in relation to the initial project, the participation level of the 34 countries.

The U.S. administration managed to get away, at the eighth FTAA Ministerial Meeting with a minimum agreement giving way to an "FTAA a la carte." This avoided the discussion of thorny and fundamental issues, disentangling the opposition and setting the conditions to sign an FTAA, with even more radical contents than the initial project. It is the FTAA+ since it opens the possibility of creating subregional and/or bilateral negotiations.[16]

From 2004 there is a turn in regional negotiations toward the subregionalization and bilateralization of these negotiations. With this, the U.S. administration managed to isolate the opposition to the FTAA and open the doors to more adverse scenarios for small economies. For example, as in El Salvador, in the negotiations for the Central American Free Trade Agreement (CAFTA), the governments of the region had nothing to do but to "bargain" their access to the U.S. market for some products and have accepted, without any discussion, all the significant aspects of the agreement stated by the U.S. negotiating team.[17]

Now there is an "FTAA a la carte menu" offered by the United States from which, theoretically, every government can select whatever they want. In practice, the main course will be chosen and served by the host of the banquet aside from the preferences and tastes of the "guests" as has been demonstrated by the Mexican experience within the NAFTA framework. After the eighth Ministerial Meeting, the U.S. government is trying to finish the FTAA puzzle through a longer process, placing piece by piece, that is to say, FTA by FTA, thus neglecting the opposition expressed by Venezuela, Brazil, and any other country against the FTAA negotiations.

For Central America, the CAFTA is the FTAA. The agreement not only fairly reproduces the FTAA principles, but covers and broadens its content. So the outcome of the Miami Meeting modified much of the current Central American situation since the governments of the region have advanced in the granting of all conditions sought by the United States in the FTAA through bilateral investment agreements, reforms to national legal frameworks, and, more recently, the ratification of the CAFTA.

As a complement to "free trade" agreement negotiations, the Central American region is promoting a set of investment mega-projects included in the Puebla Panama Plan (PPP) financed by the foreign debt and national budgets in order to build the required infrastructure to guarantee the formation and functioning of the transnational capital through a complex group of interconnection works in electricity, telecommunication, and transportation.[18]

Development Policies and Investment

For underdeveloped economies, mainly from oil nonexporting countries, the net entry of financial resources is an important component when defining their long-term development strategies to the extent in which they can compensate their permanent current account deficit and their low level in national savings. Foreign direct investment (FDI), which together with financial investment (short-term investment and portfolio) conform foreign investment, is still recognized for its potential contribution to development since it facilitates access to capital, technologies, and markets in contrast with financial investment that, due to its speculative and erratic nature, is associated with macro-financial destabilizing processes.

FDI is controlled by transnational corporations, entities with a great political and economic power allowing them to exert pressure upon the governments and monopolistic or oligopolistic markets where they act. They do this through their capacity to manipulate prices and benefits, collude enterprises to distribute control zones among them, limit the entry of new competitors, and shape the tastes and preferences of consumers. These enterprises are the protagonist actors of neoliberal globalization whose net sales greatly surpass the Gross Domestic Product of most underdeveloped countries.

There is a certain coincidence in the contribution of FDI to the macroeconomic aggregates, though the economic and social development in its relation with activities carried out by transnational corporations is highly questioned. Arguments sustained by the neoclassical approach, which identifies the FDI as the development locomotive, enunciate that its promotion constitutes a way to close the commercial gap, increase fiscal income, facilitate the transfer of technology, know how, and training of national human resources.

Nevertheless, in practice, the FDI functioning contrasts with these theoretical statements. Obviously, the concessions obtained by transnational corporations through arrangements with governments exert control and dominate local markets thus limiting the expansion of national enterprises since competition is eliminated. Besides, the FDI deregulation can cause serious economic and financial problems as, for example, the long-term reduction of foreign income that will result in the repatriation of benefits or a high component of imports in trading flows and low levels in tax collection resulting from out-of-proportion fiscal exemptions granted to foreign investment.

The empirical evidence shows that FDI benefits "depend on the use of several political strategies,"[19] and the fact that "there is not a mechanical relation between FDI presence and the transfer of technology,"[20] and this is why investment constitutes a tool and not an end in itself. The FDI statement can only be meaningful when articulated with national development projects. The historical experience of developed economies in dealing with investment shows the importance of keeping controls and regulations over FDI so as to make them compatible with the objectives of development.[21]

Investment is not a new issue, as suggested by the WTO when it stated the Singapore New Issues, but an old one with a historical tendency toward the global deregulation of capital, whose process has been progressing on four tracks. The "first track" was built with Programs of Economic and Structural Adjustment (PAE and PEE), tools that led to liberalization and deregulation of economies, as well as the establishment of incentives to foreign investment. Currently, 95 percent of all countries have already deregulated investment through changes made in their legal frameworks[22] that become more permissive with foreign enterprises and offer ideal terms for their performance, namely, tax exemptions, public services at preferential rates, low labor costs and flexible labor, and environmental standards favoring enterprises betting for a competitiveness based on low prices.

During the last decade, Central American governments made great efforts to promote free zones and fiscal zones as a way to consolidate a growth scheme based on sweat-shop activities. Today, sweat-shop activities, mainly in textiles and garments, represent one of the most dynamic and important branches in regional exports, in spite of the minor contribution in value-added activity and the significant lack of coordination with other national industrial branches. FDI, in Central America, takes the form of sweat shops that, in general terms, based their competitiveness on low labor costs.

The "second track" includes Bilateral Investment Treaties (BIT) representing an important incentive to FDI that have recently experienced an extraordinary increase. In 1950, only the BIT was known, but in the year 2000 there were already 1,857 treaties of which 1,472 were ratified during the 1990s. Besides, nowadays, 28 of the 34 countries in the FTAA are signatories of the International Centre for the Settlement of Investment-Related Disputes, though only seven countries have effective bilateral investment treaties with the United States, four have signed (yet to be ratified), and two countries, Mexico and Canada, are already subjected to regulations similar to the BIT through the North America Free Trade Agreement.

The Center for the Settlement of Investment-Related Disputes is an international court under the World Bank that provides international arbitration to investors who want their "rights or privileges" complied with, rights or privileges stipulated in accordance with subscribed contracts under the laws of the recipient country. This center has dealt with paradigmatic disputes as the one lodged by the American transnational Bechtel, when expelled from Cochabamba after the "war on water," against Bolivia that resulted in the return of water resources to the Cochabamba population.

This instrument has a great importance to deregulation processes of investment since, besides having an FTA in effect, it activates a mechanism to settle disputes between investors and the state, and acts similarly and with the same mechanisms applied by courts under the FTA and the WTO. Therefore, the adhesion to the BIT opens a door to admit many prejudices and disadvantages for small economies that have not yet ratified the FTA with countries where foreign investors are present.

The "third track" through which FDI is going includes the free trade agreements whose strategic objectives concentrate on investment and related issues, namely, intellectual property rights, access to government procurement, and liberalization of services. Treaties represent a "letter of rights" for transnational's granting them broad privileges to capital vis-à-vis no obligations, through effective mechanisms of compliance.

The "fourth track" is the FTAA. One of the main aspects of the FTAA is investment, whose treatment shows an extraordinary coincidence with the logic of deregulation, both in content and in the mechanisms already defined in treaties. In the last FTAA draft, there were eight broad and inclusive definitions of investment as shown in these two examples: investment means "any kind of activity and right of any nature" or "any property asset directly or indirectly controlled." Therefore, investment practically covers everything: estates or any other property, either tangible or intangible, bought or used to obtain an economic benefit or for any other corporate aim. This meaning of investment coincides with the statement included in the now-obsolete Multilateral Investment Agreement (MIA) and its extension is meaningful for the transnational interests that, with such a broad definition, will deregulate any activity or change made by these enterprises.

The FTAA also reestablishes the prohibition to governments to devise requirements for foreign investment. Among the eight restrictions introduced by the FTAA and other agreements there should be no obligation imposed to comply with a national content percentage of local goods and services; give preference to local goods or services; quotas or types of goods and services to be exported; the use of certain types of technology; any relation between imports, exports, and profits; the transfer of technology, productive process or any other reserved knowledge; or any act as exclusive provider of goods produced or services provided. From this logic, we can discard any possibility to link investment policies to a national development strategy.

The mechanisms for the settlement of disputes, as in the free trade agreements, expose an antidemocratic character and grant a "special right" for the use of international arbitration and the resulting substitution of the national legislation and legal courts in recipient countries for foreign investment. In North America alone, there are more than 25 cases and demands by transnational's against the states, both acquitted and solved, 11 against Mexico, 6 against Canada, and 8 against the United States.

Likewise, the FTAA broadens the definition of expropriations. Besides the traditional concept of direct expropriation, linked to the corresponding compensation, there are also indirect expropriations. According to this category any state public policy or decision that, in the opinion of the enterprise, might affect its interests and potential profits is equivalent to an expropriation and, therefore, can be denounced by enterprises at any court of dispute like the International Center for the Settlement of Investment-Related Disputes.

The FTAA proposal prevents governments from using control mechanisms against the movement of capital, a fact that contrasts with the need, increasingly acknowledged by specialists, to establish regulations to capital functioning. The investment chapter includes contributions to capital, royalties, fees and payments to intellectual property rights, as well as royalties derived from the exploitation of natural resources. A whole interpretation of the investment chapter demands a comprehensive analysis including government procurement, liberalization of services, and intellectual property rights. This allows us to examine the complementary elements to this chapter giving sense to capital deregulation.

In this regard, the FTAA, like the bilateral free trade agreements, try to grant powers and the control of basic aspects of economic and social life to the transnational's while guaranteeing foreign investment access to public services such as education, health, social security, water resources, and energy.

The European Union, Japan, Canada, South Korea, and Switzerland,[23] in their eagerness to promote deregulation of investment at the global level, are promoting an initiative in the WTO in an attempt to establish a multilateral framework for investment when retaking high protection standards for investors and harsh disciplinary measures against restrictions to the FDI free flow among WTO member countries, as the ones already in effect in the existing FTAs are to be incorporated to the FTAA.

These countries are trying to create a "fifth track" aimed at deregulating the FDI proposing the WTO to become a forum to negotiate a multilateral framework for investment. This pretension of retaking the Singapore New Issues into WTO has faced an important opposition by India, Malaysia, Zimbabwe, Tanzania, Zambia, Kenya, Belize, Uganda, and Sri Lanka, which point out that the WTO is not the ideal forum to deal with investment since it is not included in its eminently commercial competence.

With the multilateralization of investment, the European Union attempts to obtain the privileges the U.S. investors already enjoy as a result of bilateral and regional negotiations in the Americas. In this context the group of countries headed by India is questioning the statements included in the WTO proposal on investment in relation to the right to investment and the application of the national treatment principle. Besides, they are evaluating the fact that the FDI model has not been satisfactory to the interests of the recipient economies.

The FTAs: Instruments for "Adjustment" Consolidation

The mushrooming career of Central American governments to subscribe "free trade" agreements began during the 1990s after signing the first agreement between Mexico and Costa Rica (1996), a fact that coincided with the apogee of the implementation of economic and institutional reforms pushed by the World Bank and the IMF through the PAE and PEE.

This "curious" temporal coincidence between the free trade agreements (FTA) and the PAE–PEE reinforces and consolidates the adjustment process initiated at the end of the 1980s since it allowed taking simultaneous political measures with convergent purposes through two different tracks. Both are aimed at the shared objective of guaranteeing economic deregulation and the reinforcement of an accumulation basis for transnational corporations. For this purpose, they overlap their actions or act as in a relay race to give continuity to what the PAE–PEE began though from the FTA.

The economic and institutional reforms contained in the PAE–PEE, turned into demands for debtor countries through the cross-conditionality in stabilizing, which is granted by the IMF, and adjustment by the World Bank, loans are complemented and promoted when subscribing a free trade agreement, to the extent in which the contents of these agreements transform the legal framework of nations and legally seal the reforms they promote.

The theoretical ground of PAE–PEE is found in a set of "recommendations" that constitute the Washington Consensus,[24] which has been structured from several theoretical approaches,[25] and has given proof of its merely ideological basis resulting in a consensus stemming out from its critic concentrated in nature and the state participation in the economy.

This set of measures gathered the main issues of the "neoliberal" agenda and is expressly defined as an instrument to the service of transnational corporations so as to face and take advantage of the opportunity derived from the new competition in the world capitalist system. The neoliberal discourse identifies the state as a source and factor of macroeconomic instability, as well as a real obstacle to complete the "free game of market." These arguments are justified by the alleged interference by the state on the market (in both prices and amounts) since it limits competition and discourages private initiatives. Within the PAE–PEE we find the prevalence of the myth of an insurmountable contradiction between the state and the market—the belief that the private allocation of resources is "always more efficient" than public allocation.

Based on these statements, it is meaningful then that the supreme purpose of PAE–PEE is oriented to limit the state functions in economy, thus eliminating the "instability and distortion source" that will guarantee the optimal conditions to promote the greatest benefits for private enterprises. In practice, this is expressed in fiscal proposals aimed at reducing public expenditures resulting in a foreign debt, restriction of state intervention in the economy through institutional reforms, sale of assets and public enterprises, and, finally, the opening and deregulation of the economy.

The reforms promoted in the region by the World Bank and the IMF has led to important changes in the definition of the economic policy.[26] The opening and the deregulation, combined with the "modernization of the public sector," led to the reduction of competition by the state and its weakening in the economic activity. Therefore, the context was then ideal for capital accumulation processes pushed by transnational corporations.

Privatization processes, as a result of which important public enterprises were bought by transnational corporations and the large national enterprises to create private monopolies in the public service sector, as in the electricity distribution and generation, telecommunications, or the administration of pension funds, were carried out together with unilateral processes of foreign opening and tariff exemption. Policies were applied in an attempt to encourage private investment, especially foreign investment, through incentives in free zones and tax zones for sweat–shops, the flexibility of labor market, and the resulting deterioration of working conditions as an alternative to cheapen production costs and create a regime of fiscal incentives favorable to private enterprises. With these measures the progress made in the configuration of a favorable and permissive context for both investment and trade becomes evident.

Regarding taxes, with the reform of the nonfinancial public sector (NFPS) giving emphasis to efficiency, more than equity, there was an attempt to attain fiscal discipline by paying attention to expenditures and making fiscal structure more efficient.[27] However, such an objective has not been achieved. It is still an unattained goal and has the aggravating circumstance that public indebtedness levels have become a risk factor for the macroeconomic policy stability. The fiscal reform modified the basis of the fiscal system that passed from capital to labor with the corresponding elimination of some direct taxes[28] and indirect taxes, as the Value Added Tax (VAT), previous by the main source of public income.

In the process of reforms much progress was made in deregulation and opening the privatization processes. As a result, most enterprises and public assets fell into private hands. However, there are still some important public services to be privatized that are in the sight of transnational corporations who are orienting the FTA agenda to the privatization of services like health, social security, education, generation of electricity and geothermal services, the transmission of electricity, among others.

CAFTA Legal Implications

CAFTA, like many international agreements and treaties signed by governments and ratified by the Central American legislative bodies, constitutes a law of the Salvadoran Republic,[29] as they have prominence over the secondary legislation.

International treaties are signed by the executive and legislative branches in keeping with the powers vested by their constitutions. Nevertheless, these powers are neither absolute nor unlimited since the constitution itself states that treaties are subjected to the constitutional framework, especially, concerning any damage or detriment to fundamental individual rights.[30]

As enshrined by the Salvadorian Constitution, "none of the bodies can sign or ratify any treaty limiting or affecting in some way the form of government or damaging or undermining the integrity of the territory, the sovereignty, and independence of the Republic *or the fundamental rights of human beings.*"[31] This being the case, the approval and ratification of Free Trade Agreements affecting the fundamental rights of individuals would be a contradiction.

In general terms, commercial relations between countries have not concerned themselves with human rights. These commercial agreements are based on a "development model" that is not always coherent with the respect and effectiveness of human rights. It is a serious mistake, with unconstitutional implications, that establish membership in CAFTA without considering the implications on human rights.

Before the FTA negotiations, the Salvadorian state had ratified several treaties on human rights: the International Covenant on Civil and Political Rights; the International Agreement on Economic, Social and Cultural Rights; the American Convention on Human Rights; the Additional Protocol to the

American Convention on Human Rights, among others.[32] These agreements forced the state to impose the required provisions to make rights acknowledged in these treaties effective, as well as the duty to respect and guarantee the rights and liberties contained in them.

On the other hand, CAFTA, the International Labor Organization (ILO) agreements, and the Universal Declaration on Human Rights shared the same legal hierarchy, so there is no contradiction among them and much less the prevalence of one over the others. However, in practice, the FTA, with its mercantile logic, subordinates the rest of these international agreements and conventions.

This subordination is not found only in Central America but also in the NAFTA provisions derived from the Center for the Settlement of Investment-Related Disputes mandating the Mexican state to pay the American transnational Metalclad $15,500,000 as compensation for "indirect expropriation" due to the closure of the toxic garbage dump located in Guadalcázar, San Luis Potosi.[33] It was an operation generating serious health hazards among the population. Cases like Metalclad set a precedent of great concern since it shows the prevalence of a logic placing profits above anything else, so the compliance and effectiveness of the rights of peoples and communities are subordinated to the commercial interests of transnational's.

If we consider the great significance of ratifying CAFTA within the national legal frameworks and the implications for Central American countries, then we must examine the potential unconstitutional nature of these agreements to prevent them from affecting the rights of national individuals. Bearing in mind the "bias" in favor of foreign investment contained in the free trade agreements, their ratification acts as a mechanism through which a set of reforms initiated with the structural adjustment processes favoring the exclusiveness of transnational corporations are "legally sealed."

The subordination of labor rights to those contained in the FTA or the mercantilization of public services, such as education, health, and water, whose access constitutes a social right, according to the constitution, and ratified international agreements represent two axes of the privatizing reforms that are silently consolidated with the signing of these treaties. In this regard, the FTA not only lead to the mercantilization of public services but also erode public authority since they limit their involvement in the foreign enterprise performance, without any counteraction to guarantee obligations with workers and with the legal legitimatization of this situation for the worst.

The FTA: Much More than a Mere Commercial Treaty

Despite the fact that Free Trade Agreements are promoted by governments under the label of "free trade," these agreements incorporate aspects that go beyond the export and import of goods, since they also include different areas such as investment, intellectual property rights, government procurement, services, competition policies, telecommunications, and the financial sector, among others. This way they define the framework determining the orientation of public policies in the small economies subscribing to the agreement.

With these "extra-commercial" contents, the agreements invade the sovereign competences of states and affect the compliance and effectiveness of economic, social, and cultural rights of the population through the rules established in government procurement, trade on services, intellectual property rights, and investment chapters promoting the privatization of public services through concessions.

We are witness to an instrument with broad scope that incorporates, in its contents, a wide range of mechanisms combining prohibitions to governments with rights of foreign enterprises on investment, nondiscriminatory treatments, intellectual property rights, "liberalization" of services, and access to public biddings. The free trade agreements guarantee the legalization of privileges and turn them into rights for transnational corporations since their ratification by the legislative bodies of all countries they become law of the republic in Central America, with higher juridical hierarchy over the secondary legislation, which is not so in the United States. The structure and content of these chapters respond to a transversal logic granting privileges to profits over human rights and sustainability. It is distressing to note how these agreements contain a large list of rights granted to foreign enterprises, thus contrasting with the omission of mechanisms to guarantee the compliance of the economic, social, and cultural rights and the preservation of ecosystems.

The Rhetoric of the Official Discourse

The intense official campaigns in mass media and discourses made by corporate elites present CAFTA as the panacea to problems faced by the Central American small economies, the key for employment generation and a way to have access to the U.S. market of 300,000,000 people. According to these statements, it will suffice to swing the "magic wand" to ratify CAFTA and automatically experience an economic growth by exporting "cheese with *loroco*," "doughnuts," and "iguana consommé" to the large North American market, and the national welfare of the population, with the possibility of being "blessed" with employment in the maquila.

In the CAFTA justification they have missed the deep economic, technological, social, and institutional asymmetries existing among the signatory countries but, above all, the overwhelming capacity of the government of the United States to impose its interests during negotiations and dictate the outcomes. On the other hand, it is a paradox to present this agreement as an alternative to economic growth and employment generation when it reproduces the same opening and deregulating economic measures that constitute the basis of the failed "neoliberal policies" of the World Bank, the Inter-American Development Bank, and the International Monetary Fund that, during the last 15 years, have increased the structural problems of Central American economies.

For economies to grow it is necessary to devise deliberate actions to achieve this objective, but it is not enough to obtain positive growth rates of the GDP,[34] it is necessary to reach the growth threshold, with rates above 6 percent, in order to reduce unemployment and, besides, in a sustained way for a long period of time. This kind of growth is the first condition that is necessary, though not enough, to solve the poverty and marginalization problems plaguing Central America. Besides, it is necessary to have a redistribution of growth based on justice and equity that might result in a harmonic relationship with nature and environment.

The preparation of economies for development must face the scourge of inequality expressed in the high levels of concentration of wealth and the assets measured by the Gini Index, which, save in Costa Rica, is above 0.50 percent across the region, and the unequal distribution of goods showing how the proportion destined to be a worker's payment is almost the one-third part of that taken by entrepreneurs as net profits or surpluses from exploitation.

Aside from CAFTA, El Salvador needs to put its house in order, must establish the basis that will allow it to overcome the huge asymmetries that place it among the countries with the lowest human development rates. Regional integration, seen as a systemic project, and unlike the FTA, is a path that could come closer to a fair and sustainable development.

A Secret and Antidemocratic Practice

In the Central American countries there is an old tradition concerning the application of public policies with an antidemocratic nature, not only due to the negative impacts on the population, but also due to excluding mechanisms used in their formulation and implementation. Few wondered why these economic decisions are made by only a few individuals without the possibility of involving the majority in the future, due to costs and prejudices generated by such decisions.

The negotiation of trade and investment agreements and treaties have not been an exception. In spite of the impact these treaties could have on national life, due to the social and economic impacts they generate, the negotiating processes and the decision-making processes were characterized by the lack of transparency, the absence of consultations with affected sectors and the poor participation of the different economic and social sectors. The secrecy and antidemocratic character of these negotiating processes contrast with the official discourse rhetoric on the need to "establish processes of broad social involvement." According to the logic applied by governments, civil society is more or less reduced to the entrepreneurial sector, since they have presence in the teams negotiating the Free Trade Agreements, that is, made up of public officials from the ministries of economy, trade or industry, and by a representation of the entrepreneurial elite.

Treatment of Asymmetries and Access to Market

The alleged benefits derived from the foreign opening and liberalization of investment not does come automatically, nor are they distributed in an equitable form within or among countries. The unequal distribution of economic growth is determined by the ownership structures over means of production, due to imperfections found in concentrated internal markets and the asymmetric information, protectionist practices, both tariff and nontariff, besides from the huge asymmetries existing among countries which became tangible in the unequal levels of development they have.

Bearing in mind that Free Trade Agreements are not applied among homogeneous economies, but among unequal economies, with high disproportions and differences in development, production, territory, poverty, competitiveness, population, resources, power, legal, and institutional frameworks and culture, we cannot ignore the asymmetries when evaluating the impacts derived from their implementation.

The application of treaties like CAFTA contribute with very little or nothing to the development of small economies considering the fact that they operate with the purpose of favoring the accumulation processes of transnational capital that only scantily strengthen national capabilities or even reduces them. In this regard, treaties grant a poor favor to these countries since they expose them to unfair and unbalanced relations affecting the low-income populations.

The treatment of these asymmetries has been limited, within CAFTA, to the application of a timetable for tax deduction and the establishment of quotas though neglecting the huge gaps between signatory countries. In CAFTA, the United States denied the countries in the region the granting of a "special treatment" due to the size of their economies and the level of development, which means they are neglecting the great asymmetries existing and increasing them with its implementation. On the other hand, the U.S. solution to the asymmetry problem is very simple: to promote cooperation and training programs already adopted for the region by the World Bank, the Inter-American Development Bank, the United States International Agency for Development (USAID), and other financial organizations in order to prepare the area for the application of rights and obligations contained in the free trade agreement. These solutions ignore the structural determinants of these asymmetries and are concentrated on training for CAFTA rights and obligations, the response to these situations, with the resulting fiscal pressure through public indebtedness. Furthermore, this disadvantageous situation in Central America is worsened by the difficulty posed to exporters in the region who compete with the U.S. agricultural goods and have access to its market in addition to the sanitary and customs barriers limiting their entry and the subsidizing policies kept by the United States to benefit its sector.

As a proof of this lack of coherence of CAFTA with the objective aimed at "eliminating trade barriers and facilitating the circulation of goods," the United States unilaterally decided that internal subsidies should not be subjected to negotiation; "there is no way of discussing them in this or in any other trade negotiation."[35] In spite of the fact that sanitary and phytosanitary standards constitute an instrument that might contribute to guarantee the quality and safety of foodstuffs, for the benefit of consumers, in practice they operate as true protectionist mechanisms. This has been illustrated in the case of the Mexican poultry sector that, within the NAFTA framework, has "apparent" access to the market without linking it to the application of sanitary and phytosanitary measures. As a result of this, Mexican poultry exporters have not been able to comply with the sanitary requirements in 10 years so as to have access to the American market, thus eliminating the concession granted by Mexico in the treaty, while, on the contrary, the United States has entered the Mexican poultry market in an unlimited way.[36]

The Strategic Objective of CAFTA

Beyond the eagerness expressed by Central American countries to export "nostalgic products" to the American market, the true motivation of CAFTA is to promote the interests of the U.S. government,[37] which mainly concentrates on gaining access to the Central American market, services, and e-commerce, consolidation of intellectual property, investment, and increasing transparency in governmental procedures and regulations.[38] CAFTA disproportionately favors the United States because of the huge asymmetries found among the parties, but, above all, to the overwhelming ability of the U.S. economy to define the agenda and determine the outcome.

The Central American governments would be "satisfied" if CAFTA ratifies the advantages already granted by the U.S. government through the CBI and the GSP. They would also welcome because the arrival of more maquilas, these factories that generate employment for Central American economies. In addition there is the possibility for the U.S. market to be opened to receive the "nostalgic products" that would find a potential market in the Central American population living in the United States.

The U.S. government imposed a treaty that, besides allowing free access of its products to Central American markets, guarantee the best conditions for its investment in the region, without regulations and with "nondiscriminatory" treatment, and where its enterprises will be able to control public services (such as water, education, and health) thus consolidating its domination over electricity, telecommunications, ports, and airports. CAFTA is a treaty that also gives the United States preponderance in gaining procurement contacts from Central American governments and protects the patents of their enterprises to have unlimited access to natural resources and biodiversity in the region.

These considerations reveal a CAFTA favoring the United States, even over its "concern for the development" of Central American countries as was so many times expressed by American officials. For the U.S. transnational corporations, such as the AES Co., Enron, Coastal Power, Duke Energy, Constellation,[39] already settled in the region, and others interested to invest in the waste disposal treatment, telecommunications, water resources, health and social security, education, and direct investment in general, CAFTA represents an excellent opportunity due to its content, logic, and principles, turning it into a proven and efficient instrument to guarantee their interests.

Who Wins and Who Loses with the CAFTA?

The free trade agreements, like any other economic policy, are not and cannot be neutral instruments. Their implementation generates differentiated effects among signatory countries and the interiors of these countries. On the one hand, there is a select group of winners, generally, a reduced number of national monopolistic or oligopolistic enterprises and a few transnational corporations that operate or attempt to operate within the region, receiving the benefits of the scheme promoted by the treaty. On the other hand, broad economic and social sectors emerge, those who historically have been affected by the application of "neoliberal reforms," bearing the negative outcomes of the treaty.

Assuming that CAFTA provisions do not reflect the interests of most of these enterprises, micro, small, middle, and even large national enterprises, much less does it reflect the rights of workers, consumers, and population at large. But it does serve the interests of hegemonic groups of entrepreneurs who have had the possibility of participating in and shaping the negotiations that led to the treaty.

It is very difficult to list the advantages derived from CAFTA for social sectors when the contents of this treaty not only lack logic on human rights but actually contradicts them. CAFTA and other free trade treaties have neither been inspired nor constructed to serve the interests of citizens or small enterprises or for the respect of environment. Hence there is a fundamental omission of logic for labor, social, migratory, and environmental rights throughout the provisions, which is clear evidence of its bias and incompleteness. In this regard, CAFTA is contrary to labor rights of workers, rights of consumers, development of micro, small, and middle enterprises, rural development and the sustainability of the region, and, in general, to the legitimate aspiration of peoples to build their own development process without markets dictating their fate.

Undoubtedly, CAFTA's implications are so broad in scope that it goes beyond the strictly commercial sphere to impact the economic, labor, social, political, cultural, and environmental spheres. The direct and indirect negative effects on the population assume several forms: the development generated by the bankruptcy of national enterprises, the mercantilization of public services, the burden of tariffs and the increase in the price of drugs, the deterioration of environment, the consumption of genetically modified foods, the bankruptcy of agricultural and livestock production with the resulting lack of food security, and, as a result of everything pointed out before, the increase of migration to the United States and the cultural uprooting of the people.

The Links between the FTA,
the FTAA, and the PPP

The PPP is another important tool for FTAA purposes, since it allows the creation of conditions in Mesoamerica for the required infrastructure and legal-institutional framework needed by transnational corporations to enter that region of the continent through the implementation of a set of investment projects financed by international financial institutions and finally paid for by the citizens of the region. Together with the FTAA, objectives aimed at creating a liberalized energy policy,[40] a continental market for water, and an "agribusiness" sector for the profitable production of transgenic food,[41] the PPP is also leading the way to the liberalization of strategic activities that are currently controlled by the state such as oil, natural gas, water courses, forestry reserves, and biodiversity. Gaining access to these important niches for foreign private investment is a key goal of CAFTA and PPP.

There is a remarkable convergence in the content and emphasis of public investment between the initiatives contained in the PPP, the Central American Strategy for the Transformation and Modernization in the twenty-first century, and the recommendations made by Michael Porter to Central American governments,[42] since all of them agree on promoting investment in the infrastructure (roads, telecommunications, and energy), ecotourism, and the construction of a Mesoamerican biological corridor along with the importance and promotion of maquila technologies as the strategic axis for the "sustainable development of the region."

Despite the PPP, most of the rhetoric refers to projects for human development and the improvement of the people's quality of life and, thus far, the single initiative dedicated to the connectivity of the region is the construction of the Central American logistic corridor (roads, railways, maritime and coastal transportation, air transportation, and telecommunications) and the electrical interconnection (hydroelectric, thermoelectric generation, and hydrocarbons).[43]

In this regard, initiatives aimed at human and sustainable development within the plan constitute, in practice, secondary components only important to the extent to which they convey the "human and ecological face" of the PPP needed to sell and disseminate a project dominated by a mercantile logic, the transnational interests prevail over the national interests. When examining the PPP document, its mercantile project nature is evident since it pretends to achieve the regional relocation of production through economic criteria aimed at maximizing profits and using the "comparative advantage of the region" thus promoting the reduction of total costs by obtaining low direct costs (raw materials, labor force, and energy) and low transportation costs (inputs and products).[44]

It is evident that the structure of the PPP focuses on a geographic economic approach that applies some extensions of models of imperfect competition and mixed scheduling in order to identify the location of productive plants.[45] Therefore, the logic that gives coherence to the PPP is the one that justifies the maximization of benefits and minimization of corporate costs. The PPP proposes the establishment of an integrated system of transportation (road, railway, air, and maritime transportation) through road networks[46] linking the suppliers of raw materials with the nodes (assembly cities) and the exporting points in order to create an infrastructure enabling production and stimulating the preferential option of Central American governments for a regional plan based on maquilas. The idea of mobilizing unassembled pieces in containers, thus facilitating the terrestrial and maritime transportation, is closely associated with the interconnection between "assembly" cities or maquilas that will be interconnected through a road system that, by the way, will be endowed by a cheap labor force.[47]

The plan emphasizes the public investment in infrastructure mainly through the construction of a transportation system that would reduce freight costs and facilitate the transportation of goods by dry channels in circuits linking the zones in which they are produced to the transnational corporations who market the products in the Northern Hemisphere.[48] With this investment component in the infrastructure, the governments involved will guarantee the highest purpose of the PPP by achieving this connectivity in the region. Moreover, it will open the scope of investments in the hydro-agricultural infrastructure by means of irrigation projects for African palm trees in 700,000 hectares. Furthermore, the PPP establishes agreements for biological exploration and biodiversity under the current framework of the World Trade Organization and the free trade agreements already signed forcing countries in the region to comply with the provisions included in the Agreements on Intellectual Property Rights applied to Trade (TRIPS), which include the monopolistic right of up to 25 years over patents registered by transnational corporations.

These conditions open the door to transnational corporations in the chemical and pharmaceutical industries, biotechnology, and biogenetics to access the universe of wealth found in the biodiversity of the region since they can use them without any limit. The situation is worsened by those patents registered on natural resources that will return as drugs or industrial products at unaffordable prices as a result of the monopolistic power that corporations wield over their international markets.

The PPP is resorting to the legal and institutional transformations needed to complete its final and true purpose in the investment project under the political constitution of the Republics, the single and final level to which free trade agreements are subordinated within the legal framework in Mesoamerica. The elimination of the legal factors "hindering" the "development" of the southeast region of Mexico and Central America, according to the PPP study, is one of the key elements in the construction of the legal framework over which the CAFTA will be based, since it will allow the modification of the last legal obstacle to achieve the complete liberalization of investment, the region's national constitutions. With the completion of this task, CAFTA will render subordinate the legal framework of every country to the contents of the agreement.

As evidence of these "legal and institutional factors" that are "hindering the development" of the poorest regions, despite their wealth of natural resources, the advocates of liberalization are now resorting to the proposals found in the basis of the Mexican component of the PPP stating the need to modify the ownership rights over hydrocarbons and water, the elimination of the constitutional restriction to own or lease great extensions of land, and the rupture of the monopolistic control exerted by the state over strategic activities such as electricity, gas, and petrochemical industries. Therefore, the objective of these legal and institutional reforms propelling the PPP is quite evident and, undoubtedly, its completion will open a complete space for private investments in those strategic areas so far reserved for public enterprises.

Society versus Trade-investment Projects

Though we acknowledge the importance of trade and investment to carry out growth processes, these instruments cannot be applied as ends in themselves. Their importance lies in the role they have to play within national development projects so that they might contribute to the attainment of a sustainable and equitable development objective.

CAFTA, FTAA, and other free trade agreements are not the single and, much less, the best way to guarantee the adequate external insertion of small economies into the world economy since they grant to the market the sovereign right of the peoples to define their fate. It is inadmissible to subordinate the solidarity, justice, and equity principles to the search for maximum profits and minimum costs.

Obviously, the scope of the WTO processes and those promoted by the FTAA and CAFTA initiatives exceeds the local capacities toward the transformation of both logic and content, but this demands, above all, to reaffirm our conviction that the transformation of this unfair and unsustainable "order" is possible and that Central Americans can never renounce their right to define their own destiny.

These proposals constitute a great challenge to our world society. A challenge demanding the greatest creativity and audacity, as well as a close coordination among citizens at the local, national, and international levels. The dream of "another world is possible"—the theme of many grassroots meetings—especially the Social Forum of the Americas stems out from the bottom-up and inside-out construction. Though there are no models or recipes that could be used as a global alternative, there are basic principles that must be put into motion, responding to particular realities and others which are more general. For example, it is imperative to affirm the role played by the state in regulating economic activity and in development planning. We consider that it will not be possible to achieve a fair and sustainable development without the presence of a sound entity to guide the way and guarantee the process. The promotion of alternative proposals demands the definition of our own national development project to be structured on the basis of democratic participatory principles, sustainability and the bridging of inequality gaps, age, gender, social, ethnic, and geographic, thus guaranteeing the compliance to and insurance of human rights.[49]

It is clear that CAFTA is not a viable alternative for Central American countries and the historical and structural problems of the region will never be solved through it. Therefore, the pressing task for Central Americans is to put their own houses in order. This includes the reaffirmation of national development projects toward the integration of Central American countries as a tool to encourage a sustainable and equitable development. Men and women in this hemisphere have been submitting proposals, from an alternative perspective, aimed at democratic participation, the reduction of inequalities, the sustainability and reaffirmation of the people's right to promote their own development projects.[50] For all those who acknowledge, from an ethical and technical viewpoint, the insurmountable systemic limitations imposed by neoliberalism, resistance constitutes the key element in the construction of another world. "We are still on time to revert this abandonment and massacre."[51]

Notes

1. According to the Stockholm Institute of Peace Research (SIPRI) in the year 2002 military expenditures increased for the fourth time consecutively at a 6 percent rate equivalent to $794,000,000,000. The United States is still the largest manufacturer of weapons in the world; its production is estimated at $335.7 trillion corresponding to 43 percent of the world supply. See *SIPRI*, "The 15 Major Spender Countries in 2002," http://www.rebelion.org/internacional/031112sipri.htm. Accessed on September 20, 2005.

2. United States Department of State, the United States National Security Strategy. Washington, D.C. September, 2002, p. 23.

3. Ibidem, pp. 18–19.

4. Cited in Osvaldo León, "Movilización Continental contra el ALCA," in *ALAI*, January 24, 2002, http://alainet.org/docs/1698.html.

5. The term NAFTA + means that the FTAA includes transnational scopes and privileges for capital that go beyond the limits container in NAFTA.

6. The WTO was created in Marrakech, Morocco, on April 15, 1994.

7. See Raúl Moreno, "Visibilizando los Impactos del Comercio e Inversión en los Consumidores y Consumidoras," *Consumers International-Centro para la Defensa del Consumidor*, Santiago de Chile, 2002.

8. Wolfang Kreissl-Dorfler and Melanie Quandt, "La Organización Mundial de Comercio. Cinco años después de su Fundación: un Balance Provisional," in *Libre Comercio. Promesas versus Realidades*. Ediciones Henrich Boll, El Salvador, 2000.

9. Ibid.

10. See Raúl Moreno, "La Ronda de la Organización Mundial de Comercio en Seattle: un Caos que Evidencia la Necesidad de la Participación Ciudadana," in *Revista Eslabón*, MS Denmark, Managua, 1999.

11. See Martin Khor, WTO: "The New Threats to Developing Countries and Sustainability," *Third World Network*, Geneva, 2003.

12. In the planned FTAA Project, 34 tour economies of the hemisphere would participate, save Cuba, and they represent a potential market of 800,000,000 individuals; the third part of the Gross Domestic Product (GDP) of the world and more than the fifth part of global trade.

13. There is a new opportunity for transnational corporations to participate in tenders covering areas such as health, hospital care, primary and secondary education, museums, libraries, water services, insurances, tourism, mailing services, transportation, and others.

14. After the Miami Meeting (1994) there were the Summits in Santiago de Chile (1998), Québec in Canada (2001), and Mae del Piata in Argentina (2005).

15. The "deep FTAA" promoted by the United States, El Salvador and Chile includes the FTAA original content: elimination of restrictions to foreign investment, liberalization of public utilities, broadening of intellectual property protection and American agricultural protectionism; while the "light FTAA" promoted by Brazil, preserves the principles and essence of the FTAA with some concessions especially in access to both market and intellectual property.

16. In the FTAA Ministerial Declaration, 8th Ministerial Meeting of Trade in Miami, United States, November 20, 2003, it is explicitly stated that ". . . reiterate that the FTAA can coexist with bilateral and sub-regional agreements . . .," p. 1.

17. The negotiating strategy of Central American governments was reduced to consolidate the tariff advantages already in effect for some products in the area by the Caribbean Basin Initiative (CBI) and the Generalized System of Preferences (GSP) to expand the sweat-factory investment and project the U.S. market to exporting "nostalgic or ethnic products" among the national population living in the United States, while the U.S. interests look for access without any limitation to our markets, elimination of any regulation to investment, consolidation or its intellectual property rights, access for its transnationals to government procurement and privatization of public utilities.

18. Raúl Moreno, "Desmistificando el Plan Puebla Panamá: los impactos económicos y sociale," *Oikos Solidaridad*, mimeo, San Salvador, 2002.

19. See UNCTAD Report on Trade and Development, 2000.

20. Note from the WTO Secretariat, Report on the Meeting held on March 7–8, 2001, WGTI/M/14, p. 6.

21. Despite nowadays many developed countries argue that "free trade" and "free investment" have been the main way through which they have reached their current status and that developing countries should encourage these policies, a historical study on experiences made by the United States, Great Britain, France, Germany, Finland, Ireland, Japan, Korea,and Taiwan shows that these countries have had strong foreign investment regulations according to national interest. See Chang Ha-Joon. "Kicking Away the Ladder," *Anthem Press*, London, 2002.

22. Jaime Stay, ALCA, *el paraíso de los inversionistas*, Puebla Autonomous University, mimeo, Puebla, 2002.

23. "Mapa político de posiciones de los países en la discusión sobre inversión" at the WTO. WWF Internacional and Oxfam, Geneva, April 22, 2003.

24. The Washington Consensus constitutes a set of guidelines of economic policies which form the basis of "consensus" neoliberalism between the political, economic, military, and academic complex.in the United States.

The consensus is structured on the basis of the work by John Williamson (1990): "Lo que Washington quiere decir cuando se refiere a reformas de las políticas económicas," It includes ten "recommendations" for measures, namely, fiscal discipline, focalization of public expenditures, fiscal reform, financial liberalization, competitive exchange rates, liberalized commercial policies, promotion of foreign direct investment, privatization of public enterprises, economic deregulation, and intellectual property rights.

25. The monetary approach of the balance of payments, absorption theory, quantitative money theory, supplying approaches, among others. See Osvaldo Rosales, "El debate del ajuste structural en América Latina," ILPES, ECLA, Santiago de Chile, 1979.

26. See Raúl Moreno, "Los impactos de los programas de ajuste estructural en la niñez salvadoreña." Save the Children, Imprenta Criterio, San Salvador, 2000.

27. Raúl Moreno, "La reforma fiscal en El Salvador; una exigencia impostergable," Ebert Foundation. Imprenta Criterio, San Salvador, 1999.

28. The fiscal reform carried out in El Salvador led to the elimination of equity taxes imposed on exports so practically one single direct tax was left: the income tax.

29. The "international treaties signed by El Salvador with other States or with international bodies constitute a law of the Republic when they come into effect in accordance with provisions enshrined in that treaty and this Constitution." See Constitution of the Republic of El Salvador, Article 144.

30. Abraham Abrego, "Consideraciones jurídicas sobre los Tratados de Libre Comercio", mimeo, FESPAD, San Salvador, 2001, p. 1.

31. Constitution of the Republic of El Salvador, Article 146.

32. Abrego, "Consideraciones jurídicas," p. 2.

33. See Hilda Salazar et al, "Impactos socio ambientales del TLCAN," RMALC, Mexico D.F., 2001

34. According to the vice president of the Republic of El Salvador; "There are serious studies showing that CAFTA will increase 50 percent in a 10 year period, the GDP per capita of Salvadorians. This has a scientific base showing that this is the great opportunity for Central America to fight and reduce poverty rates." This shows the frailty of governmental arguments used to sustain CAFTA. Besides, he said that "We are going to adequately sell to the largest consumer in the world and that is the market where 2.000.000 Salvadorians are living," as an act of magic. See "La Prensa Gráfica," San Salvador, May 9, 2003.

35. Ibid.

36. "La Prensa Gráfica," San Salvador, April 30, 2003, www.laprensagrafica.com. Accessed on September 25, 2005.

37. Taken from a document prepared by the Office of the Commercial Representative of the United States (USTR) dealing with the interests to be taken into account by negotiators in the Bush administration. See http://www.elsalvador.com/, October 9, 2003.

38. Ibid.

39. After the privatization process of the electricity sector a group of transnational corporations of American capital control a large part of the electricity generation and distribution in Central America, save Costa Rica, where the electricity sector is still in the hands of the state, though the CAFTA-U.S. is threatening with the privatization.

40. Controlled by transnational corporations to generate, transmit and distribute energy.
41. See "El Observatorio Internacional," FUNDE, San Salvador, year 2, first quarter 2001, pp. 1–8.
42. See the proposal made by Michael Porter and Lucia Marshall: "Estrategia para el Desarrollo Sustentable de Centroamérica," submitted by INCAE, Alajuela, 1998.
43. www.iadb.org/regions/re2/ppp. Accessed on October 1, 2005.
44. Ibid.
45. Santiago Levy, Enrique Davila, Georgina Kessel, "El Sur Tambien Existe: UN ensayo Sobre el desarrollo regional de Mexico," *Economica Mexicana*, 11, 2 (Segunda Semestre de 2003): 205–206.
46. In Mexico, the main road networks are: a) Matamoros-Tampico-Veracruz-Villahermosa-Campeche-Mérida; b) Tapachula-Arriaga-Salinas Cruz-Acapulco-Lázaro Cárdenas; c) The link between Tuxtla Gutiérrez and Cárdenas—Tabasco; d) The ports at Progreso, Salina Cruz and Coatzalcos.
47. The PPP Hill generate the decomposition of the "social fabric," an interview made by *La Jornada*, Mexico D.F. to Dr. Andrés Barreda, in http://www. jornada.unam.mx/2001/jun01/010627/oriente-ppb-htm. Accessed on October 8, 2005.
48. Ibid.
49. Raúl Moreno (Coordinator), "Cumplimiento y Vigencia de los DESC in El Salvador," 2003, p.110.
50. See www.asc_hsa.org. Accessed on October 10, 2005.
51. Ernesto Sabato, *La resistencia*, Seix Barral, Buenos Aires, 2000.

Chapter 9

Social Movements, Hegemony and Resistance

Harry E. Vanden

The history of subaltern social groups is necessarily fragmented and episodic. There undoubtedly does exist a tendency to (at least in provisional stages) unification in the historical activity of these groups. . . . It therefore can only be demonstrated when an historical cycle is completed and this cycle culminates in a success.
Antonio Gramsci, *Selections from the Prison Notebooks*: 54–55[1]

The emergence of new political and alternative movements despite their scant participation in [traditional] political life marks the start of a new way of conducting politics which responds to the legitimate demands of the marginalized majorities.
Juan del Grando, Mayor of La Paz greeting rise of the new political movement MAS and its leader and Coca Growers Federation head, Evo Morales
(*Los Tiempos*, July 2, 2002)

Introduction

Since the initial rebellions by the native peoples against imposed European rule, there have been innumerable uprisings and other forms of resistance by the exploited masses in Latin America. With the notable exception of the slave uprising in Haiti led by Tousant l'Oveurture, most have been brutally and successfully suppressed and the particular offending segment of the masses repressed and returned to their subaltern position. But even these outbreaks were rare. The daily hegemony exercised by the ruling classes generally managed to avoid such unseemly eruptions of popular anger.

Seen against this background, the backlash against economic neoliberalism and the globalization process is all the more interesting.[2] As has been the case in the United States, the national and international economic elites have used all the mechanisms of intellectual domination at their disposal to exercise hegemony and convince all classes of Latin Americans of the virtues of globalized neoliberalism. Despite their best efforts, even the *New York Times* and other mainstream English press like *the Economist, the Financial Times,* and *Newsweek* began to catalogue a different reaction by 2003. Several of these publications went on to note a resultant change in Latin American politics, which they initially saw as a resurgent populism or simply a turn to the left.[3] Yet, the progression of events suggest that there is a realignment that is much more profound and that may well represent a sea change in politics in the region.

Ever since the Caracazo in 1989, there have been different forms of popular protest against austerity measures and elements of the conservative economic policies that came to be called neoliberalism in Latin America. These new repertoires of protest actions[4] have been manifest in diverse forms: the Zapatista rebellion in Mexico from 1994 on, the neopopulist Movimiento V República led by Hugo Chávez in Venezuela beginning in the 1990s, the national indigenous movement led by the Confederación de Nacionalidades Indígenas del Ecuador (CONAIE) in Ecuador, and the growth of its related party, Pachakutik, the Movement of Landless Rural Laborers (MST) in Brazil, the Asambleas de Barrios, the Piqueteros, and other protest organizations in Argentina and the Indigenous Peasant Federation and Federation of Cocaleros and its linked political movement, MAS in Bolivia. The election of Lula and the strength of the Partido dos Trabalhadores (PT) in Brazil, the more recent strong popular vote for Evo Morales in Bolivia and Tabaré Vasquez in Uruguay—and even the support that Nestor Kirchner enjoys in Argentina—can also be seen as part of a strong popular reaction to neoliberal policies advocated by the I.M.F. and other international financial institutions, and a further indication of a movement away from traditional politics and an authoritarian political culture to new forms of popular democratic participation.

Electoral alternatives to politics as usual have not always been present, and even progressive parties such as PT (the Workers Party in Brazil) have not always been trusted by new social movements like the M.S.T. in Brazil. Though not always well or precisely articulated, new demands are being registered. They have not always been addressed to the political system per se, but to society more generally, since there have been growing questions about the system's relevancy and legitimacy. Indeed, much of the struggle to form a consensus and determine hegemony has been occurring in civil society rather than the halls of government. Nor has the populace in most nations looked to armed struggles and revolutionary movements to remedy their problems (Colombia is the significant exception here, but it remains to be seen whether the masses see either the FARC or the ELN as actually articulating their needs). The populace seeks something different. Different groups are looking for new political structures that allowed for if not encourage their participation. Civil society is becoming the new locus of conflict and contention. Specific segments of the population are seeking forms of political organization that they can call their own. There is a search for new structures that can respond to the perceived—and not always clearly articulated—demands being formulated from below by the popular sectors.

A broad segment of the population (from the lower and middle classes) has begun to mobilize and seek new and different political involvement and responses in parties, governmental structures, and social movements. They want something that works for them. Indeed, the increasing promotion of democracy and democratization tells them that their voices should be heard and that the political system should somehow respond to them. Many become disillusioned and angry when it is unclear how, their votes count and (if at all they do) whether the political class is responding to their hue and cry. Similarly, the return to democracy after authoritarian military rule or the strengthening of democratic government institutions during intense democratization convince broad sectors of the population to expect better, cleaner, more efficient, and hopefully a less corrupt government. In this respect, the political culture is beginning to change. If nothing else, elections are not expected to be fraught with fraud and the resultant governments are expected to be a bit more responsive and a little less corrupt. Similarly, the populace is generally becoming less tolerant of some of the traditional vices in Latin American politics: corruption, ineffective rule, and nonsubstantive political discourse (*politiqueo*). Thus, political regrouping has begun.

Chiapas: Regional Victory

In Southern Mexico, local and community organizations began to resist the dire economic consequences engendered by globalization and globalized integration through free trade and even NAFTA. It is argued that similar forms of resistance have occurred throughout the hemisphere since the region was interjected into the international capitalist economic system. Yet, these previous struggles were more akin to traditional peasant or indigenous rebellions in that they did not spawn strong national or international links and as such were easily marginalized or defeated. Indeed, localized resistance had bubbled to the surface sporadically since the time of the conquest. This certainly had been the case in southern Mexico and the Yucatan as well. Perhaps stimulated by this tradition of rebellion, in the 1980s the indigenous rural population in Chiapas began to resist and organize against the traditional land inequity and the hardships that the commercialization of agriculture and Mexico's further integration into the global market structure caused them. Racial identity and unequal land distribution helped to solidify the movement and led to the formation of a social movement that eventually spawned the Zapatista Army of National Liberation, (EZLN). Unlike some other groups, the Zapatistas were successful in linking their struggle to a growing continental indigenous identity and the disastrous effects of globalized free markets on local small farmers. Their ingenious use of the internet, the mountain mask, public relations, marches, and mobilizations kept their cause before the Mexican nation and the international community. They were able to create a highly politicized movement with considerable regional power and national visibility. However, they were not able to link their struggle to other large politicized social movements to form a national coalition. Nor were they able to mobilize their support behind a nation-wide new political party or new political movement (as would be done in Ecuador and Brazil) which would be sympathetic to their demands once it achieved national power or that would at least ensure adequate space in civil society to continue to mobilize support and pursue their demands as would be done in other places such as Bolivia.

Beyond Populism

In previous times, populism like the one championed by Getulio Vargas in Brazil had offered some alleviation of similar dissatisfaction. Indeed, populism lent itself well to the process of hegemonic control exerted by different sectors of the dominant classes. But even traditional populism and its hegemonic underpinnings seemed unable to staunch the growing mobilizations in Ecuador, Brazil, Venezuela, Argentina, and Bolivia. One might even conclude that traditional populism had run its course. It had responded to a time of increasing enfranchisement, growing literacy, and increased political knowledge. Higher levels of education, ever wider suffrage and greater female gender equality, more sophisticated political culture, and a widespread involvement in politics had called for other forms of political participation. This was beginning to develop in places such as Chile under Allende, Brazil, El Salvador, and Guatemala before the onset of bureaucratic authoritarian regimes and military run repression. Other responses included authoritarian Nasserite reformism in Peru under Juan Velasco Alvarado and a military populist form of the same in Panama under Omar Torrejos. Although both military regimes did pay attention to popular needs, both Velasquismo and Torrejismo were, top-down authoritarian movements that did not provide adequate effective political institutions to incorporate demands from below and the growing political assertiveness and participation of large sectors of the population. Their nationalist populism did, nonetheless, mobilize segments of the masses—albeit in pro-government forms—and served to keep political expectations high in their own and in other countries. It also suggested that progressive nationalist sectors of the militaries would and could respond to the growing restiveness of the masses and at least some of the economic and social problems undergirding it. These ideas would later find resonance in Venezuela from the 1992 coup attempt on and in Ecuador after the January 2000 coup. Indeed, coup leaders in both countries were later elected president (Chávez and Gutiérrez), even though their policies differed greatly after they were in office.

Right Wing Populism in Peru

The legacy of Velasquismo was very mixed in Peru. The military had retreated to the barracks by the end of the 1970s and taken much of their nationalist vision of development with them. By the 1980s, Peru was again suffering from a profound economic crisis and the populist variant of

Aprismo under Alan García. Warmed-over Aprismo without Haya de la Torre proved unable to lead the country out of the quagmire. This in turn led to the de-legitimization of the political system, with the concomitant growth of political movements that represented nontraditional options. Though there were social movements, they remained relatively small and did not reach national proportions. Rather, political competition developed among a violent Maoist guerrilla group, Sendero Luminoso (Shining Path), a Fidelista guerrilla group, the MRT (The Tupac Amaru Revolutionary Movement), and a rising political movement led by Alberto Fujimori. The latter had broken away from traditional party groupings and created his own ad hoc political coalition that later evolved into a brand of right-wing populism. As the 1990s progressed, dissatisfaction with traditional political leaders and traditional political parties became more widespread as did a growing trend to doubt the legitimacy of the political system itself.

In Peru and throughout the region, traditonal personalismo, clientelismo, corruption, and personal class and group avarice became subjects of ridicule and anger if not rage. The effects of neoliberalism and continued racism amidst ever stronger calls for economic and racial equality began to be felt. Traditional parties like APRA and attempts at leftist unity in Peru had fallen before political newcomer Alberto Fujimori and his ad hoc political movement, Cambio 90. Yet, the Fujimori government became increasingly authoritarian in the face of continued success by Shining Path and eventually closed down congress and altered the supreme court as it pursued an extremely brutal—but ultimately successful—war against the guerrillas. After experiencing some popularity for stopping the guerrillas and restoring calm, Fujimori was discredited for corruption and forced into exile in Japan. However, by late 2003, the neoliberal policies championed by the successor government of Alejandro Toledo were also under attack as economic conditions worsened and his government lost support. There were no strong national social movements or new political grouping to offer alternatives and the legitimacy of the political system was again being questioned. Amid strikes and demonstrations, Shining Path once again became active.

The Bolivarian Republic and the Rise of Chavismo in Venezuela

When the voting populace is presented with what they perceive as a real choice that they believe could actually generate policies that would counteract the most economically and socially damaging aspects of economic globalization and neoliberalism, voter turnout often tends to peak and reformist leaders and their parties or coalitions regularly reap the benefits.

This was certainly the case in Venezuela with the strong antiglobalization campaign to create a new Bolivarian republic led by Hugo Chávez Frias. The identification of the two traditionally dominant parties (Acción Democrática and COPEI) with the status quo and neoliberal policies connected to economic globalization led to their resounding defeat in the 1998 election (neither was able to achieve double digits in the presidential election). After a spirited campaign and a somewhat demagogic appeal to the 80 percent of the population which Chávez classified as poor, his Movimiento V République and the Polo Patriótico coaliton made a strong showing in the polls and won a resounding victory in the December presidential elections (56.5 percent). Voter turnout increased for the first time in recent years to 64 percent of the registered voters. More remarkable was the fact that the main competitor (Henrique Salas Rómer) was from neither of the two main parties. The popular classes had responded with enthusiasm to Chávez's antineoliberal, Bolivarian rhetoric and program. Although his political movement was not well organized at the national or grass-roots level, his criticisms of Venezuela's self-indulgent and increasingly corrupt political elite and the neoliberal policies they were pushing on the people paid big dividends at the polls. Indeed the political momentum of the election and the popular mobilization that made the Chávez victory possible carried the new government to a majority in a constituent assembly (approved in a popular referendum) and the subsequent new presidential elections under the new constitution in 2000. Here Chávez got 59.5 percent of the vote, though voter turnout was much lower.[5] Since then the resonance of his attacks against the wealth, the corrupt traditional political class and neoliberal policies that promote economic globalization can still be seen in the support among the poorer segments of the population. It was precisely his ability to mobilize these sectors in the face of growing opposition from traditional political groupings and their upper and middle class allies that thwarted a temporarily successful coup attempt in April of 2002, placing Chávez back in the presidential palace after he had been removed to a military base by the coup leaders. A subsequent strike by the managers and some pro-Acción Democrática employees of the state oil company PEDEVESA was ultimately unsuccessful, though it did engage the Chávez government in a struggle with some opposition controlled unions. An even more concerted attempt to remove President Chávez through a referendum in 2004 was also unsuccessful and helped to consolidate the Bolivarian Republic. This was also done at the grass-roots level through the organization of Bolivarian Circles and pro government community and neighborhood movements.[6]

Ecuador

Southern Mexico was not the only place where the effects of neoliberal policies and the globalization process generated innovative responses. Since Incan times, local indigenous communities have been marginalized from important decision-making processes in Ecuador. This practice was extended to virtually all indigenous people after the conquest and continued during the republic. Yet, by the 1990s the traditional struggle for land, power, and some modicum of justice for the indigenous, mostly peasant masses was gradually transformed from local, community based struggle to a national struggle coordinated by the Confederación de Nacionalidades Indígenas del

Ecuador (CONAIE). The Confederation of Indigenous Nationalities of Ecuador had become a national organization that was able to mobilize thousands of its people in land takeovers and marches. It connected different ethnic and regional groups and used modern means of communication to forge a national social movement. In the process it became a major power contender that could challenge governmental action by the late 1990s. After the disastrous dollarization of the economy and imposition of other neoliberal economic policies by President Jamil Mahuad, CONAIE was able to mobilize tens of thousands of its constituents for a march on Quito that culminated in the taking of the congress building and—backed by a few progressive army officers and civilian politics—the formation of a short-lived junta. This was the first time indigenous people had governed substantial parts of Ecuador since the conquest. Their victory was, however, short lived. Although some horizontal contacts with other organizations had been made, the CONAIE militants were not part of a broad-based national coalition that could retain power. With the support of the United States, the traditional political class was able to retake power and negotiate the exit of Mahuad by placing Vice President Gustavo Noboa in power. Once moblilized, CONAIE learning from the experience, initiated a national political strategy, and even started an affiliated political party, Pachacutik. In the 2002 elections they continued to cultivate their now highly politicized national social movement, but were also able to field successful local and congressional political candidates. Eventually they rallied their support behind Lucio Gutiérrez, the army colonel who had been part of the short-lived junta in January of 2000. Thus they helped to elect Gutiérrez to the presidency, though their support was not unconditional. They maintained their autonomy, but ensured that their demands would at least receive a hearing at the highest level, and might even be received with some sympathy. Ultimately, however, many sectors of CONAI were coopted by the Gutiérez government. When he too was driven from office because of his adherence to neoliberal policies, the power of CONAIE suffered a significant setback.

Local Struggles and New Social Movements at the Local and Regional Level

In Bolivia the simultaneous national mobilizations of several new social movements in the national political arena and their common alliance (and support for national political alternatives) contributed to massive popular mobilizations in 2002, 2003, and again in 2005, and successful regime change. However, long before such national mobilization occurred, local communities often formed their own organizations to fight some aspect of globalization that was impacting them at the most local level. This reaction can be seen in the strong grass roots movement against the privatization of the public water supply in Cochabamba, Bolivia, in 2000. The Coordinadora de Defensa del Agua y de la Vida, remained locally rooted.[7] Yet their struggle was always framed in an international and national context. They championed their cause through the internet and sent delegations to international meetings like the World Social Forums in Porto Alegre, Brazil. Further, they were not only very aware of the international dimensions of their struggle and of its globalized causes, but were equally aware of the possibilities of international links with similar struggles and the international antiglobalization movement generally. This awareness and their electronic and personal links to other movements in Bolivia and outside later facilitated their integration into the broad national coalition that set forth a national agenda through support for Evo Morales and his MAS Party in the 2002 presidential election and in subsequent actions in 2005. Their extensive networking with other new social movements allowed their movement and other local or regional movements to become part of a near unstoppable national mobilization that, as will be discussed in the following sections, toppled the Sánchez de Lozada government and later that of his predecessor Mesa. By linking the local effects of the neoliberal privatization of the water supply in Cochabamba to global policies and national politics, they linked their struggle to a growing regional and international consensus, and to a national movement with concrete, achievable objectives.

National Social Movements and
the Bolivian Crisis

The intensity of the politization of social movements in Bolivia was demonstrated by the massive protests and the popular mobilizations that rocked the nation in 2003 and again in 2005. As had occurred in Ecuador in 2000, the popular mobilization of indigenous peoples and rural peasants through a newly formed peasant indigenous federation that called for the blockading of roads and popular mobilizations. They had quickly been joined by the Cocaleros of the now famous Coca Growers Federation led by Evo Morales, who had finished barely a percentage point behind President Gonzalo Sánchez de Lozada in the 2002 elections. Other groups like the Cochabamba movement against the privatization of water and a similar movement in El Alto also joined. An ongoing economic crisis and a crisis in traditional politics combined with strong U.S. pressure to open Bolivian markets and virtually eliminate the centuries-old cultivation of coca leaves, to stimulate the masses to heed the calls of the social movements for action. The precipitating event was a U.S.-backed plan to sell Bolivian natural gas through a Chilean port that land-locked Bolivia had lost to the former in the ill-fated War of the Pacific (1879–1881). The disastrous failure of the neoliberal model that U.S. educated President Sánchez Lozada had so strongly advocated added to the widely shared perception that this new trade deal was but one more ruse to extract wealth from the nation and leave the indigenous masses even more poverty-ridden. In the words of one protester, "Globalization is just another name for submission and domination. We've had to live with that here for 500 years and now we want to be our own masters."[8] The indigenous federation and the Cocaleros were soon joined by the Coordinadora de Defensa del Agua y de la Vida in Cocabamba, urban unions, and students as they mobilized in massive demonstrations in La Paz and then other major cities. The government futilely tried to repress the demonstrators, causing the loss of 80 lives. This enraged the opposition even more and increased the president's isolation. Bolivian miners and their unions also joined the protests and decided to march on the capital. As his political backers dropped away in the face of the mass mobilization Sánchez de Losada was forced to resign and leave the country. The new social movements in Bolivia had been able to take politics out of the presidential palace and halls of congress where traditional politics—and the traditional political class—dominated and into the streets and rural highways that they could control. They had been able to forge a broad national coalition that cemented the president's downfall and established the viability of their social movements as key political actors whose demands had to be heeded. Unlike Ecuador in 2000 and the Bolivian revolution of 1952, they had done so without seizing power themselves, but had demonstrated just how effectively they could use and mobilize massive political power on a national scale. They had done so "from below," through a broad coalition of social movements with strong identities and deep democratic ties to their constituencies. The mobilization to force Carlos Mesa from power in 2005 was even stronger, wider, and more sustained. Not only did the mobilized movements force Mesa from office they also forced the government to agree to an election and a constituent assembly and vest the temporary government in the hands of the president of the supreme court rather than the constitutional prescribed congressional leaders. These concessions paved the way for the strong vote that placed Evo Morales in the Presidency in the first round of voting in December 2005.

Argentine Manifestation

The strength of the reaction to neoliberal policies and the loss of confidence in traditional institutions of governance and their susceptibility to corruption and personal/corporate/small group appropriation of public resources is manifest in various contexts throughout the region. For instance, in Argentina popular mobilizations, street demonstrations, strikes, and neighborhood *Asambleas Populares* (or *Asambleas Barriales*) shook the political system and the political class to the core at the end of 2001 and occasioned the resignation of elected president, Fernando de la Rúa, and the rapid replacement of three other appointed presidents (the vice president had already resigned). In early 2002, a declared anti-neoliberal Peronist president Eduardo Duhalde was voted in office by the Argentine Congress. The unresolved economic crisis, default on the foreign debt and Duhalde's perceived need to make some concession to the International Monetary Fund (IMF), other international financial institutions and U.S. policy kept the population angry and mobilized.[9] Demonstrations and protests continued through early 2003 as the Argentine nation groped to find a political force capable of ending the crisis. There was so little confidence in traditional parties or politicians that one could frequently hear a popular refrain among many Argentinians—*que se vayan todos*! Throw them all out! Both the economic and political system were losing their legitimacy, with many of the nations' problems being blamed on the IMF and neoliberal policies and a corrupt and incompetent political class. The situation remained chaotic in 2003 as a wide array of candidates competed in a new presidential election amid continued demonstrations, strikes and economic uncertainty. The different new social movements were united in their anger with economic conditions and political leadership, but were unable to put together a national coalition that coalesced into a national political movement or favored one political candidate. Ironically, former President Carlos Menem was seen by some as a stabilizing force amid the chaos and managed to finish first in the first round of voting. However, as the second round developed and the antiglobalization forces united against him, his comeback faltered as the millions protesting economic and political failures remembered his identification with neoliberal policies. Ultimately his showing was so low in the polls that he pulled out of the second round before the vote could be taken. The winner by default was the left-wing Peronist candidate Néstor Kirchner, who had been much more critical of IMF recommendations and neoliberal policies and seemed to respond to the demands made by the highly politicized social movements that had toppled previous governments. Indeed, the popular support he enjoyed from the masses enabled him to ignore pressure from the international financial institutions and chart an anti-neoliberal policy for the Argentine government that began to show strong signs of success by the beginning of 2006.

Initial Analysis

The nature of the massive protests that have continued to rock Buenos Aires and other Argentine cities and that deposed Bolivian President Sánchez de Lozada in October of 2003 and Carlos Mesa in 2005 suggest the political sea change that is sweeping across Latin America. Although these movements have many new characteristics, they are also a recent and vociferous manifestation of the specter of mass popular mobilization against the governing elite that has haunted Latin America since colonial times. In the last few years, a great many of the masses—and some of the middle class—seem to be hit by a feeling that the much touted return to democracy, celebration of civil society, and incorporation in the globalization process has left them marginalized economically if not politically as well. The reactions in Argentina, Mexico, Ecuador, Bolivia, Brazil, and Venezuela are strong and significant and, in varying ways, make one wonder if indeed the political project is working for the common people. It is also quite possible that it is the democratization and celebration of civil society that allow—some would say encourage—the political mobilization that is manifest in the widespread emergence of new social and political movements.

Dissatisfaction seems widespread. Selected abstention rates are indicative of growing disillusion with government and the political system. In the 2001 elections in Argentina in, around 41 percent of the voters abstained, or cast annulled or blank ballots.[10] The 1998 national elections in Brazil saw a similar phenomenon, with 40.1 percent of the electorate either abstaining, or casting blank or annulled ballots.[11] In the Mexican presidential election of 2000, the abstention rate alone was 36 percent.[12]

There are many who wonder if the new political project is indeed working for the common people. As the region democratizes, there is greater discussion of the emergence of a new(er) political class. Such talk is, however, coupled with a growing consensus that the political class' new political enterprise is leaving behind the great majorities, and further marginalizing specific groups within those majorities. Such groups include indigenous people in southern Mexico and Ecuador, rural laborers and the poor in Brazil, the rural peasants and indigenous people in Bolivia, those who live in the slums and who have been left out of the diffusion of oil wealth in Venezuela, as well as large segments of the lower and middle classes in Argentina. Indicators of the growing malaise are many: not only the growing abstention rates in elections, but the abandonment of traditional political parties for new, more amorphous, ad hoc parties, the upsurge of new more political social movements and mass organizations, and a plethora of national strikes, demonstrations, and protests such as those that swept across Argentina at the end of 2001, the beginning of 2002, and spread across Bolivia in 2002, 2003, and 2005.

New Elements, New Movements

The current mobilizations seem to be different. The systems of mass communication and related communication technology, and easy, low cost access to the internet have combined with higher levels of literacy and widened access to higher education and much greater political freedom under the democratization process.[13] The result has been a new wave of highly political social movements that are often different in their organization and strategy from traditional movements and endeavor to articulate popular needs in new ways. This has occurred when ideas of grassroot democracy, popular participation and even elements of Liberation Theology and Christian Base Community organization have been widely disseminated. Likewise, there is a growing belief that racial, gender, and economic inequality should not exist and that systems which perpetuate such inequality need to be changed.

Unlike movements of the last few decades, these new movements do not employ or advocate the radical, revolutionary restructuring of the state through violent revolution. Rather, their primary focus is to contest power by working through civil society to push for modification of the existing political system, and push it to the limits to achieve needed and necessary change and restructuring. Although there have been some exceptions like the initial Zapatista uprising of early January 1994 and CONAIE's very brief participation in a junta that held the Ecuadoran Congress building overnight in January of 2000, they were short-lived and both movements quickly changed tactic from trying to insert themselves as the regional or national rulers to negotiating power with existing national political elites (while at the same time trying to change the composition of the national political class).[14]

These new political movements all contest power, but do so in a political environment that is substantially different from what it has been historically. National level political participation was quite limited at the time of independence. Mass political movements like the one led by Hidalgo failed, while those led by the less popularly oriented members of the *criollo* elite like Iturbide succeeded and set the stage for the elitist politics of the nineteenth and much of the twentieth centuries. The franchise—and concomitant political participation—were gradually widened during this period. This in turn challenged the political elite to seek mechanisms to incorporate (if not manipulate) ever wider segments of the population. This eventually led to the emergence of mass based parties, reformist and revolutionary parties, and the emergence of populism as a means of incorporating the masses into a national project led by a political elite. Some reformist parties such as Liberación Nacional in Costa Rica and Acción Democrática in Venezuela were able to bring about economic and political structural change and incorporate wide sectors of the masses into national society and competitive two-party dominant political systems. A few populist projects like Peronism in Argentina were also able to achieve significant economic redistribution, break the oligarchy's economic domination, and incorporate the laboring masses and segments of the middle class into the (one party dominant) party system, albeit under the somewhat demagogic leadership of Juan and Evita Perón. The Cuban revolution challenged traditional elitist rule in a different way, but left little space for the development of autonomous social movements, though it did respond to the needs of the masses and developed mechanism of *poder popular* (popular power) that did foment active participation at the neighborhood and local level. The widespread rebellion against Anastacio Somoza in Nicaragua helped to make it possible for the Sandinista-led revolution to take power and for the FSLN-led government to begin an economic, social, and political restructuring of the Nicaraguan nation. Indeed, the strength and relative autonomy of many of the mass organizations in Nicaragua in the early 1980s was significant and helped to show that new organizational structures and political movements that supported them could radically change the way power was exercised in Latin America.[15] Likewise, the strength and dynamism of neighborhood and community-based movements that began to flower all over Latin America in the 1980s (even under repressive military regimes), redefined the parameters of political activism and suggested new repertoires of action for emerging social and political movements.

Thus one might conclude that the traditional political institutions seemed too far removed from the masses spatially, politically, class-wise, and in regard to political culture. Likewise, as suggested above, growing abstention rates suggested a general dissatisfaction with the political system. For instance, in Venezuela, the abstention rate for local elections had reached 55.8 percent in 1992, the year of the first coup attempt.[16] There was also growing resentment of the political class and their distance from the conditions of the masses on the part of many military officers.

New Social Movements and
New Politics: the MST

The radically different nature of these new social movements and the new politics can perhaps best be seen in the largest of the social movements in Latin America, the MST or Movement of the Landless Rural Workers in Brazil. Their ranks exceed 200,000 and on one occasion they were able to mobilize 100,000 people for a march in Brasilia. Their views are well articulated. In a draft document on the "Fundamental Principles for the Social and Economic Transformation of Rural Brazil," they note that "the political unity of the Brazilian dominant classes under Fernando Henrique Cardoso's administration (1994–2000) has consolidated the implementation of neoliberalism [in Brazil]," and that these neoliberal policies led to the increased concentration of land and wealth in the hands of the few and the impoverishment of Brazilian society. The document goes on to say that "Popular movements must challenge this neoliberal conceptualization of our economy and society."[17] In a pamphlet titled "Brazil Needs a Popular Project," the organization calls for popular mobilizations, noting that "All the changes in the history of humanity only happened when the people were mobilized." And that in Brazil, "all the social and political changes that happened were won when the people mobilized and struggled."[18] Their political culture and decision-making processes break from the authoritarian tradition. The movement has been heavily influenced by Liberation Theology and the participatory democratic culture that is generated by the use and study of Paulo Freire approach to self-taught, critical education.[19]

The MST itself was formed as a response to long-standing economic, social, and political conditions in Brazil. Land, wealth, and power have been allocated in an unequal way in Brazil since the conquest in the early 1500s. Land has remained highly concentrated and as late as 1996, 1 percent of the landowners who owned farms of over 1,000 hectares owned 45 percent of the land.[20] Conversely, as of 2001 there were some 4.5 million landless rural workers in Brazil. Wealth has remained equally concentrated. In 2001 the Brazilian Institute of Government Statistics reported that the upper 10 percent of the population averaged an income that was 19 times greater than the lowest 40 percent.[21] The plantation agriculture that dominated the colonial period and the early republic became the standard for Brazilian society. Few owned the land, reaped the profits, and decided the political destiny of the many. Slavery was the institution that provided most of the labor on the early plantation system and thus set the nature of the relationship between the wealthy landowning elite and the disenfranchised toiling masses who labored in the fields. Land stayed in relatively few hands in Brazil, and the agricultural laborers continued to be poorly paid and poorly treated. Further, after the commercialization and mechanization of agriculture that began in the 1970s much of the existing rural labor force became superfluous. As this process continued not only were rural laborers let go, sharecroppers were expelled from the land they had farmed and small farmers lost their land to larger family or commercial estates. This resulted in growing rural unemployment and the growth of rural landless families. Many were forced to migrate to the cities to swell the numbers of the urban poor while others opted for the government sponsored Amazon Colonization program whereby they were transported to the Amazon region to cut down the rainforest and begin to cultivate the land. Few found decent jobs in the city and the poor soil of the former rainforest would allow for little sustained agriculture. As conditions deteriorated, the landless realized that they were fighting for their own existence as a group and as such they were the authors of their own destiny. As one analyst observed, it is possible to classify them as did Eric Hobsbaum, in the context of the nineteenth-century working class as one of the groups that came to have a conviction that its social salvation is in its own hands. "The landless become social subjects to the extent that they constituted a collectivity that brings with it . . . the struggle to guarantee its own social existence as workers on the land."[22] The origins of the organization harken back to the bitter struggle to survive under the agricultural policies implemented by the military government. The landless in the southern Brazilian state of Rio Grande do Sul began to organize to demand land. Other landless people soon picked up their cry in the neighboring states of Paraná, and Santa Catarina. These were the beginning of the MST.[23] They built on a long tradition of rural resistance and rebellion that extends back to the establishments of *palenques* or large inland settlements of runaway slaves and to the famous rebellion by the poor rural peasants of Canudos in the 1890s. In more recent times it included the famous Peasant Leagues of Brazil's impoverished Northeast in the 1950s and early 1960s and the Grass Wars in Rio Grande do Sul and the southern states in the 1970s.[24] When the MST was founded in southern Brazil in 1984 as a response to rural poverty and lack of access to land, wealth, and power, similar conditions existed in many states in Brazil. Indeed, there were landless workers and peasants throughout the nation. Thus the MST soon spread from Rio Grande do Sul and Paraná in the south to states like Pernambuco in the northeast and Pará in the Amazon region. It rapidly became a national organization with coordinated policies and strong local participatory organization and decision making, and frequent state and national meetings based on direct representation.[25] By 2001 there were active MST organization in 23 of the 26 states.[26]

This type of national organization had not been the case with the Zapatista movement because conditions and identity were much more locally rooted. Yet, in both cases traditional politics and traditional political parties had proven unable and unwilling to address the deteriorating economic conditions of the marginalized groups who were suffering the negative effects of economic globalizaton. Their response was grassroots organization and the development of a new repertoire of actions that broke with old forms of political activity.

Developing organization and group actions began to tie individual members together in a strongly forged group identity. They were sometimes assisted in this task by progressive organizations concerned with economic and social justice. In the case of Brazil and the Landless, this role was played by the Lutheran church and especially the Pastoral Land Commission of the Catholic Church. Although these organizations assisted the Landless as did some segments of the Workers Party (PT), the organization never lost its autonomy. It was decided from the onset that this was to be an organization *for* the Landless Workers that would be run by the Landless Workers for their benefit as they defined it. They engaged in direct actions such as land takeovers from large estates and public lands, the construction of black plastic covered encampments along the side of the road to call attention to their demands for land, and marches and confrontations when necessary. They even occupied the family farm of President Fernando Enrique Cardoso to draw attention to his land owning interests and the consequent bias they attributed to him. They were at times brutally repressed, assassinated, and imprisoned, but they persevered, forcing land distribution to their members and others without land. Their ability to mobilize as many as 12,000 people for a single land take over or 100,000 thousand for a national march suggested just how strong their organizational abilities were and how well they could communicate and coordinate at the national level. They also created a great deal of national support and helped to create a national consensus that there was a national problem with land distribution and that some substantial reform was necessary.[27]

The Landless were well attuned to the international globalization struggle and considered themselves part of it, helping to organize and participating in the World Social Forums in Porto Alegre and sending their representatives to demonstrations and protests throughout the world. Indeed, at least one recent work suggests that this was part of a developing global backlash against economic globalization.[28] Struggles that were once local and isolated were now international and linked. The news media and growing international communications links like cellular phones and especially electronic mail greatly facilitated the globalization of struggle and the globalization of awareness of local struggles and support and solidarity for them. This and the dramatic actions like the massive land takeovers by the MST also generated considerable support at the national level and helped to define what might have been considered a local problem as a national problem that required national attention and national resources to remedy it.

The interaction between the MST and the PT is also instructive. Although relations between the two organizations are generally excellent at the local level, with overlapping affiliations, the national leaderships have remained separate and not always as cordial. The MST has maintained a militant line in regard to the need to take over unused land and assert their agenda, where as much of the PT leadership has wanted to be more conciliatory. Thus the Landless backed and supported Lula (Luiz Inacio "Lula"da Silva) and the PT in most local campaigns and the national campaign for the presidency. In this way they helped to achieve significant regime change in Brazil, where Lula was elected with 61.27 percent of the vote in the second round of voting in 2002. Indeed, realizing the PT's historic challenge to neoliberal policies and elitist rule, the landless turned out heavily in the election to join around 80 percent of the registered voters who participated in the voting in both rounds.[29] Once the election was over, the Landless did not press to be part of the government. Rather they continued to press the government for a comprehensive land reform program and a redistribution of the land and the wealth. There would be no return to politics as usual. The PT would press its "0 Hunger" program and other social and economic initiatives and the MST would press the PT government for the structural reforms (e.g., comprehensive agrarian reform) that it considered necessary.

Conclusion

As suggested by the example of the MST, as these new social movements grow and are politicized, they come to represent a clear response to the neoliberal economic policies that are being foisted on Latin American nations by international financial institutions and the U.S. government. They have become bulwarks in the resistance to the process of neoliberal globalization advocated by the Washington Consensus and have aggressively resisted the implementation of neoliberal policies. In the process they have changed the way politics is conducted in most Latin American nations. They have been fundamental in breaking the cultural and political hegemony that the traditional ruling classes and their Washington based allies in the U.S. government and the international financial institutions have long exercised. Their growth and militancy have generated whole new repertoires of actions that include national mobilizations so massive that they can topple governments and/or force them to change their policies. They have left the traditional parties far behind as they forge new political horizons and create a nonauthoritarian, participatory political culture. Such movements also use existing political space to maximum effect. In the process they strengthen participatory democratic practice substantially.

They have vigorously resisted the corporate-led economic globalization process that many are heralding as the panacea to underdevelopment and poverty. Indeed, the economic realities that the masses of people all over Latin America are living has provided a potent empirical antidote to the universal prescription to globalize. The formulation of highly political social movements and the participatory democracy they practice provide a new and potent response to globalization in a time of neoliberalism. Further, these responses represent a substantial change from previous forms of political action—one that is transforming the conduct of politics throughout Latin America.

Notes

1. Antonio Gramsci, "*Selections from the Prison Notebooks*," ed. and trans. Quintin Hoare and Geofrey Nowell Smith. (New York: International Publishers, 1971).
2. Professor of Government and International Affairs, University of South Florida. The author wishes to thank his many friends, informants and participants in rallies

and demonstrations in Venezuela, Brazil, Argentina, Ecuador, Bolivia and Mexico for sharing their knowledge of events and perspectives with him.

3. Shifter, M. "Latin America's New Political Leadership: Walking on a Wire," *Current History*, 102, 661 (February 2003): 51.

4. Sidney Tarrow, "*Power in Movement, Social Movements and Contentious Politics*," (Cambridge: Cambridge University Press, 2003).

5. Elliner, Steve and Daniel Hellinger, *Venezueln Politics in the Chávez Era: Class Polarization and Conflict*. (Boulder, Colorado: Lynne Rienner Publishers, 2003).

6. Jonah Gindin, "Chavistas in the Halls of Power, Chavistas on the Street," *NACLA: Report on the Americas*, 38, 5 (March–April 2005): 27–29.

7. Jim Shultz, "Bolivia: the Water War Widenns," in *NACLA, Report on the Americas*, 36, 3 (January–February 2003): 34–37.

8. Larry Rohter, "Bolivia's Poor Proclaim Abiding Distrust of Globalization," *New York Times*, October 17, 2003, A2.

9. Andrés Gaudin, "Thirteen Days that Shook Argentina—And Now What? In "Who Owns Knowledge?" *NACLA, Report on the Americas*. 25, 5 (2002): 6–9.

10. Purcell Kaufman, Susan, "Electoral Lessons," *América Economía*, December 6, 2001, p. 40.

11. Banco de Datos Políticos das Américas: 1998.

12. Dirección Ejecutiva de Organización Electoral, "Estadística de las Elecciones Federales de 2000," www.ife.org.mx/wwworge/esta2000/gcprepcn. Accessed on April 9, 2002.

13. United Nations Development Program, "*Human Development Report 1999*," (New York and Oxford: Oxford University Press, 1999), pp. 3–9.

14. Jennifer N. Collins, "A Sense of Possibility, Ecuadors's Indigenous Movement Takes Center Stage," in "!Adelante! The New Rural Activism in the Americas" *NACLA, Report on the Americas* . 33, 5 (2000): 40–46.

15. Harry E.Vanden, and Gary Prevost, "*Democracy and Socialism in Sandinista Nicaragua*," (Boulder: Lynne Rienner, 1993).

16. Fátima García Díez, "The Emergence of Electoral Reforms in Contemporary Latin America," 27th ECPR Point Sessions Workshops, Designing Institutions, Mannheime, p. 26.

17. The Landless Rural Workers Movement (MST), "Fundamental Principles for the Social and Economic Transformation of Rural Brazil," Translated by Wilder Robles, *Journal of Peasant Studies*, 28, 2 (January 2001): 153–154.

18. *O Brasil Precisa de um projecto popular*. Cuartilla 11 São Paulo: Secretaria Operativa de Consulta Popular, 2000, p.29.

19. Paulo Freire, *The Pedagogy of the Oppressed*. (New York: Herder and Herder, 1970).

20. Petras, James "The Rural Landless Workers' Movement," *Z Magazine*. March, 2000, p. 35.

21. Brazilian Institute of Statistics, *Statistical Report 2001*, as cited from "Pais Termina Anos 90 Tão Desigual como Comenou," *Folha de São Paulo*, April 5, 2001 in Tom Lewis, "Brazil: The Struggle Against Neoliberalism," *International Socialist Review*, 18 (June–July 2001). Online, accessed on September 4, 2006.

22. Roseli Salete Caldart, *Pedagogia do Movimiento dos Sem Terra*, (Petrópolis: Vozes,1999), p. 25.

23. João Stedile Stedile, and Bernardo Mançaano Fernandes, *Brava Gente: a Trajetória do MST e a luta pela Terra no Brasil*, (São Paulo: Fundacão Perseu Abramo, 1999).

24. Elide Rugai Bastos, *As Ligas Camponesas*, (Petópolis: Vozes, 1984).

25. Sue Bradford and Jan Rocha, *Cutting the Wire*, (London: Latin American Bureau, 2002).

26. Author's interview, Gerald Fontes (Member of National Coordinating Council of Landless Movement). São Paulo, September 17, 2003.

27. See Rohter in Notes 8 for strong Bolivian reactions to (now deposed) President Sánchez de Lozada's globalization and neoliberal free trade policies in Bolivia and the movement to force him from office. Most tellingly, Rohter notes that "Two decades of free-market reform leave many resentful."

28. Robin Broad, ed. *Global Backlash, Citizen Initiatives for a Just World Economy*, (Laham, Maryland: Rowman and Littlefield, 2002).

29. IFES. 2003 at ifes.org/eguide/turnout2002.htm. Accessed on March 24, 2003.

Chapter 10

Geostrategic Resources in Latin America and U.S. Control Mechanisms

David Alejandro Alvarez Dieppa

Geostrategic resources are those natural components that are indispensable for the development of life on the planet; they are usually divided into three groups: biodiversity, petroleum, and water. These resources are extinguishable, nonrenewable, and irreplaceable (with the exception of petroleum). The scarcity and high demand of these resources lead to the creation of diverse means for their exploitation.

Biodiversity

Biodiversity includes species, ecosystems, knowledge, beliefs, traditions, and cultural customs. It is important because it comprises genes and chemical substances. For this reason it is a resource frequently used in different industries such as biotechnology, pharmaceutical, cosmetics, and bio-informatics industries, among others, for which markets have wide global dimensions exceeding billions of dollars; and hence these branches are extensively developed in the United States, Europe, and Japan.

A huge part of the progress of modern agriculture depends on the genes obtained from organisms of natural ecosystems. The 20 best-sold medicines in 1988, in the States, with worldwide earnings of $6 billion were based on plants, animals, or microorganisms for their development. The top ten pharmaceutical companies on the planet had earnings of $243,300 million in 2003. Approximate calculations show that 25 percent of all prescribed drugs come from botanical sources, and every wild plant providing the chemical bases to develop new drugs is projected to generate an average of $290 million per year. According to the United Nations Environment Program (UNEP) biological resources represent at least 40 percent of the worldwide economy.

In 1988, Dr. Russel Rettemeier, basing his research on prior studies made about the endemism of species, determined that there were four "mega-diverse" countries in the world; that is, four countries containing on their territories a high percentage of all the species existing on the planet; Brazil and Colombia are on top of this list. The most relevant issue is variety and the endemism of plants. Most endemic plants are located in countries such as Peru, Mexico, Bolivia, Ecuador, Venezuela, and, as previously mentioned, Brazil and Colombia; these countries are among the top 10 on a global scale.

In 1997, the number of mega-diverse countries increased from 4 to 17 (map 10.1), due to the addition of new parameters. This allowed other countries such as the United States to join the list. Even though its levels of endemism were not as high as the ones from the countries of the Amazon territory, it does possess, due to its territorial extension, a wide topographic variety, which was the main reason for its inclusion on this list.

Seventy percent of biodiversity resources are found in these 17 countries. The Amazon territory has the biggest extension of tropical forests on the planet (56 percent) and is the holder of a great biological variety of ecosystems, species, and genetic resources. There are close to a million and a half known species and it is estimated that there are more than 10 million total.

It is quite peculiar that the main corporations depending on the resources of biodiversity are not from underdeveloped countries, rather they are from the United States, which is mega-diverse and has the major quantity of these corporations, but, as stated before, its mega-diversity is not due to its richness in species and its endemism but for its variety of soils.

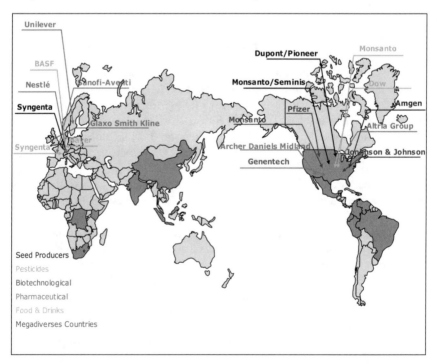

Map 10.1   Principal Corporations that Depend on Biodiversity and Megadiverse Countries
Source: Elaboración propia a partir de datos de ETC Group 2005 y Quezada 2004.

Conclusions

- Biodiversity is extinguishable, nonrenewable and irreplaceable.
- Its main reservoirs are located in undeveloped countries, mainly tropical, most prominently in South America.
- Currently, biotechnology is one of the strongest branches of science, basing its development on the use of natural genes. It is widely developed in the United States, Europe, and Japan.

Petroleum

Petroleum is the core of the worldwide economic system. Our society is totally dependent on this product. In 1880, its global production was generated almost exclusively by the United States, with amounts under a million tons. Now, production exceeds the three and a half billion tons (figure 10.1). Experts foresee that this demand will continue growing in a short period of time. The U.S. Department of Energy anticipates that the global demand of oil will increase 61 percent during the next 25 years, in relation to the demands of 2003.

The distribution of this resource in the world is not equal. The eleven OPEC member countries possess 70–77 percent of petroleum reservoirs found in the world.

The Wood Mackenzie Report of 2004, aside from admitting the reservoirs of Alberta, found the existence of heavy oil in the Orinoco Area of Venezuela, making this country the most important reservoir in the world.

The important thing is not how many reservoirs exist. One has to take into account that petroleum, like water and biodiversity, is a limited, nonrenewable

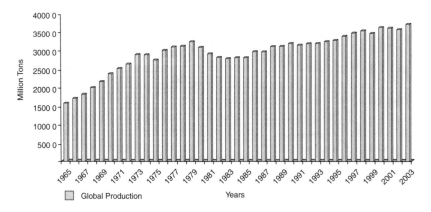

Figure 10.1   Global Production of Petroleum 1965–2003

Source: Excerpt from B.P. Statistical Review of World Energy, June 2004.

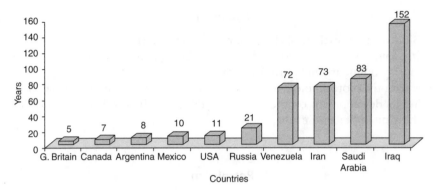

Figure 10.2   Longevity of the Main Reservoirs of Petroleum
Source: Excerpt from B.P. Statistical Review of World Energy, June 2004.

natural resource, and it is close to extinction. Technology and the pattern in which these reservoirs are discovered nowadays are actually decreasing. During the decade of 1981–1991, global reservoirs grew at a rate of 45.5 percent whereas during 1991–2001 they grew by only 4.9 percent.

The more exact numbers are those referring to the reservoirs per country. The U.S. reservoirs are supposed to be extinguished in 11 years, judging from the extractions made during 2003 (figure 10.2), though if it were to produce all the oil consumed there, its reservoirs would be consumed in only 4 years.

The United States accounts for 25 percent of the world's total consumption of oil, which makes it a major consumer and the biggest atmospheric contaminant in the world. Importing 53 percent of its oil, its main suppliers are Mexico, Venezuela, Canada, and Saudi Arabia. The United States also accounts for 20.2 percent of the refining capacity, which shows that it tries to control the most important areas of the strategic branches.

Conclusions

- Petroleum is extinguishable, nonrenewable, and irreplaceable.
- The Middle East is the richest area, though Venezuela is on top of the list of countries with the biggest reservoirs.
- The United States consumes 25 percent of the oil production in the world and its reservoirs are predicted to be drained in 11 years considering the pattern of exploitation of 2003.

Water

The total volume of water on the planet is estimated to be 1,400 million of km^3. Out of this amount, 97.5 percent is salt water and the 2.5 percent left is fresh

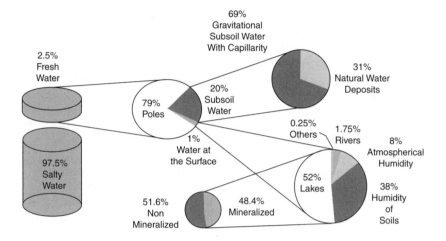

Figure 10.3   Water Distribution to the World

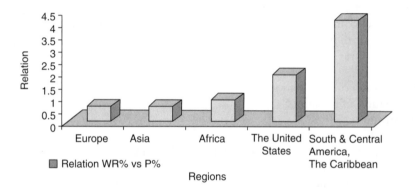

Figure 10.4   Relation between Water Reservoirs and Levels of Population, year 2003

Source: Excerpt from: FAO 2004 Martin Oinco, Las batallas del agua en America Latina.

water (figure 10.3). The water deposits whose volume is 10.53 million km³ are the most important reservoirs for human supplies, from which over two billion people in the entire world profit.

The worldwide situation is critical; some experts affirm the world's next wars will be for water. Estimates indicate that in 2025, 2.5 billion people will not have access to fresh water.

The situation in Latin America is the best, taking into account the reservoirs of this resource and population levels (figure 10.4). Despite this, the fact is that in this geographic area 77 million people have no access to fresh water.

Once again the United States presents itself as the major predator of the geostrategic resources of the planet. Its citizens consume an average of

400–600 gallons of water per day, the highest average in the world. The country spends 479 km^3 per year, which exceeds the consumption of the rest of the countries in the continent combined. In addition, 40 percent of its rivers and lakes are contaminated and its water deposits are being affected by several problems such as reduction of water levels, infiltration of salt water on the coastal water deposits, and the erosion of the soil. This results in the existence of a deficit of subsoil water estimated to be 13.6 billion liters.

Conclusions

- Water is an extinguishable, nonrenewable, and irreplaceable resource.
- Latin America is the wealthiest region of this resource in the planet.
- The United States, despite being a country with large water reservoirs, presents serious problems in its usage.

Control Mechanisms

The previous section underscores the challenges faced by the United States in the twenty-first century to maintain its resource flow in the face of changing geopolitical circumstances. To carry out its program, the United States turns to various control mechanisms.

There are three main control mechanisms:

- Manipulation of information
- Privatization of resources
- Militarization

It is important to mention that these mechanisms are not necessarily applied separately. Commonly they are complemented or one leads to the other in order to achieve the final goal—to obtain the resource.

The first of the three mechanisms, manipulation of information, is clearly shown in one of the most notorious examples related to the Amazon Rainforest in the book *An Introduction to Geography* (figure 10.5)

> Since the mid 80s the most important rain forest in the world was passed to the responsibility of the United States and the United Nations. It is named FIN-RAF (Former International Reserve of the Amazon Forest), and its foundation was due to the fact that the Amazon is located in South America, one of the poorest regions on earth and surrounded by irresponsible, cruel and authoritarian countries. It was part of eight different and strange countries, which are in the majority of cases, kingdoms of violence, drug trade, illiteracy and an unintelligent and primitive people.
>
> The creation of FINRAF were [*sic*] was supported by all nations of G-23 and was really a special mission of our country and a gift of all the world, since the possession of these valuable lands by such primitive countries and people should condemn the lungs of the world to disappearance and full destroying [*sic*] in a few years. (p. 76)

As it is clearly stated on the text shown above, the United States manipulates the information to justify the incorrect appropriation of a region over which they have no rights, misinforming even their own children, stating that the countries of South America have no ability to protect their land.

Concerning the privatization of resources, one has to begin with the fact that not all resources are the same; since petroleum is an economic good, it can be treated as such, but water and biodiversity are natural human rights and their exploitation as merchandise should be forbidden.

Biodiversity

The privatization of this resource is done through patents, bio-prospecting, and bio-pirating, which have no respect for history, culture, or the millennia of knowledge of the regions that are submitted to plunder. Transnationals and governments apply these methods only taking into account the possible earnings. The assignation of intellectual property rights to wide transnationals corrodes traditional knowledge systems and jeopardizes biodiversity.

The most diabolic part concerns human beings, where aboriginal communities receive, once again, the worst part, since they are targets due to the historical isolation in which they live. This situation propitiates the existence of certain genes within them, which are widely converted. Bio-pirating of human genes and other parts of the human body turns us into potential sources of genes. We go from subjects to objects.

Petroleum

In the case of petroleum, privatization is done through the control of sources of the resource or through the management of the product itself; despite this, at present nearly 90 percent of the oil is in public hands. Its eminent extinguishment has begun an escalation of pressure from transnationals to their governments, mainly in the United States, asking them to compel those countries where reservoirs are located to privatize the wells. Even though in many countries hydrocarbons are controlled by the state, these countries have significant arrangements with private transnationals which are characterized by the nonfulfillment and violation of the established contracts, and also by misappropriation of the resource.

Water

In this case, privatization manifests itself in the same way as with petroleum, and it is possible only due to the abandonment by governments when they decide to participate in agreements like the WTO or free trade agreements. In these cases the management of the water resource is transferred to the

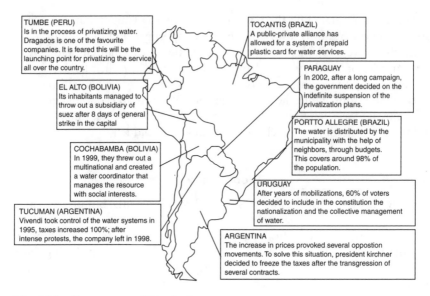

Map 10.2 Consequences of Privatization

Source: Martin Oinco, Las batallas del agua en American Latina

private sector claiming "the need to improve the poor services provided by the state trusts" and "the absence of public funds." The privatization of the infrastructure brings in many cases: an increase in taxes, inefficiency of the service, cut in the supplies, low quality of the product, bribes, corruption, and, of course, huge benefits for the transnationals. This has led to several confrontations in the South American region (map 10.2).

On the other hand, the business of bottled water has a bigger volume, per liter, than oil. It is a market that has grown exponentially in an unregulated way. Since 1995, the sales have been increasing 20 percent per year, and 25 percent is commercialized and consumed outside of the country in which it was produced.

Militarization

Militarization, the last mechanism mentioned in this chapter, and in no way less relevant, is done through the installation of military facilities in strategic zones. This tactic has its origins on the appropriation of the Panama Canal by the United States at the beginning of the twentieth century. To the already well-known military bases one has to add antidrug and antiterrorist units, training camps and military exercises between countries, which are useful to the United States to ideologically denationalize the military troops

Map 10.3   Main Military Bases in Latin America

Source: Martin Oinco, Las batallas del agua de America Latina.

from the region, and train them under the doctrines generated in Washington.

One of the clearest examples is the pressure generated by the United States over the governments of Argentina, Brazil, and Paraguay, demanding a greater control of the region comprising the Triple Frontier, claiming the presence of sleeping cells of international terrorism, and more recently of the presence of Al-Qaeda, a frequently used pretext to justify military interventions (map 10.3).

The CEMIDA (Prodemocratic Military Center of Argentina) came to the conclusion that the goal of this pressure is to achieve the military intervention of the U.S. army in the region and, through this, control the water deposit of Guarani.

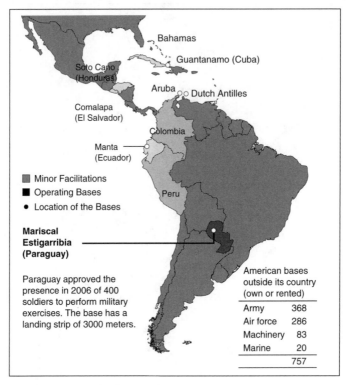

Map 10.4   Military Base Mariscal Estigarribia

Source: El de militarización: Es elaboración propia, a partir de Ana Esther Ceceña Mariscal Estigarribia: *El Clarin*, Base STRUCTUS, Report 2006.

This pressure has apparently gained results as the Paraguayan Congress approved entrance of over 400 U.S. soldiers with diplomatic immunity until December 2006, with the intention of advising the local officers on how to combat urban terrorism and to give humanitarian medical assistance to the poor. Many people consider this a prior step to the installation of a military base in northern Paraguay. The selected base is Mariscal Estigarribia (map 10.4), whose geographic location is strategic since all the relevant and troublesome targets of the region can be monitored from there, such as Bolivia, the water deposit of Guarani, or the Triple Frontier.

General Conclusions

It can be stated that the Latin American countries possess geostrategic resources of all kinds: the Guarani water deposit, the Amazon Rain Forest, and the oil line of the Orinoco, just to mention an example of each resource. Besides, it has been clearly demonstrated that all these goods are almost extinguished in the world, and the situation of resource needs in the world is getting worse and worse per day, approaching the state of crisis with each passing day. All this has led to an unmeasured race to obtain, by any means, the control of any source of these goods, including the so-called preventative wars, joint military exercises, and the creation of military bases on strategic territories that would allow them to not only control the resources but to prevent situations such as the one that occurred in Cochabamba, Bolivia, where the local population blocked a water privatization scheme.

Chapter 11

Drinking Water—the New Strategic Resource of the Twenty-First Century: the Particular Case of the Guarani Aquiferous

Elsa M. Bruzzone

The United States security is the most dangerous institution of the world.
Roque Peña Saenz

Frequently we hear and read that drinking water will be the most scarce resource in the coming years, and that, unlike oil, have no substitutes, therefore, whoever controls it will be controlling the universal economy and the life on the planet in the near future. It is also known that 3 percent of the earth's drinking water is found on the planet surface. The rest is below it and it has been stored there for more than 10,000 years.

The most optimistic data reports that by the year 2025, around 3,500,000,000 individuals will suffer from drinking water shortage, whereas the most pessimistic scientists have estimated that water scarcity will affect 7,000,000,000 children, women, and men in our planet of the 8,000,000,000 that will exist by then. Suffice it to take a look to the hydrologic maps of the world to notice the size of the problem approaching us and to understand why drinking water is a strategic resource, not only of this century but of the coming ones.

Drinking Water in Europe, Asia, Africa, and Oceania

When observing the European continent we see that almost all the countries are in a condition ranging from serious to critical. Out of the 55 rivers, only 5 are not polluted. The water shortage is critical in Spain, Southern Italy, Greece, the Balkans, Germany, the Netherlands, and England. In the rest it is considered serious. The irrational exploitation of resources, the pollution produced by petrochemical industries, the use of agro toxic products, and the devastation of forest and natural leafy glade have contributed to this disaster.

The situation in Asia is worse. In Asia Minor, the Middle East, the Arabian Peninsula, Iran, Afghanistan, Pakistan, India, Central Asia, and part of China, Japan, and Korea the conditions are critical. Turkey and Iraq are affected by the sources of Tigris and Euphrates, where the Turks hope to build a dam to divert the water of these rivers. The background of the Israel-Palestine war has to do with the decision of Israel to take over nearly all the resources that both countries share, even water from Lebanon and Syria. The rivers of India are totally polluted. Likewise the Yellow River, the heart and life of China, and the rivers that feed the Northern plateau are seriously polluted although the Chinese government has undertaken measures to change the situation. China's underground reserves were also affected, especially between 1991 and 1996. The Aral Sea, located in Uzbekistan and Kazakhstan, is drying up because of the pollution caused by chemical elements used in Uzbekistan to wash cotton, the main economic product of the country. This pollution has killed all the life that flourished around the Aral, thus affecting the health of the region's inhabitants, bringing about different types of cancer, spontaneous abortion, and children born with serious physical and mental problems.

Australia is suffering from serious problems in the South. The over-exploitation of rivers and of the reserves of underground water is concentrating great amounts of salt on the surface. The Australian attempt to deviate the course of some rivers toward the south of the country ended up bringing about an ecological disaster irreversible in every sense, not only for vegetation and animal life but also for humans, as arable lands suitable for agriculture were lost.

Africa, despite its two huge aquifers (reserves of underground mineral drinking water that are found at different depth of the surface), in Nubia (Sudan) with a volume of 75,000 km^3 (a km^3 is equal to a trillion liters of water) and in Northern Sahara with 60,000 km^3 is in a critical state. This happens in the north, part of Somalia, Eritrea, and Ethiopia, and in the south of the continent. All its rivers and lakes are polluted because of human over-exploitation, especially for economic reasons. A cruel paradox! A continent with drinking water reserves that once was compared with Paradise, is today dying of thirst because its great aquifers are still unexplored.

Drinking Water on the
American Continent

Our continent, with 12 percent of the world population, has 47 percent of the drinking water reserves in the world, both on the surface and underground. In North America the situation ranges from serious to critical. Two hundred million people depend on underground water for domestic use, and scientists have determined that it plays an important role in the conservation of rivers, lakes, wetlands, and aquatic systems. Surface and underground waters interact in such a way that changes in underground water levels can have significant effects in critical habitats of the riparian vegetations and wildlife that depends on them. Canada has 9 percent of the fresh and renewable water of the world, the majority of which is underground. It has been estimated that its volume is 37 times greater than the water in lakes and rivers of the country. It is known that underground water supplies 22 percent of Lake Erie and 42 percent of Lakes Huron and Ontario. Over a fourth of Canadians are supplied with underground water for domestic use. Although they have so much drinking water, the population has access to only 40 percent of it. In many regions underground water is used more rapidly than the discharged capacity. Canada is facing problems of pollution in some areas due to the petrochemical industry, pesticides, sewage waters, nitrates, chemical waters, and bacterias. Pollution in aquifers can be deadly to the population, especially children. Underground water is transformed into a lethal weapon because of acquired toxic poisons and bacteria.

The United States has a pollution rate of 40 percent in its rivers and lakes. The famous Love Canal of Niagara Falls that for Americans is like the Devil Throat in our Iguazu Falls, suffers from a high level of pollution as do the American aquifers. The Ogallala—which spreads out through eight states, from South Dakota in the north to Texas—has seen its waters reduced because of the overexploitation of the great prairies, the heart of cereals in the country. The use of agro-toxic products such as glyphosate as a defoliant by the American troops during the war in Vietnam has consequences of which has affected the environment and Vietnamese population and chemical wastes, and drains have seriously polluted the Ogallala. In some areas, the aquifers have dropped 30 m of their volume.

Half of the U.S. population depends on underground water. The extraction at a greater pace than nature can recharge has brought about a decrease of the water level in the Chicago region, Milwaukee, the Albuquerque Basin in New Mexico, in the Sparta aquifers of Arkansas, in Louisiana, and in Mississippi. Furthermore it has produced the intrusion of salt water in the coastal aquifers (from the Atlantic coast of Cape Cod to Miami, Long Island, New York, and the central coast of California), the sinking of the soil (San Joaquin Valley, California, Houston, Galveston in Texas, Baton Rouge in Louisiana, Phoenix in Arizona) and the reduction of discharges of superficial water in rivers and wetlands. The subsidence process of the soil is irreversible because sediments in the aquifer are compacted and the storing capacity is reduced forever. Today the United States has an annual underground water deficit of 13. 600, 000,000 m^3, the majority of which is accumulated in the Ogallala aquifers. The overexploitation has also changed the Everglades systems in Florida and caused a rupture in the ecological balance in the region. The cross-border aquifers between Canada and the United States, the Abbotsford, is also polluted. Septic systems, underground storing tanks leakages, spills of industrial chemical substances, and leaks of dumping sites of solid and dangerous waste have polluted the resources. Waste lands lie where at one time there were industries like smelting and distillation plants of tar coal and are today highly polluted. Nitrates, pesticides, and bacteria have altered the surface quality and underground waters.

In Texas, the construction of a radioactive waste plant and other dangerous elements is being assesed, which could eventually pollute the Rio Bravo or Rio Grande, the natural border between Mexico and the United States.

In some parts of Florida, in San Antonio, Texas, and in Albuquerque, New Mexico, underground water is the only available source of drinking water. Water shortages are leading to disputes among users and suppliers because in the United States drinking water is a commodity, it is therefore an object of supply and demand and not a social asset and a human right linked to health and life. Pumping costs increase more and more and wells produce ever less. In the High Plains, farmers have started abandoning irrigation agriculture. Changes of water resources are affecting international relations in the northern and southern border (Canada) and (Mexico) of the United States, where the shared basins are bringing disputes, despite the Binational Agreements on Shared Waters. The agreement between Canada and the United States goes back to 1909 and it controls the San Lorenzo River Basin, the Great Lakes, and the Great Plains of Columbia and Yukon.

The agreement with Mexico dates back to 1944 and rules the use of the Colorado, Tijuana, and Bravo rivers. The treaty allocated 1.85 billion m^3 annually to Mexico (with 246,700,000 additional m^3 in times of abundance), 10 percent of the average annual flow of the Colorado river, but the water quality is not mentioned. Mexico is getting salt water due to the evaporation of reservoirs, the transfers out of the basin, and industrial and urban uses in the American territory. Regarding the Tijuana basin, there is no agreement on the distribution of its water, but it does exist regarding the Bravo River. Mexico should deliver a quota of the river tributaries to the United States. In the past and due to water volume problems, the country could not meet the commitments. Because of this a dike in the Colorado River is being built to prevent its waters from going to Mexico. For the basin of the Santa Cruz and San Pedro Rivers there is no binational agreement. In 1977, an agreement was signed on cross-border underground waters.

In 2002, American governmental sources assessed the cost of modernization of water treatment facilities at $2.7 billion and the renewal of the drinking water network at $2.65 billion, and the depollution of superficial and underground waters at several billion dollars. This explains why the United States has looked southward for possible new sources of water. One of the Santa Fe IV premises' "The Hemisphere's natural resources are available to respond to our national priorities. A 'Monroe Doctrine' if they want."

Sixty-six percent of the Mexican population receives underground water. Out of the 449 aquiferous of the country, 130 are polluted, suffer overexploitation, or are threatened by the latter. The Ciudad Juarez-El Paso aquiferous, on the U.S. border could support 1.5 million people living there. If this situation is not reverted, it will inevitably deplete in the year 2018. The whole area of San Pedro River, fed by underground water which becomes a river in the Sonora desert in Mexico and reaches Arizona in the United States has been affected because its volume is reduced. The situation is likewise critical in the Lerma and Chapala basins. The panorama changes in the south of Mexico. Majority of the country's rainfall is concentrated there as well as the bigger aquifers: Tabasco, Chiapas, Oaxaca, Veracruz, and the Yucatan Peninsula. The availability of drinking water is one of the main attractions of the region. Add to this the richness of animal and vegetable species, and Mexican oil. These resource issues underscored the importance of NAFTA to the United States.

In Central America there are plentiful rivers and aquifers and genetic biodiversity. In Guatemala the presidential representative to the Plan Puebla Panama (PPP), was a Shell official and shareholder together with the high-ranked military influential in Guatemalan water projects. All the countries in the region have surface and underground water. Regrettably water projects are often in the hands of U.S. and European multinationals with the support and intervention of investment from the World Bank. Therefore, neither the population interests nor the environmental balance is considered, so necessary for the human, vegetable, and animal life, because drinking water is seen as a commodity and not as a social asset.

In Costa Rica the Barba Aquifer supplies the Central Valley population in the high lands of the country and is located in the high and middle part of the Virilla River Basin. Its use, through wells and springs, began hundreds of years ago, long before the Spaniards arrival in the region. Its waters are used for human and industrial consumption. It is recharged with rainfalls, rivers, and superficial aquifers. It is connected to the other aquifers of the Central Valley and at the same time feeds the Colima Aquifers under which it is located. All the aquifers of the region form part of the great aquifers of Central America, from Yucatan to Panama. Despite all this richness, the majority of the Central American population has no direct access to drinking water.

All this explains the proliferation of the American bases in the region— among them is Curacao, Soto Cano, in Honduras; Liberia in Costa Rica; Comalapas in El Salvador; Vieques in Puerto Rico; Guantanamo in Cuba, and Reina Beatriz in Aruba. In addition there is pressure exerted over the local government to accept the PPP, a simple extension of NAFTA and now CAFTA too. Both instruments ensure military and economic control for the United States in the region whose political control is already established. South America is not less rich. Fresh water is abundant everywhere. To the rivers, lakes, estuaries, marshlands, lagoons we must add aquifers and among them the third largest of the world: the Guarani Aquifers, shared by Brazil, Paraguay, Uruguay, and Argentina.

In Colombia few urban and rural areas are totally supplied with underground water. There is almost no knowledge about the total capacity of this resource. Because of this, only 19.5 percent of underground water is used to supply the population. Most of the time the assessment and control of exploitation is not done. There is a pilot project for the Integral Management of underground water in the valley and for the protection of the Morro Aquifers in the department of Sucre in Guajira and Risaralda.

Ecuador and Peru share the aquifers of the Zarumilla River Valley. Although it has been under exploitation for years, its evaluation is virtually nonexistent. The Binational project has taken shape without the support of institutions from abroad. The respective atomic energy commissions are involved in this project. Papers have been drafted on isotopic hydrology and the Puyando Tumbes Project. It is expected that 40,000 inhabitants of the bordering area will benefit and the plan is to irrigate 50,000 to 70,000 hectares distributed between both countries.

At the same time, both countries have their own aquifers. In Ecuador, they are located in heavily populated areas: Cayambe, Tabacundo (at present they are under study together with those of the Chillos and Tumbaco Valleys), and Quito that recharge in the hillside of the Pichincha Volcano, on the side of the mountain where one of the greatest battles was waged for independence from Spain. It is believed that its development is the solution for the supply of drinking water and irrigation to the region.

In northern Peru the high basin of the Piura River has an underground aquifer considered to be of great capacity but its characteristics are practically unknown. At present the aquifer supplies water for 30,000 hectares of farming, and it may be the same one that supplies the cities of Piura and Catacaos. The water quality, pollution level, and vulnerability are unknown. However, it has been estimated that it could directly benefit 650,000 inhabitants (130,000 families) of the area and indirectly 30,000 more families.

In South America there are big basins of the Amazon, Orinoco, and Plata Rivers and the green lung of the planet, the region with the greatest biodiversity and genetic richness of the world, the Amazonia. In the Amazonia Plan, sketched in 1950, important U.S. interests threatened to establish control of its great reserves of drinking water in the region. In the northern border they encouraged the indigenous independentist movement of Yanomanis with the aim of segregating important sectors of the Brazilian territory. Years later the United States established a military base in San Pedro de Alcantara. However, Brazil responded quickly to the danger thus preventing the segregation and establishing a line of military bases along its northern border, where they built roads to the forest and moved its capital to Brasilia in the Amazonia. In an affirmation of its sovereignty, a more recent and complete strategy was implemented, including SIVAM (Surveillance System of the Amazonia), the SIPAM (Protection System of the Amazonia), and the closing of the Alcantara base by the United States.

However, the United States does not surrender easily. They changed their battleground and unsuccessfully tried to settle with a coup d'etat in Venezuela, to take over their oil, another resource considered strategic by the United States. Furthermore, Venezuela is one of the main doors to the Amazonia. Under the excuse of struggling against the drug traffic, they established Plan Colombia and it was completed with the Andean Regional Initiative, to have an active military presence in the region through the installed bases throughout the Amazonian border, like the Tres Esquinas, Larandia, and Puerto Leguizamo in Colombia. The most important one the Manta Base in Ecuador. Moreover, it has been exerting pressure on the governments of Argentina and Bolivia to install military bases in the province of Misiones in Argentina close to the known zone of Triple Border, and on the shore of the Itonamay River, in Bolivia. Thanks to this strategy, the siege has been closed on the Amazonia, and the United States controls their periphery militarily and they are ready to have a predominant role whenever their natural resources are exploited. They operated in a same way against Iraq in the case of oil.

The Guarani Aquiferous

The Guarani is the third biggest aquifer in the world. It extends throughout the basins of the Parana, Uruguay, and Paraguay Rivers. It has an approximate surface of 1,194,000 km^2, of which 839,000 belong to Brazil; 226,000 to Argentina; 71,700 to Paraguay, and 59,000 to Uruguay, representing 10 percent of the Brazilian territory, 6 percent of Argentina, 18 percent of Paraguay, and 25 percent to Uruguay. It has been established to date that the greatest length of the deposit is approximately 1,800 km and its greatest width has been estimated at 900 km. In the north it connects with the Pantanal that in turn links with the Amazonia. The western limit of the aquifer is unknown in Paraguay and Argentina, although it has been estimated that in Argentina it extends toward the Bermejo basin and beyond the Mar Chiquita Lagoon. The southern limit is also unknown in Argentina, but it has not been ruled out that it continues to the Pampas and Patagonian regions and it could connect to the area in the foothills of the Great Lakes.

Some geological characteristics of the Guarani have been known for more than 50 years by the YPF and exploration in Brazil, Argentina, Paraguay, and Uruguay. In 1974, the first important hydrogeologic study on the region was published in Brazil. The aquifer's volume has been estimated at 55,000 km^3.[1] The annual recharge has been estimated between 160 and 250 km^3, if 80 km^3 (a rational exploitation could reach up to 100 km^3 annually) around 720,000,000 people could be supplied with 300 l daily per inhabitant. Considering that the current population of the Americas is 5.5 million, it could supply not only nations of the aquifer, but also to others of the Southern Hemisphere that lack drinking water. In vast regions it surges naturally. The most common thickness of the aquifers is 200 m. It reaches 800 m alongside the Uruguay River and it reaches 1,000 and 1,200 m in areas of Brazil and Argentina. Water found at 500 and 1,000 m of depth have volumes of more than 500,000 in l/h and in some cases 1,000,000 in l/h. The water temperature varies depending on depths.

The recharge and discharge areas of the Guarani and the areas where there is a high concentration of uses and consumers are considered hot spots: Concordia (Argentine)–Salto (Uruguay): Rivera (Uruguay)–Santana do Livramento (Brazil); Riberao Preto (Brazil). But the most important and main recharge and discharge is in the border corridor between Paraguay, Brazil, and Argentina, the Triple Border area.

When observing the area the feeling one gets is of a kingdom of river waters. The magnitude of the Parana River contributes to this in the convergent point with the Iguazu, boosted in the north by the Itaipu dam and decorated in the east by the Iguazu Falls. It is surrounded by the huge basins of the Paraguay, Uruguay, Pilcomayo, Bermejo, Grande, Parapema, San Lorenzo, Apa, Negro, and other rivers that are, at this point underexploited resources. Known as the Plata Basin, it has great energy possibilities and communication.

According to official figures, the population of the Triple Border is around 470,000 grouped in Iguazu Port (Argentine) 30,000; Foz do Iguazu (Brazil) 270,000, and Ciudad del Este (Paraguay) 170,000. Together the figure is significant but in each case it is a small percentage of their respective countries and almost insignificant in relation to the population of the three countries.

The region shows different characteristics in different countries. In Argentina, the north of the Misiones Province has been organized as a National Park to preserve the original species where no commercial or tourist activity is allowed. In Brazil where the original forest has disappeared, its relative larger population is devoted to rural activities and there is an important tourist flow in the Iguazu Falls area. In Paraguay, tourism is the main commercial activity, derived from all sorts of business created in Ciudad del Este, and although it doesn't have direct access to the Falls, it uses the tourist flow to trade in whatever possible. In the surrounding areas there is little population and it takes care of rural activities, lately increased by the soya crop. The original forest has been severely damaged and is practically nonexistent.

Argentina, Brazil, and Paraguay have deployed security measures in the region to prevent eventual criminal actions from threatening the very vital industry of tourism. Puerto Iguazu, Foz do Iguazu, and Ciudad Del Este have significant detachments of National Police, branches of intelligence organs, customs police, and private surveillance agencies for hotels and other tourist facilities. It can be said that in a not very extensive geographical space and with a moderate permanent population, these means of surveillance and security are more than enough to keep a near absolute control of the zone and their inhabitants and to immediately detect any important anomaly. To this we must add the immediate or almost immediate availability of military garrisons of regional importance, mainly Brazil and Paraguay and a bit further in Argentina, as well as the deployment of its respective intelligence services typical of bordering regions.

In the Brazilian and Argentin territories, the tourist, commercial, and social activities are quite organized and controlled, though some looseness is observed on the petty smuggling practiced by the permanent residents and some tourists. But it is always under the control of authorities that do not allow disorders. The situation is somewhat different in the Paraguayan territories. They do not possess the attraction of the waterfalls, an Argentine-Brazilian privilege, which is why they called for a trade of goods and merchandise that takes place in public areas, where all kinds of elements can be obtained. All this in the middle of a situation that some may think it is chaotic but is not as bad. Paraguay obtains its resources from activities that sometimes are not very clear but they have a degree of strict control: large scale smuggling, purchase-sale of stolen objects especially cars from Brazil and Argentina, activities related to the crossing of all type of merchandise and objects through places out of the control of the border control posts and even minor actions of drug trafficking. All these resources are managed by a corrupt military political power that has historically organized and controlled it. That control is secretive and infallible.

In Ciudad del Este, a Syrian-Lebanese community has settled down dedicated to trade, developing their activities in a very controlled and peaceful way. They, together with the Arab community of Foz do Iguazu, have been accused by some, of being a center to plan terrorist actions and raise funds to finance and coordinate all kinds of criminal actions to obtain those funds. We can say that in this frame of reference, these denunciations are irrelevant and ridiculous. The poor Arab community dare not break the order established through the years. They work in the established trade framework through the order created and yet pay out large sums of money to be able to do it.

The relation of the aquiferous with the Parana River and its effluents is not well known, although it has been estimated that the recharge can be high in the areas close to the river bed and its effluents and above all in the areas flooded by the existing reservoir in its basin and at the same time the aquiferous discharges in the Parana. It has been determined that there are areas of direct recharge in the Southwest of the Misiones Province, around San Ignacio and in the center of the Corrientes province, in Curuzu Cuatia and Mariano Loza and that one of the most important discharges of the Guarani takes place in the Ibera estuary that continues in Paraguay.

The region in the Guarani has 15,000,000 inhabitants. The aquifer is the main source that supplies drinking water for the urban, industrial, and agricultural regions of Brazil, where over 300 cities of between 3,000 and 500,000 inhabitants are totally or partially supplied by it. Its use began in 1930. In Paraguay around 200 wells have been registered that supply the population of the three eastern regions of the country. Uruguay has over 135 wells used for the public supply and thermal baths. In Argentina, 9 thermal wells are under exploitation of fresh water in the eastern province of Entre Rios and in the Province of Corrientes, some towns and areas of Quintas have started to use the water. It is known that the waters are of excellent quality for human, industrial, hydro thermal consumption, and for irrigation and that the cost-benefit relation is extremely favorable when compared to the demand of surface water treatment. With the construction of aqueducts as was done in the past by the big civilizations of the continent, the Huarpes in the Cuyana area and the Argentine Diaguitas in the north, the big and small cities and the population of the Mesopotamic provinces in the northeast, northwest, Cordoba, Federal Capital, and Gran Buenos Aires could be supplied with pure water and also water for irrigation. If they assemble with the Bermejo Basin, the provinces of the Northeast and Northwest could develop. The population could have access to drinking water—a very scarce resource for the majority of the Argentinean people—at a very low cost and in unlimited amounts. If the connection of the Guarani with the Patagonic basins is confirmed, we will be at the doors, if we were lucky to have the political leaders committed with real interest of the countries to accomplish the exploitation of resources that could finance the whole development of our people and of our Latin-American brothers, by transforming our deserts into oasis.

The Guarani Aquifer Project was prepared by national universities of the four countries. The final cost was estimated to be $26,760,000, but the governments of the region gave it to the World Bank. The World Bank immediately accepted it and decided that it would be used to preserve the Guarani from pollution and to achieve its sustainable development. This in First World terms means the local inhabitants will have no access to that resource and therefore will not be able to use it freely. Furthermore the project provides that the governments will pay its partners in "kind" (an euphemistic term given to the aquiferous water), that is to say, with the privatization of that resource. The project therefore does not take into account the needs of Argentina, Brazil, Paraguay, and Uruguay, or the needs of their inhabitants. In the year 2000, Brazilian technicians submitted a proposal to the World Bank for the creation of a Monitoring Network for the Guarani Aquiferous with the purpose of improving the technical and scientific level of knowledge to carry out a sustainable action. This project proposes not only the monitoring of certain wells, but also the elaboration of maps: of cities and towns, of the soil, of the vegetation, water courses: rivers, dams, lakes, lagoons; structural drainage; of ways of access: routes, main and secondary roads, waterways, railways; of oil pipelines and gas pipelines; of exclusion areas; perimeters in areas marked out in the environmental zones as the areas of permanent preservation (APP), of environmental preservation (APA), of permanent conservation (ACP), of restoration (AR), as well as historic sites and areas of spring protection and all kinds of physical and chemical analysis. This proposal was accepted and was implemented during the year 2004. The elaboration of a new base map as well as studies of hydro-geo-chemistry, isotopic, geo-physic, geology and use of resources is immediately foreseen. In one word, the Brazilian proposal served the World Bank to get hold of the resources with the conspiratorial silence of the governments of Argentina, Paraguay, and Uruguay.

The International Organization of Atomic Energy at the request of the World Bank has carried out isotopic studies of the aquiferous waters. They have determined that it is rich in different chemical elements, such as deuterium, used as fuel in astronautics and military rockets—part of the mix of propulsion gases—of tritium, used in thermonuclear tests since 1952 that penetrates the earth in the aquiferous through rainfall; uranium, thorium, and silicon are also found on the earth whose properties are similar to that of the titanium making it suitable for the space and aeronautic industry. They have committed funds of $300,000 for the year 2004, destined to transportation and laboratory tests for water sample isotopes of the Guarani. Coca Cola and Nestle have already done this in their regional plants to separate these elements. As we may observe, they are preparing a fortunate future for their empire. The Paraguay National Secretariat for Environmental Cleaning

Up (SENASA) dumps all the aquiferous information of Paraguay in the Dutch Regis Data Bank. We do not know if the change of government caused the situation to be reverted.

The Project Secretariat has its headquarters in Montevideo, and every year in March and September it must inform the World Bank about their progress. They and the Protection of the Global Environment Fund (GEF) determine the guidelines that the secretariat will follow in its operations and they must check what they have done with them and with UDSMA/OAS. The World Bank periodically supervises and determines the new guidelines to be followed. We do not know what they will continue to order in the future, but we can imagine.

The World Bank created a Citizenship Fund of $240,000 to support the promotion of courses, training, and spreading events in relation to underground waters, especially with the Guarani Aquiferous. They have also implemented a Fund for Universities of $370,000, destined to finance two year research university projects on the Guarani. Nine projects were approved that will be directly supervised by the World Bank. The universities selected are University of Sao Paulo, Federal de Santa Maria, from Brasilia, Mato Grosso, Minas Gerais, Rio Dos Sinos Valley, Federal de Parana (Brazil); National University of Litoral, National Technology of Entre Rios, from the Center of the Buenos Aires Province (Azul), Buenos Aires and Catolica de Santa Fe (Argentina); University of the Republic and Faculty of Engineering of UDELAR (Uruguay), Faculty of Exact and Natural Sciences of San Lorenzo (Paraguay), and the National Autonomous University of Mexico. The following also will participate: the Belo Horizonte Center for the Development of Nuclear Technology (Brazil), the National Direction of Environment (Uruguay), and the National Institute for Water, and its subsidiary, the Regional Litoral Center (Argentina). Contracts stipulate that the researchers respond directly to the World Bank and must abide by their rules. All the papers drafted will be the responsibility and the intellectual property shared between the World Bank, the OAS and the recipient of the projects. The worst thing is that those appointed are proud for those nominations, not understanding or not wanting to understand what it is all about.

The creation of a data centralized system has been foreseen. With that purpose the aquiferous was divided into two areas for the study, north and south. National, provincial or state and local data centers are created. In those centers, also called nodes, all the information obtained should be dumped on the physical, economic, and social characteristics of the countries involved in the project. The results of new researches on the Guarani and all related information with the deposits will only be processed and managed by the World Bank.

Now everything becomes clear: the unexpected presence of American military soldiers in the region, the mushrooming of false reports, the terrorist action from the Triple Border, the groundless charges against the Arab community, the constant combined armies of the American military forces with the regional forces, the constant pressures on the government of Argentina to install an American military base in the province of Misiones. It would be good to ask the inhabitants near the navel base of Mazaruca, in the Entre Rios province, what they know about the American marines and ask the governor of the area what happened in April 2003 when that illegal presence was denounced and systematically infringed the Constitution of Argentina.

Furthermore, there is a project in Argentina to build eight bases, apparently under the UN supervision, and a scientific laboratory, that will be part of the Control Network of the Treaty for Comprehensive Banning of Nuclear Tests of which Argentina is a signatory. The United States does not want to sign this treaty because they cannot do anymore nuclear explosions and would limit their capacity to develop new atomic weapons. It should be recalled that in the past 50 years the United States, Russia, China, and France made around 2000 explosions of this type. The eight bases and the laboratory will be part of a 321 piece system that will be built in 89 countries "to verify that no one will make underground, maritime or atmospheric nuclear explosions, especially tests for new weapons." The main headquarters is in Vienna. The places designated are Tolhuin, already under advanced construction according to denunciations of the area's inhabitants, Ushuaia in Tierra del Fuego, Bariloche and Paso Flores in Rio Negro, Villa Traful in Neuquen, Salta in Salta, Coronel Fontana in San Juan, and two bases in the city of Buenos Aires where since March 2001, their "radionucleic" station is working (to measure the radioactive air) in the headquarters of the National Commission for Atomic Energy. The bases of Tolhuin and Villa Traful will be for "infrasound," the Ushuaia, Paso Flores and Coronel Fontana will be for "seismology," the Bariloche, Salta, and one in the City of Buenos Aires (the other one will be a "laboratory") will be for "air measuring." All these will be under the supervision of the Nuclear Regulatory Authority (ARN) and the National Institute for Seismic Prevention (INPRES) in coordination with the Ministry of Foreign Affairs. It is a good way to disguise their military presence in the area where the fundamental strategic resources of the twenty-first century are located.

The Annual Report on World Terrorism was drafted by the American State Department on April 30, 2003, determining that in the Triple Border there were no cells or terrorist bases and specially mentioning the 3 plus 1 Antiterrorist Dialogue. Accomplished due to the pressure exerted on the governments of the region by the empire, the 3 plus 1 Antiterrorist Dialogue, also known as the Agreement 3 plus 1 signed by Brazil, Argentina, and Paraguay with the United States, was designed to control and monitor the region. Reports published on December 3, 2003, ratify this information. These reports speak about new agreements made such as joint patrolling of the Itaipu Lake and adjacent waters by Brazilian and American military, migratory computerized integrated control, design of controls for cross-border transportation of values, implementation of a new information matrix on money laundering, financing of terrorism and cargo flights to the Triple Border, implementation of an Intelligence Center in Foz do Iguazu, formulation of national antiterrorist laws, and the training of soldiers in the United States.

On February 7, 2004, a report from the U.S. State Department confirmed the existence of terrorist cells in the area. The important thing for the United States is having recognized the area in advance on the basis of a possible use of military forces in more or less the immediate future if the government of the region change their selling-out behavior followed until now.

The ineffectiveness of local governments has been clearly exposed, always paying attention only to their particular interests and not the national ones, to prevent the incessant advance of the empire. This issue becomes ever more consolidated to defend the sovereignty of our countries over the aquiferous and the region that is increasingly threatened.

This threat has been ratified these days in the report submitted by the Pentagon to the U.S. government. In it, mention is made to the devastating effects caused on the planet as a result of global warming, the most important of which is the lack of drinking water for the near future. Moreover, it is suggested that the United States should get ready to take over this strategic resource found anywhere, when the right time comes. It must be remembered that in 2001 the United States withdrew from the Kyoto Protocol that controls the emission of gases responsible for global warming, which for the treaty to come into effect, the countries responsible for 55 percent of those emissions must approve, which Russia said they will not ratify because they consider it to be a threat to their economic growth. The United States in the Special Conference on Hemispheric Security, held in Monterrey, Mexico, October 2003, refused to sign the resolutions related to the environmental protection. This Special Conference is part of the System of Hemispheric Security created by the United States to guarantee the control of the region's strategic resources and the combined use of military forces to jointly fight against those considered as enemies. All this has been detailed in the "Document for the 4th Bolivarian Anfitionic: The Latin American-Caribbean National Defense: Past, Present and Desirable Furure."[2]

Conclusions

The strategic resources of United States should be in the hands of the American people and should be exploited for their needs and interests. For this it is necessary to be conscious, to mobilize, and exert pressure ceaselessly on the governments that have the habit of looking in the opposite direction. The defense of American national heritage is indispensable to maintain the survival as peoples and nations and its identity. They should not and cannot remain on the margin of these present and future problems. All sectors of U.S. population should be informed about such important matters. They should not tolerate the presence and actions of national prophets who brag about their denationalized actions much less foreign armed forces in our territories. Argentinean Manuel Ugarte, a firm fighter for the unity and integration of America wrote: "Peoples who expect their lives or future from a legal abstraction or from the will of others are in advance sacrificed peoples."

It would be desirable that the American governments preserve the natural resources for their nations and peoples and not to allow foreign interference in their proximities, particularly military. If they would have futurology plans, exploitation, and maintenance plans of strategic resources for the long, medium, and short term, they should only coordinate among themselves the way to exploit the shared resources. It is shameful that the research of that richness is in most of the cases organized and financed by the empire and they get second hand information.

It would be desirable that the armed and security forces do not fraternize with soldiers of the imperial power no matter how important the benefits they offer may seem. Their only place is beside their peoples, of which they are a part, to safeguard their economic, social, cultural, and historic heritage.

None should forget what Gustavo Cirigliano said: "When an empire proclaims peace it brings war, when it enhances solidarity it hides an attack, when it claims for adhesion it plans to give in and when it offers friendship, it distributes hypocrisy."

Notes

1. Remember that each cubic kilometer is equal to a trillion liters of water, it means one with 12 zeros following it.
2. See www.geocities.com/cemida_ar. Accessed on October 15, 2005.

Chapter 12

Latin American Integration and Environment

Antonio Elizalde Hevia

Introduction

The hypothesis of this work is the existence of deep interactions between integration and environmental processes in Latin America and the Caribbean based on two key questions to be answered. Is the environment a decisive element for the integration of Latin America and the Caribbean? Is integration a key element in the environmental sustainability of Latin America and the Caribbean? According to Julia Carabias,

> Over one third of terrestrial natural ecosystems have been lost in Latin America and the Caribbean. Nevertheless, it is still the region with more closed forests[1] and with the greatest biodiversity in the world. Eight percent of its surface has been transformed for agricultural activities and 30% for livestock purposes. Every year some 5.8 million hectares are deforested, and 95% of this deforestation takes place in the tropics. (UNEP-ECLA-2001)
>
> The regional deterioration has been widely documented: deforestation, erosion, salinization, extinction of biological species, modification of hydrological cycles at national, regional, and local levels so there is now an increasing concern and social demand.[2]

The deterioration process described by Carabias is the outcome of long-term, systematic economic decisions made over the course of the last century by the region's political and economic elites.

The economic ideas prevailing within the region stress increasing economic growth rate as the way through which the existing poverty could be alleviated, as well as the moment when they will promote institutional and collective behaviour aimed at protecting and preserving the environment. This notably reductionist view is the one that prevailed within the academic framework, the political decision-making process, the corporate circles, and the main mass media. In this regard, Gabaldón and Rodríguez stated thus;

> Every day more importance is granted to subregional integration programs promoting the creation of common markets which, according to some of its guidelines, should play a key role in the search for an environmental sustainability in the economic internationalization processes. Programs like the Central American Common Market established in 1960, the Andean Community founded in 1969, and the Caribbean Community in 1973 have several decades in existence, while Mercosur was recently created. In the midst of these agreements there are different environmental activities (agreements, standards, protection programs, etc.) sometimes with broad implications for signatory countries. However, registered environmental advances have been moderate as a whole when they are measured against the new pressures exerted on the environment by the integration processes. Once again, environment has been placed as a secondary issue against the priority given to the regional economic growth.[3]

The "hegemonic" diagnosis of our past poor behavior when dealing with economic growth has emphasized some key elements to explain it, namely, the reduced size of our domestic markets as well as "institutional rigidity."[4] From this point of view, the solution seems to be the liberalizing recipe: that is, privatization, labor flexibility, deregulations, integration to the global market by eliminating subsidies and protection to domestic production, and fiscal asceticism in order to create favorable conditions for foreign investment.

Therefore, the economic growth panacea, in the mind of political and corporate elites, is one achieved thanks to foreign investment oriented to the production of goods and services for an increasing global market. In this case there is the logical priorization that places environmental protection in the last position, well below economic growth and poverty reduction. The most advanced example of this developmental route is the Chilean case.

These ideas are not new in economic thinking. Suffice it to remember the economic growth stages stated by W.W. Rostow during the 1960s or what was contemptuously called at that time the "trickle down" theory. The new factor in these ideas is that an additional factor has been added, that is, the constitution of a global market and/or the phenomenon of so-called globalization.

Globalization, a term widely discussed in the social sciences,[5] can be characterized as a growing internationalization process of financial, industrial, and commercial capital due to new information and communication technologies. These developments have generated new international political relations and the emergence of transnational corporations as an answer to the constant readjustment needs of the capitalist system of production from which the new and geographically displaced production, distribution, and consumption processes have originated, as well as the record-breaking expansion and intensive use of technology. While this economic, political, and social process is not new, it has been refocused by placing more emphasis on developing countries as a specific strategy to achieve economic growth and to eradicate poverty. Though this phenomenon was never conceived as a model of economic development, in fact, it has emerged as a regulatory framework for international economic relations among countries.

Such is the situation in which globalization is considered, by its advocates, and also by many means of communication, governments, and universities as an inevitable and out-of-control force of nature, a fait accompli derived from economic and technological forces that have evolved through centuries up until its current form. Therefore, the only thing possible to counter it would be to accept it with resignation, to adjust to it, or try to take advantage of this process, to a certain extent, in order to serve one's own purposes.

Consequently, many have turned globalization into a defining argument in every public political sphere. An example of this is what Jerry Mander[6] criticizes in relation to environmental issues:

> Among the many preposterous arguments, those advocating for economic globalization point out that, in the long term, it will increase environmental protection. This theory states that to the extent in which countries are globalized, usually by exporting resources such as forests, minerals, oil, coal, fish, wild life and water, their greatest wealth will allow them to save a greater part of nature against potential devastation and, will allow them to introduce technical elements to mitigate negative environmental impacts derived from their own increase in production. However, there is strong evidence that when countries increase their apparent profits within a global economy, most of them will go to global corporations with few incentives aimed at environmental protection. Instead of doing this, they drag the country into an even greater exploitation or they simply keep the money and quickly escape from the country. Such is the normal corporate behavior within the global economy.

Globalization and Environment

It is worthwhile clarifying which interactions can be found between globalization and environment. Nevertheless, in a succinct analysis it will be possible to identify the following dynamics: Globalization produces a global monoculture; this is the result of an obsession for hyper-growth; leading to an absolute mercantilization of social and natural existence; everything is based on export-oriented production resulting in the destruction of agricultural economy, and small agricultural production.

The utopia of globalization advocates is the integration and merging of every economic activity in all countries of the planet into just one single market, a unique homogeneous model with a unique and centralized super system. In that way, countries with different cultures, traditions, and economies like Thailand, Guinea Bissau, Guatemala, Brazil, Finland, and others would have the same lifestyle, values, and preferences. Humankind as a whole is now facing that fate, toward the "McDonaldization" of the world as some have called it. In this regard, Mander states that:

> Such a homogenized model directly serves the efficiency needs of big corporations. Acting on a global sphere they can duplicate their production and marketing efforts in an increasingly expanding field and achieve high efficiency

without any frontiers. It is like the railway network from past centuries. Or, as we currently say, a "computer compatibility." One of the first objectives of broad trade treaties and bureaucracies is to dictate rules to ensure no obstacles through the flow so as to allow global corporations to move freely in every country and accelerate economic homogenization and integration.[7]

If one observes the press and, in general, written means of communication in any country as well as public statements and/or comments made by different political and social actors, you will notice that they do not mention economic growth. Nowadays, the prevailing cultural purpose at the global level is to achieve a faster and unlimited economic growth, which we could call hyper-growth, encouraged by the constant search for access to new resources, new and cheaper labor sources and new markets.

In order to achieve hyper-growth, as Mander points out, emphasis should be placed on the ideological core of the globalization model, the free market, accompanied by the deregulation of corporate activities, and the privatization and mercantilization of as many areas as possible. They include the previously pristine global and common elements that so far have kept completely alien to the trading system, those areas that many of us believe will continue to be an inalienable right of every human being, not to become mercantilized.

We have reached a point in which there is no limit or moral, ethic, political, or cultural standard to mercantilization in the search for growth. Everything must have a price and should generate an economic growth. Mander believes that nowadays

the genetic structure of our bodies, throughout life, is now being incorporated in the commercial system of goods, through biotechnology, a fact closely supported by standards in the intellectual property rights of the World Trade Organization. Another example can be found in native seeds that for millennia were developed and freely shared by agricultural communities. Now they are subjected to the monopolization by the transnational corporations through the patent system of the WTO. Recent protests against TRIPS (Intellectual Property Rights related to the WTO trade system), organized by agricultural workers in India and by AIDS victims in Africa and other places in the Third World, have began to shed light on these problems. We are also witnessing a similar pressure on fresh water, rivers, lakes, watersheds. These are perhaps the most basic element for human survival and an element that has always been considered as part of the "common goods" available to every living being but also an element which will soon become part of the global trading system. At least, this is what will happen if FTAA, NAFTA and WTO member countries advance their plans. All these aspects of human life, which were previously public and of free access, are being privatized and mercantilized very rapidly as part of the globalization process. The logic is to place more raw materials and more territories (both geographically and biologically) at the disposal of corporate access, investment access, development and trade.[8]

Another myth of global thinking affirms that in an increasingly internationalized world where a world market is emerging, the most convenient thing for every economy, either local, regional, national, or continental, is to increase exports, since this will mean more foreign exchange to be devoted to increase their imports and, thus, be able to consolidate a more prosperous economy.

In this regard, in a work written more than a decade ago,[9] the author questioned the real occurrence of what this myth affirms, and I asked myself, How much value do producers receive from what they produced? Data obtained from a study conducted in Guatemala indicate that for every dollar from a watermelon coming from Central America bought in the United States, producers only received one cent of that dollar.[10] Data from a research conducted in Chile corroborates that out of the total exports of fruits from the country, producers only receive 1.6 percent of the price, in wholesale markets or 3.4 percent of the money received by the country in exchange for the fruit.[11]

On the other hand, export-dependent economies are mainly unstable and vulnerable to market fluctuations. Hans Singer[12] showed that at the beginning of the 1950s through a data series covering more than 70 years, there is a tendency for commodity prices to fall, in relation to prices of industrial products exported by more developed countries. Besides, globalization allows multinational corporations to move to cheap-labor countries looking for greater benefits while workers do not have comparative advantages since they cannot leave their countries. Similarly, the Economic Commission for Latin America (ECLA), headed by Raúl Prebish, in several works proved what it called a sustained trend of deterioration in the exchange terms.

The most important factor in this analysis is the high environmental costs that this model yields at the global level. Irrationality is absolute from the energy point of view. What was easy to produce in one part of the planet, close to consumption areas, is now produced at much higher costs many kilometers away. As a result there are huge energy expenses to transport that good across great distances to the consumption areas. The study conducted by the German Wuppertal Institute on the miles a foodstuff must travel from its origin point to the dinner table has become a classic work. It states, for example, that the average components of a 150 gm strawberry yogurt consumed in Europe has to travel around 2,000 kms before being processed and then shipped to the consumer destination points. The strawberries come from Poland; corn flour and wheat from the Netherlands; marmalade, sugar beet, and yogurt itself from Germany, and the plastic and paper containers come from several countries.

According to Mander, it is estimated that, nowadays, the ingredients in an average meal served in U.S. households travel some 1,500 miles from their origin point to the table. Every mile of such a transportation process in this global economy implies huge costs for the environment; costs that are externalized in our own efficiency measures, that is, costs that eventually are subsidized by those paying taxes.

Similarly, in the case of products with certain requirements of preservation, transportation across the sea also means an increase in refrigeration and a significant contribution to the depletion of the ozone layer and

climate change and an increase in packaging methods and the use of wood
pallets to load the goods. The latter is not so notorious, but they do constitute important factors that increase pressure on forests worldwide. Again,
Mander argues;

> Another environmental problem inherent to the exporting model though not
> quite known, is the production of monocultures which cause many environ-
> mental complications. Monocultures reduce biodiversity not only because they
> eliminate the microscopic life in soils through the constant use of chemical
> products, but also because they reduce the production of goods to one or two
> exporting varieties. For example, where the Philippines once planted thousands
> of rice varieties, today they only cultivate two varieties which account for
> 98 percent of the production. The others are disappearing. Mexico has lost over
> 75 percent of its original corn varieties. Among the potato growers in the
> Andean region, where thousands of potato varieties were grown, production
> has been reduced to 4 or 5 used for intensive production at large scale.
> According to the United Nations Food and Agriculture Organization (FAO),
> the world has already lost around 75 percent of its agricultural products due to
> the globalization of the industrialized agriculture.
>
> Besides, we must consider the external costs of industrial agriculture. Today it
> is important for its alleged higher efficiency compared to small-scale agriculture.
> Nevertheless, no attention is paid to the cost of air, water and soil pollution, the
> increasing use of fossil fuels, pesticides and herbicides, the loss of organic matter
> due to intensive and mechanized production, and the problems in public health
> resulting from diseases caused by foodstuffs coming from factory agricultural sys-
> tems like *salmonella, e coli, listeria* and many others. Without mentioning the
> mad-cow disease and diseases like foot and mouth disease et al.[13]

Mainly the small local producers are the ones who suffer the most traumatic
consequences of economic globalization since the change of economies
based on diversified and small-scale agricultural production models to industrial exporting models imply the systematic destruction of agricultural and
small agricultural production economies. The outcome is terrible: famines,
mass migrations, and general impoverishment.

As Mander affirms,

> Almost half of the world population depends on land, cultivating foodstuffs for
> their families and communities. They pay special attention to basic commodi-
> ties and other combined products and replant them with several varieties of
> indigenous seeds using crop rotation and shared use of resources like water,
> seeds, labor force and so on. With this system they have been able to survive
> for a millennium. But as I already mentioned, local systems constitute an anath-
> ema for global corporations. Therefore, companies like Monsanto, Cargill
> and Archer Daniels Midland are leading a unanimous chorus of corporate,
> governmental and bureaucratic voices, frequently expressed in million dollar
> advertisements affirming that small agricultural workers are not "productive"
> or "efficient" enough to feed a hungry world. Global corporations are the only
> ones who can do it.[14]

Almost every WTO and financial banking investment rule, and many others recently proposed, decisively favor global corporations and monocultures to the detriment of diversified local agriculture for self-sufficiency. Land where thousands of farmers used to cultivate foodstuffs for consumption now belongs to the largest corporations, who for the sake of global development are turning the land into luxurious single-variety monocultures managed by absentees.

Mander states,

> These companies do not cultivate foodstuffs for consumption of the local population. Globalized corporations are experts in luxurious products with high prices and high margin—flowers, plants in vases, meat, shrimp, cotton, coffee— that they export to already overfed countries. Concerned people who used to live in the countryside cultivating their own commodities are now being dragged from their lands and they are not employed. As these corporate systems perform a highly intensive agricultural production with large machine and chemical pesticides, they generate very few employment opportunities. So those who used to feed themselves are left without lands, without money, without shelter, dependent and hungry. Communities which were once self-sufficient are disappearing and the farmers and their families are moving to overcrowded urban slums. There, without a community, without cultural support, they try to compete for the poorly paid urban employment. Families who were once self-sufficient become a public burden for society while the big corporate landowners become wealthier with exports.
>
> Some landless farmers are also crossing the borders. Certainly, we have experienced this within the context of trade between Mexico and the United States, since the creation of NAFTA. For the Mexican Mayan farmers who used to cultivate corn and who supported themselves through the cooperative system called *ejido* for almost a century NAFTA has become a death sentence. In order to join NAFTA, Mexico had to eliminate the *ejido* system and open the doors of the Mayan agricultural lands to foreign investors, thus evicting Mayans from their lands. These landless farmers, without shelter, without money, have frequently escaped, crossing the American border looking for seasonal jobs like the collection of grapes and strawberries and they have found xenophobia and violence.[15]

The above-mentioned dynamic that constitutes the creed of neoliberal globalization has resulted in the following in Latin America:

1. destruction of biodiversity;
2. destruction of linguistic diversity and loss of cultural identities;
3. general impoverishment;
4. increased foreign indebtedness evidenced in both social debt and environmental debt;
5. higher wealth concentration up to unbelievable levels (the continent with the worst income distribution);
6. hunger and insomnia. Paraphrasing Josué de Castro: "Three quarters of the continent's inhabitants cannot sleep due to hunger, the other quarter cannot sleep fearing the hungry";

7. increasing violence and insecurity; and
8. systematic destruction of life and creation of expendable humans. Thus, the market "ideology" has been instilled in the collective mind and this is undermining the basis of life and human existence as a whole; by destroying languages and cultures; by destroying biodiversity and creating expendable humans in broad sectors of the Latin American and Caribbean population which is transformed from surplus population, or reserve army as Marx said, into expendable population; whole countries like Haiti, territories like the northeast region in Brazil or groups as those displaced by the armed violence in Colombia.

All the above-mentioned show a generalized deteriorating situation in life quality, a permanent threat to life, and a progressive process of inhumanity.

Integration: Why and What for?

In a context like the one just described, it might seem naïve to ask ourselves why should there be integration. But with it we can find many frequent phenomena in which we are implied and against which we have no other reaction than to go passively to where they might lead us. At most, we adhere to one or the other potential alternative, not so much by our own conviction, but rather because to the imaginary politician or philosopher with whom we identify, this or that idea constitutes a constituent motto. So in many cases we do not even ask ourselves if that to which we adhere, in the sphere of political proposals like in this case, is the most adequate or rational way of attaining to the kind of society we want to build.

Why is integration necessary for our countries? Because if we are not integrated in today's world, then life will become much more difficult for all of us, things will be more expensive, money and jobs will be harder to obtain and, therefore, our quality of life will be reduced. Let us think in terms of the facilities we have to move from one place to another, for example in Europe. Every person can cross the border without any kind of restriction, there are no extensive and difficult customs or migratory controls like in Latin America. If you do not find a job you can go to some other place. Maybe someone might think that this is something benefiting just a few, specifically those who can travel. But this is precisely the case; in Europe everybody can travel without problems from one place to another across the continent.

Anyway, this is not the most important point. The fact is that in the European Union welfare policies are universal and that implies that all citizens in the European Union have guaranteed basic rights, education, health, and minimum income. Any EU citizen can request social security benefits no matter where he or she is within the territory.

Likewise, the EU citizenship value is different from the one in the United States. An effective protection of social and political, and economic rights that does not exist in our countries.

But, most of all, integration is necessary because it could mean something on the international scale. Currently, the relative demographic weight of small countries like those of Latin America is practically nil at world level, save Brazil and Mexico that surpass a population of 100,000,000 inhabitants.

Importance of Latin America and the Caribbean in the World

In the year 2001, while the world population was 6.13 billion, population in the Latin American and Caribbean subregion was estimated at 526 million, that is, 8.58 percent of the total. In the year 2004, the Latin American and Caribbean population was estimated at 546 million and the world population at 6.45 billion—so their share in the world total has decreased to 8.46 percent.

From the economic point of view, the situation is even worse. As can be seen in table 12.1, the gross geographic product (GGP) in the Latin American and Caribbean region in the year 2000 was only 6.21 percent of the World Product and decreased to 6.1 percent in the year 2001.[16]

Likewise, from the table 12.1 it is possible to see that Brazil and Mexico alone are the single countries in the region contributing with over 1 percent of the world product. Together both countries contribute about half of the regional product. If we examine other indicators, in this case biodiversity, the regional situation, in terms of its importance at world level, is completely different. In fact, Latin America, which only occupies 16 percent of the planet surface and has only 8 percent of the world total population, accommodates 27 percent of all mammals known in the world, 37 percent of the known reptile species, 43 percent of known birds, 47 percent of known amphibians, and 34 percent of known flowering plants. Likewise, it has over 700 million hectares of arable lands, 570 million hectares of natural grazing lands, over 800 million hectares of forests and almost 27 percent of the surface fresh water existing on the planet.

Table 12.1 Share in the World GGP

Year	World GGP	Latin America & The Caribbean	%	Brazil	%	Mexico	%
1970	3,252,943	206,029	6.33	67,090	2.06	39,611	1.22
1980	11,932,132	932,304	7.81	245,938	2.06	207,663	1.74
1990	22,854,534	1,156,945	5.06	438,256	1.92	262,710	1.15
2000	31,375,763	1,949,802	6.21	601,732	1.92	580,121	1.85
2001	31,041,311	1,893,911	6.10	508,994	1.64	617,181	1.99

Source: http://unstats.un.org/unsd/snaama/SelectionBasicFast.asp

Bárcena and Guimaraes, when referring to the document drafted by ECLA and the United Nations Environment Program Regional Office for the Latin American and Caribbean Regional Conference in preparation for the World Summit on Sustainable Development (Johannesburg, 2002), stated the following:

> In environmental terms, despite the overwhelming ecological potential of the region, pollution is showing worrying signs of deterioration resulting from economic and demographic growth and increasing patterns of production and consumption. In general terms, the causes of the increasing air, soil and water pollution in the region and its consequences on health are associated with the unplanned urbanization process and agriculture (UNEP 2000). The significant urban growth has caused many people to suffer the consequences of the worsening of air quality, pollution by solid and dangerous residues, deterioration of coastal zones and water pollution. The overcrowding and lack of an infrastructure result in an increasing exposure to pollutants, that is why the poorest classes are the ones who suffer most the polluting effects.[17]

There are some factors that are fundamental from the planet sustainability point of view that, consequently, can give our nations a better treatment in the international realm. Factors that have emerged since the end of last century are as follows:

First, the strategic value of biodiversity and environmental services for development processes. Latin America's natural resources can give us an advantageous position in relation to the rest of the world. This is something we should utilize for our development. There are environmental benefits such as the capture of carbon dioxide by our tropical and temperate forests that should be examined and used as a negotiating factor. Similarly, the increasingly scarce resource of surface fresh water also provides negotiating capital.

Amazonia: the World's Lungs?

In a monopolar scenario like the one emerging after the fall of the Berlin Wall and the collapse of the socialist bloc as a result of the Cold War, which resulted in the weakening of the national states of developing countries, in general, we find that many of the existing resources in the Latin American and Caribbean region are now considered strategic resources for the national security of the major powers. It is relevant to ask the question posed by Cristobam Buarque, Brazil's former ambassador to the United States: Is Amazonia a global heritage of mankind or is it a national asset of the countries crossed by it? A few months ago a map was produced on the website that is being used by American schools, in which the Amazonia appears under similar conditions as the Antarctic. But following Buarque's question, why isn't oil internationalized? Or financial capital? Or the large museums across the world, beginning with the Louvre? Or nuclear arsenals?

> In fact, as a Brazilian, I will simply speak against the internationalization of the Amazonia. In spite of the fact that our governments do not pay due attention

to this heritage, it is ours. As a humanist, knowing the risk of environmental degradation in the Amazonia, I can imagine its internationalization, as well as everything which is important for humankind. If the Amazonia, from the humanistic viewpoint, is to be internationalized, then let us internationalize also the world oil reserves. Oil is as important for human welfare as the Amazonia for our future. In spite of this, the reserve owners feel they have the right to either increase or decrease oil extraction and its price. Similarly, the financial capital of wealthy countries should also be internationalized.

If the Amazonia is a reserve for all human beings, it cannot be burnt just as a result of one owner's or country's will. Burning the Amazonia is as serious as unemployment caused by the arbitrary decisions made by global speculators. We cannot allow financial reserves to be used to burn whole countries for the sake of speculation. Before the Amazonia, I would like to see the international-ization of every museum all over the world. The Louvre should not belong to France alone. Every museum in the world constitutes the custodian of the most beautiful artworks produced by human genius. We cannot allow that cultural heritage, like the Amazonian natural heritage, to be manipulated and destroyed by just one owner or country. Not long ago, a Japanese millionaire decided to be buried together with a painting by a great painter. To keep that from hap-pening, we should have had that painting internationalized. During this meet-ing, the United Nations is holding the Millennium Forum, but some presidents have encountered difficulties attending the meeting due to restrictions at the U.S. border. That is why I believe that New York, as the venue of the United Nations, should also be internationalized. At least Manhattan should belong to all of humanity. The same applies to Paris, Venice, Rome, London, Rio de Janeiro, Brasilia, Recife. . . . Every city in the world, with its specific beauty and history, should belong to the world at large.

If the United States wants to internationalize the Amazonia, because they do not want to run the risk of leaving it in the hands of Brazilians, then let us internationalize the U.S. nuclear arsenals. They have already demonstrated that they are capable of using those weapons and causing a thousand-times bigger destruction than the regrettable burning of Brazilian forests. During the debates, current members of the US administration defended the idea of internationalizing the forest reserves around the world as an exchange for debt. Let us start using that debt to guarantee every child in the world the possibility of eating and attending school. Let us internationalize children, treating them all, despite their country of origin, as a heritage deserving the attention of the world at large, even more attention than the Amazonia. If leaders treat children like a heritage of humanity, they will not allow them to work but to attend school, they will not allow them to die but live. As a humanist, I do defend internationalization of the world. But, as long as the world treats me as a Brazilian, I will struggle for the Amazonia to be ours . . . Ours only"![18]

The Value of Water

According to the above-mentioned work by Bayón, Latin America has almost 27 percent of the existing surface fresh water on the planet. Several authors have pointed out that most of the future wars would be waged because of continental waters. Water may become the main geopolitical conflict of the twenty-first century since it is expected that in the year 2025 the demand for this important element of human life will be 56 percent higher than supply and those having water could become the target of a forced plundering. It has been estimated that for the 6.25 billion inhabitants we have now, we will require an additional 20 percent of water. The conflict is between those who believe that water should be considered as an exchange commodity or asset (like wheat, oil, or coffee) and those who state that water is a social asset associated with the right to life. The scope of national sovereignty and legal tools are also part of this conflict.

In South America, to the abundance of fresh water rivers, lakes, marshlands, estuaries, glaciers, lagoons, and ponds we must add the largest aquifer in the world, the Guaraní Aquifer extending to the watersheds in Paraná, Uruguay, and Paraguay. It has 1.194 million km^2 in surface representing 10 percent of Brazilian territory, 6 percent of Argentinean territory, 18 percent in Paraguay, and 23 percent in Uruguay. Its volume is 55,000 km^3 and, in turn, every cubic kilometer is equivalent to one billion liters. Just by exploiting 40 km^3 annually it would be possible to supply 360 million individuals at 300 liters of water daily per inhabitant.

This is such an important resource that it could become the target of political battles. Dams, irrigation channels, purifying and desalinization technologies, sewerage systems, and waste water treatment may be seen as business opportunities. We should not forget water bottling since this is a business with higher profits than the pharmaceutical industry. Between 1970 and 2000, bottled water sales increased more than 80 times. In 1970, 1 billion were sold. In the year 2000, sales accounted for 84 billion. Profits were estimated at 22 billion dollars.

The origin of this water marketing dates back to November 2001 when natural resources, like health and education, became the object of negotiations at the World Trade Organization. The final goal is the liberalization of utilities as soon as possible. This might sound boring and dense, but it could be simplified: what has been regulated by nation-states so far, will be regulated now by free markets.

Within this context, there are two potential scenarios:

1. Territorial appropriation: This could be implemented through the purchase of lands with natural resources (water, biodiversity) and even through a military conflict. The latter hypothesis takes us to the war in Iraq (March 2003) and the appropriation of Iraqi resources by the big oil companies from the United States. We cannot ignore the fact that they might have wanted to control the water resources from the Euphrates and Tigris rivers, two large rivers located in the driest zone of the planet.

2. Privatization of water: Large corporations have been seeking control of water in many parts of the world and, reportedly, in the coming years, a handful of private companies will get a monopoly on almost 75 percent of this vital resource for human life in the planet.

Two Potential Integration Models

With certainty, we can affirm that in the integration processes taking place in Latin America and the Caribbean, there are two quite distinctive projects that are practically incompatible. On the one hand, an almost purely economic project that is completely coherent with the hegemonic concepts in the political and corporate sphere; and on the other a project emphasizing the cultural and political dimensions in the search for an integration that will promote the unification of the Great Homeland dreamed of by Bolivar.

The first model, known as the subordination model, is mainly an economic model that was to conclude in the year 2005 with the hemispheric supermarket from Alaska to the Tierra del Fuego within the framework of the objectives of geoeconomic and geopolitical strategy and the huge corporate interests contained in President Bush's Initiative for the Americas and better exposed during the Miami summit. This is the "modern" new version, though more sophisticated and tempting, of Pan-Americanism, the Monroe Doctrine, updated by the post–cold war era. This is integration led by capital and, more specifically, by the financial empire of business, mercantilism, savage competition of materialist economy, global enterprises already emerging, and enterprises that will dominate the immediate future.

This integration model will consolidate the supremacy of materialism over people, deprived of any kind of sensitivity, neither human nor social. This is a completely unfavorable project for men and women who need a job to live, for the workers, and for their representative organizations. This model expresses the interests of a highly satisfied minority which excludes the majority of Latin Americans and Caribbeans who are deeply immersed in poverty and social injustice—in the garbage of society. In practice, this is the mechanical summation of what neoliberalism is already imposing on all peoples of the region. This is a project completely regulated by blind and irrational market laws within a vacuum, where it generates its most dangerous perversities and aberrations.

This model accommodates passive and subdued integration into the globalization process as part of the neoliberal project for a new civilization and world order. However, it detaches our peoples and our nations from their roots.

The Autonomous Integration Model

In opposition to the neoliberal model adopted by corporate and political elites claiming our subcontinent as their own, the dream of a Great Homeland, as a unifying utopia of the continent, still survives in the most popular spaces, among intellectuals, in an important sector of artists, among the youth, in ecological groups and in ethnic groups. This idea of integration has been instilled in the Latin American progressive imagination since Independence times. There is a book by Gregorio Recondo[19] entitled *El sueño de la patria grande. Ideas y antecedentes integracionistas en América Latina* (The dream of a great nation: Ideas on the integration of Latin America), that in its title summarizes the main utopia of Latin American and

Caribbean peoples, the building of the Great Homeland dreamed of by Bolívar.

This project has a communal nature and scope, and it deals not only with the simple elimination of tariffs or customs barriers but also to build a community of nations associated with and united by geographic, historical, and religious bonds and by the same fate; a community of nations to be soundly integrated within an economic, social, political, cultural, ethic, and spiritual framework.

It is rooted in the dream of Bolivar and other champions of political independence in the nineteenth century. This is the project of the second independence of Latin America and the Caribbean that completes, deepens, and culminates political independence as a new form of national, social, and cultural independence not regionally closed off, but opened to the world at large. This is the best answer and proposal for a creative and active insertion of our own identity and determination into the inevitable process of globalizing interdependence. It envisions a different world order, not only more free but also democratic and fair, visions that could culminate with the unity of the human family within an atmosphere of fraternity and love. Latin America, turned into the Great Homeland, has a lot to give to this new world.

Fernando Noriega points out this:

> If Latin America integrates within its own axis, it will become the fourth most powerful economy in the world, surpassed only by the United States, Japan and the European Union. It will concentrate the negotiating power of one third of the foreign debt of low and middle income countries, the main countries demanding international financial resources. It will have the third largest market in the world, surpassed only by China and India.
>
> The strategic importance of Latin America in the world economic scenario will be translated into its immediate negotiating power within the international financial system and will become the economic bloc having the largest biodiversity ecosystems in the world. Joint management of natural resources, mainly oil, mining and forest resources, will allow it to participate with incredible advantages in the negotiation of production quotas and prices.[20]

Is an autonomous model possible? The previous question leads us to ask ourselves whether a political project, like the one inspired by the Bolivarian utopia is now possible. This will lead us to ask: with which actors? The state was the main actor in the constitution of our societies, but the present conditions under which the Latin American societies are living are leading to a gradual decline of the nation-state sovereignty concept.

Nation-state sovereignty was the main factor of imperialism that built the European powers. They built and imposed new territorial borders to ensure the purity of their own identity and to stigmatize everything that was different. First, the European colors, then that of the United States, enshrine imperialist history. Negri and Hardi[21] suggested that the new political subject is the empire, which is completely different from imperialism. In opposition and contrast with imperialism, the empire did not establish a center of power and did not need limitations or fixed borders. It is a nonterritorial dominating apparatus that is gradually assimilating the rest of the world beyond its fixed borders.

As they accurately stated: "The Empire is characterized by the absence of borders. This is not a metaphor. It is a theoretical concept. No border limits the Empire's kingdom. The Empire has no limitations. It describes a regime covering the whole "civilized" world space . . . The empire does not conquer; it emerges as a new order which wipes out history. It establishes the eternity of "forever."

From the above-mentioned framework, it might seem that there is no possible alternative, save passively resorting to subordinated integration. Seemingly, these times do not generate heroic epic campaigns that force the great powers to guarantee something better. The political pragmatism now in effect will even suggest to us, to be politically correct, to join the hemispheric supermarket. However, there is a potential loophole in the promise made by Boaventura to Sousa Santos,[22] formulated as a "new paradigm of subordination, acknowledgement and redistribution," which implies the solidarian and participatory reinvention of the State and the reinvention of democracy.

In my opinion, which are the key ideas to be rescued from Boaventura's proposal? As a starting point, he refers to an essay by José Martí entitled "Nuestra América". His first statement is that there are two Americas: the European America and the mestiza America. The America dreamed of by Bolívar is diametrically opposed to the European America, the synthesis between European, indigenous and African blood. Likewise, he points out that his mixed roots gives birth to an infinite complexity, a sort of universalism that enriches the world. Martí states that there is no racial hatred since there are no races. Likewise he affirms that our America needs an authentic consciousness capable of assessing and acknowledging ourselves. The battle, he says, is not between civilization and barbarism, but between false erudition and "nature" [sic]. Finally, he realized that political thinking far from being nationalist should be internationalist, consolidated by an anticolonial and antiimperialist stance oriented towards Europe in the past and to the United States in the present.

Against what the neoliberal discourse affirms, the national state is not under extinction, on the contrary, it is still a decisive struggling space. The erosion of its sovereignty and its capabilities for action takes place in a completely selective way and only within the scope of the citizens' providence. We must move forward to redefine the state without fearing the utopian character it might imply. This reinvention has a strong anticapitalist content and it will be hard to realize it by using traditional representative democratic mechanisms. We must devise new democratic practices. The democratic struggles cannot be exhausted by national space-time. The national struggle for a redistributive democracy should be added to the struggles for new, more democratic, participatory, and decisive international law and for the defense of the most common and public issues that are now at risk by the neoliberal model: our environment, our own planet.

Notes

1. Closed forests are those with over 40 percent woodlands and plants.
2. Julia Carabias, "Conservación de los Ecosistemas y el Desarrollo Rural Sustentable en América Latina: Condiciones, Limitantes y Retos," in *La transición hacia el desarrollo sustentable. Perspectivas de América Latina y elCaribe*, Enrique Leff, Exequiel Ezcurra, Irene Pisanty, and Patricia Romero Lankao (compilers.) (UNEP, Mexico D.F.; INE/SERMANAT; Autonomous University of Mexico; 2002), pp. 258–259.
3. José Gabaldón and Manuel Rodríguez, "Evolución de las Políticas e Instituciones Ambientales: ¿Hay motivos para estar satisfechos?," in Enrique Leff et al., *La transición hacia el desarrollo sustentable. Perspectivas de América Latina y el Caribe.*, p. 44.
4. Read: incipient development of welfare and its sequels, labour legislation with a relative protection to workers´ rights, right to unionizing and strike; social security systems, etc.; the existence of subsidies to national production; tariff barriers; public enterprises in areas with natural monopolies, among many others.
5. For more details on this issue, see my recent article entitled: Antonio Elizalde. "Globalización, Mundialización," in Pensamiento Crítico Latinoamericano. Conceptos fundamentales. UCSH Editions, Santiago de Chile, 2005, 3 volumes.
6. Jerry Mander, "Globalización Económica y Medio Ambiente," in *Globalización y sustentabilidad. Desafíos y alternativa,*. Sustainable Chile Program, Santiago de Chile, 2002, p. 59.
7. Cited work page 61.
8. Ibid.
9. Antonio Elizalde, "Desarrollo y Sustentabilidad. Límites y Potencialidades. (Una Mirada desde la Perspectiva del Sur)," in *Documentación Social. Revista de Estudios Sociales y de Sociología Aplicada*, Madrid, 89, (October–December 1992): pp. 67–83.
10. See "Nuevos Dilemas para Guatemala: Agricultura no Tradicional, Ecología y Globalización", AVANCSO/PACCA, City of Guatemala, 1992.
11. Eduardo Pavese, "Fruta de Exportación. Problemas de Madurez," *La Nación*, Santiago de Chile, Sunday, October 18, 1992, p. 19.
12. Hans Singer, "The Distribution of Gains Between Investing and Borrowing Countries," in *American Economic Review*, 40 (May 1950): 473–485. See other authors, above all, Raúl Prebisch, Anibal Pinto, Osvaldo Sunkel, and Pedro Paz, Celso Furtado.
13. Mander, cited work, pp. 67–68.
14. Ibid., p. 66.
15. Ibid., p. 67.
16. Ricardo Bayón, J. Steven Lovink and Wouter J. Veening, "Financiamiento de la conservación de la biodiversidad," Interamerican Development Bank, Sustainable Development Department, Environment Division, 02.2000, ENV-134, E, S, p. 1.
17. Alicia Bárcena and Roberto Guimaraes, "El Desarrollo Sustentable de América Latina y el Caribe desde Río 1992 y los Nuevos Imperativos de Institucionalidad," in Enrique Leff et al., *La transición hacia el desarrollo sustentable. Perspectivas de América Latina y el Caribe*, INE/SERMANAT; Autonomous University of Mexico; UNEP, Mexico D.F. 2002.

18. The official version in Portuguese can be found in http: //www.educacao. gov.br/acs/pdf/al60203.pdf. Accessed on June 15, 2004.

19. Gregorio Recondo, *El sueño de la patria grande. Ideas y antecedentes integracionistas en América Latina*, CICCUS Editions, Buenos Aires, 2001.

20. Fernando Antonio Noriega Ureña, "América Latina: las razones de la integración," in Alberto Acosta (compiler), *El desarrollo en la globalización. El reto de América Latina.* ILDIS/Editorial Nueva Sociedad, Caracas, 2000, p. 160.

21. Toni Negri and Michael Hardt, *Imperio* (Barcelone: Paidós, 2002), p. 43.

22. For more details see chapter 4 in *Boaventura de Sousa Santos, La caída del Angelus Novus: Ensayos para una nueva teoría social y una nueva práctica política*, ILSA, Bogotà, 2003), pp. 81–122.

Further Reading

Acuerdo de Cartagena—Junta. *Coordinación entre el Grupo Andino y el Tratado de Cooperación Amazónica.* Lima. Junta del Acuerdo de Cartagena, 1990 (mimeo).

Albright, Madeleine. "Focus on the Issues: The Americas." Remarks to the Council of the Americas, United States Department of State, Bureau of Public Affairs, May 4, 1999, Washington, D.C., on www.state.gov/www/focus_index.html.

———. "Building Hemispheric Democracy." Address at Trinity College. United States Department of State, January 22, 2001, Washington, D.C., on www.state.gov/p/wha/rt/soa/.

Alert@ Económica. "Revista virtual." Lima, January 19, 2005.

Alvarez, Sonia, Evelina Dagino, and Arturo Escobar, eds. *Cultures of Politics, Politics of Cultures, Revisioning of Latin American Social Movements.* (Boulder, CO: Westview, 1998.)

Amayo Z. E. "Da Amazônia ao Pacífico cruzando os Andes—Interesses envolvidos na construção de uma estrada, especialmente dos EUA e Japão." Estudos Avançados 17. Revista do Instituto de Estudos Avançados—Universidade de São Paulo, January–April 1993, p. 119.

———. "La Ciudad de Lima: de Perla del Pacífico a 'Calcuta de América Latina'." In Antropología: Estudios de Medio Ambiente y Urbanismo. Instituto de Investigaciones Antropológicas—Universidad Nacional Autónoma de México, México D.F., 2002, pp. 81–103.

———. "La Política Británica en la Guerra del Pacífico," *Editorial Horizonte*, Lima. 1988.

———. "La Transoceánica Perú—Brasil: los contradictorios interes de Estados Unidos y Japón." Allpanchis. Revista del Instituto de Pastoral Andina, Year XXVII, No. 45, First Semester 1995, Cusco, Peru, pp. 37–89.

———. "Lima na história da América Latina." PUC—VIVA. Academic and Informative Publication from the Professors of the Catholic University of São Paulo. Year II, No. 7, São Paulo, Brazil, December 1999, pp. 27–40, São Paulo, Brazil.

———. "Why to study the historical formation and main current problems of Amazonia?. The indigenous question, democracy, diversities and bio-piracy." Paper presented at the International Political Science Association—IPSA XVIII World Congress, Quebec, August 1–5, 2000.

Amazon Cooperation Treaty. *Amazonía sin Mitos.* (Washington DC: TCA—Interamerican Development Bank, 1992.)

———. "Diagnóstico de los Recursos Hidrobiológicos de la Amazonía." SPT-TCA, No. 32, Lima, October, 1994. p. 123.

Arróspide M., R. *La Bioceanidad del Perú—Vía transcontinental peruana.* (Lima: Instituto de Estudios Histórico Marítimos del Perú, 1990).

Arróspide M., *Via Interoceánica Peruana*. Revista del Instituto de Estudios Histórico Marítimos del Perú. Lima, No. 13, July–December 1994, pp. 51–82.

Ayerbe, L. F. *O Ocidente e o "Resto."* *A América Latina e O Caribe na Cultura do Império*. (Buenos Aires: CLACSO—Latin American Council of Social Sciences, 2003).

Betti, M.S. *Mark Twain: Escritos Políticos*. Patriotas e Traidores: Antiimperialismo, Política e Crítica Social. (São Paulo: Fundação Perseu Abramo, 2003.)

Borges, F. *Os possíveis impactos do "Plano Colômbia" no Brasil*. Aspectos econômicos, estruturais e diplomáticos. Dissertation (under my supervision) for Bachellor in Economics—Department of Economics, Faculty of Arts & Sciences, Campus of Araraquara, University of the State of Sao Paulo—UNESP, Brazil, December 2003.

BP Statiscal Review of World Energy, 2002, 2003, and 2004. www.bp.com/statisticalreview2004.

Brack, E. A., *Perú: diez mil años de domesticación. Peru: ten thousand years of domestication*. Legado, No. 3, Año 2, Lima, 2003, pp. 16–29.

Brazil—*Comissão Interministerial para a Preparação da Conferência das Nações Unidas sobre Meio Ambiente e Desenvolvimento (CNUMAD)*. Subsídios Técnicos para a Elaboração do Relatório Nacional do Brasil para o CNUMAD. Draft. Brasilia, 1991.

Brazil. *Ministério das Minas e Energia, Secretaria Geral. Projeto Radambrasil-Amazônia Legal*. Map Made for the National Integration Program, 1983.

Burns, B.E. *A Documentary History of Brazil*. (New York: Alfred A. Knopf, 1966).

Bush, George W. "President Discusses War on Terror at National Endowment for Democracy." October 6, 2005, Washington, DC.

———. http://www.whitehouse.gov/news/releases/2005/10/20051006-3.html

Cadji, Anne-Laure. "Brazil's Landless Find Their Voice," in "¡Adelante! The New Rural Activism in the Americas." *NACLA, Report on the Americas* 33: 5, 2000.

Da Cunha E. *À Margem da História*, (São Paulo: Martins Fontes, 1999).

——— *Obra Completa em Dois Volumes*. Organizer: Afranio Coutinho, Rio de Janeiro, Editorial José Aguilar, 1966.

"Declaração Ministerial Área de Livre Comércio das Américas, oitava reunião ministerial," November 20, 2003, Miami, EUA, on http://www.ftaa-alca.org/Ministerials/Miami/declaration_p.asp.

"Declaração de Cuzco Comunidade Sul-americana de Nações." on http://casa.mre.gov.br/declaracoes/Cusco.doc. Accessed on December 9, 2004.

Delgado Ramos, Gian C. "El privilegiado y gran negocio del agua embotellada, El Catoblepas, número 25," March 2004.

———. *Privatización y saqueo del agua dulce de Mesoamérica*, August 2005.

Dourojeanni, M. J. *Amazonía. Que Hacer?* Centro de Estudios Teológicos de la Amazonía, Iquitos, Perú, 1990.

Eckstein, Susan, ed. *Power and Protest: Latin American Social Movements*. Berkeley: University of California Press, 2001.

The Economist Pocket—World in Figures, 2001 edition, London.

Ellner, Steve and Hellinger, Daniel. *Venezuelan Politics in the Chávez Era: Class, Polizaration and Conflict* (Boulder, CO: Lynne Rienner, 2003).

Encyclopedia Britannica. 2003 Book of the Year. Events of 2002. (Chicago, London, New Delhi, Paris, Seoul, Sydney, Taipei, Tokyo: Encyclopedia Britannica, Inc. 2003).

Encyclopedia Britannica do Brasil. Geopédia Volume II. Encyclopaedia Britannica do Brasil Publicações Ltda. Rio de Janeiro—São Paulo, Brasil, 1990.

The New Encyclopedia Britannica. 15th Edition, 1990.

Escobar, Arturo and Alvarez, Sonia E. *The Making of Social Movements in Latin America: Identity, Strategy and Democracy* (Boulder, CO: Westview Press,1992).

Fernando P. Luis. "Megadiversidad." March 2005, on www.biiotech.biioetica.org/apuntes.html.

Folha de S. Paulo—FSP. "Amazônia: radar do SIVAM pode vigiar a Colômbia. Repasse de informações ao país vizinho depende de assinatura de acordo; dados podem ajudar ao combate ao narcortráfico." Folha de S. Paulo, March 24, 2003, p. A7.

———. "Discurso do Presidente Luiz Inácio Lula da Silva durante o ato de posse no Congresso Nacional." Folha de S. Paulo, January 2, 2003, p.1.

———. "Peru tem a cidade mais antiga da América. Datações revelam que o sítio de Caral, na costa central de aquele país, é anterior às grandes pirâmides do Egito— Por Claudio Angelo." Folha de S. Paulo, April 27, 2001, p. A14.

Gleza, Fernando. "El peligro terrorista en la triple frontera 'hace agua,' 2004.

Gott, Richard. *In the Shadow of the Liberator, Hugo Chávez and the Transformation of Venezuela.* (London: Verso, 2000).

Instituto Moreira Salles—IMS. "Canudos." Cadernos de Fotografia Brasileira. No. 1, December 2002, IMS.

———. "Euclides da Cunha." Cadernos de Literatura Brasileira. Edição Especial Comemorativa do Centenário de *Os Sertões*. No. 13 and 14, December 2002, IMS.

Lauredo, Luis. Remarks at the Conflict Prevention and Resolution Forum, September 12, 2000, Washington DC, on www.state.gov/p/wha/rt/soa/.

———. "Toward the Quebec City Summit." Remarks to the Institute of the Americas. March 2001, Washington, DC, on www.state.gov/p/wha/rt/soa/.

Levine, Robert M. *Father of the Poor? Vargas and His Era* (Cambridge: Cambridge University Press, 1998).

Loza V.M.G. *El refuerzo hegemónico de los EEUU en América Latina: la complementación geopolítica de los Planes Colombia y Puebla—Panamá y el inicio del "Comando Norte."* Final paper for my course "Teoría Social e Relações Internacionais. A Importância Estratégica da Amazônia Sul-Americana em perspectiva mundial." Graduate Program of Sociology, Faculty of Arts and Sciences, Campus of Araraquara, University of the State of São Paulo—UNESP, Brazil, Second Term 2002.

Magalhães Ramon, I.V. *A Amazônia e a integração ao Pacífico. Euclides da Cunha: no Centro da História?* Master Thesis (under my supervision)—Graduate Program of Sociology, Faculty of Arts and Sciences, Campus of Araraquara, University of the State of São Paulo—UNESP, Brazil, May 2004.

Mahon, James E., Jr. "Good-Bye to the Washington Consensus?" *Current History.* 102: 661 (2003), pp. 58–64.

Mander, Jerry and Goldsmith Edward, eds. *The Case Against the Global Economy and for a Turn Toward the Local* (San Francisco: Sierra Book Club, 1996).

Ministério das Relações Exteriores do Brasil, 2005. "Declaração conjunta dos presidentes de Argentina, Brasil e Venezuela." http://www.mre.gov.br/portugues/imprensa/nota_detalhe.asp?ID_RELEASE=2860.

Moreley, Samuel A. *Poverty and Inequality in Latin America, the Impact of Adjustments and Recovery in the 1980s* (Baltimore: Johns Hopkins University Press, 1995).

National Geographic—Brasil. "Peru: uma estrada do Brasil ao Pacifico por Ted Conover." *National Geographic—Brasil,* Sao Paulo, June 2003, pp. 98–117.

National Geographic—Brasil. South America Map. Produced by the Geographic Division, Washington, DC, October 1972.

Natsios, Andrew. Testimony before the Senate Appropriations Committee, Subcommittee on Foreign Operations, May 8, 2001 on www.usaid.gov/press/spe_test/testimony/2001/ty010508.html.

Navarro, Zandler. "Breaking New Ground: Brazil's MST in !Adelante! The New Rural Activism in the Americas." *NACLA, Report on the Americas.* 33:5, 36–39, 2000.

Noriega, Roger. "The Bush Administration's Western Hemisphere Policy," January 6, 2004, on http://www.state.gov/p/wha/rls/rm/27975.htm.

———. "The Summit of the Americas. Rescuing the Reform Agenda."

American Enterprise Institute, October 27, 2005 on http://www.aei.org/publications/pubID.23385,filter.all/pub_detail.asp.

O Estado de S. Paulo, "Bush aprova plano de Lula para liderar AL." Estado de S. Paulo, June 22, 2003, p. A6.

———. "Caral pode ser a 1ª. Cidade da América. Sítio no Peru mostra que civilização na região era mais antiga do que se pensava." O Estado de S. Paulo, April 30, 2001, p. 12.

———. Começa construção de Rodovia Interoceânica." O Estado de S. Paulo, 2005.

———. "Mark Twain contra a Guerra. Sai no país seleção de textos do autor das 'Aventuras de Huckleberry Finn,' entre os assuntos tratados pelo escritor, que foi vice-Presidente da Liga Antiimperialista, está sua resistência a ações dos EUA na virada do século 19 para o 20." O Estado de S. Paulo—Cultura—Caderno 2, February 03, 2003, p. D1.

Oxhorn, Philip D. and Ducatenzeiler Graciela. *What Kind of Democracy? What Kind of Market?* (University Park, PA: The Pennsylvania State University Press, 1998).

Peru, "Cámara de Diputados de la República del Perú. Acuerdo de Interconexión Vial entre el Gobierno de la República del Perú y el Gobierno de la República Federativa del Brasil." Lima, Press Release. Madre de Dios Forum. Highway Perú-Brasil, 1991.

———. "Instituto Nacional de Planificación—INP. *Atlas Histórico Geográfico y de Paisajes Peruanos.* Presidencia de la República—INP—Asesoría geográfica." Lima, 1969.

Portillo, Lubis. "El Eje de Desarrollo Occidental obedece a los interés del ALCA." January 26, 2004.

Powell, Colin. "Remarks at the Council of the Americas' 31st Washington Conference." May 7, 2001, Washington, DC, on www.state.gov/secretary/ rm/2001/.

———. "Testimony to House Appropriations Subcommittee on Foreign Operations, Export Financing." May 10, 2001, Washington, DC, on www.state.gov/secretary/rm/2001/.

Quehacer, De Brasil a Japón pasando por el Perú. Una entrevista con Enrique Amayo por Alberto Adrianzén. *Quehacer,* Bimonthly Review, Lima, March–April 1991, No. 70, pp. 72–80.

Quehacer, Brasil—Perú: un gran proyecto de integración. Entrevista con el Embajador del Brasil por Alberto Adrianzén, *Quehacer,* Bimonthly Review, Lima, May–June 1991, No. 71, pp. 62–66.

Reyes, José. *Venezuela's Economic Growth: The Highest in Latin America.* US Embassy of Bolivarian Republic of Venezuela, 2005, on www.embavenez-us.org/economic_development_sep2005.pdf.

Rojas, Aravena Francisco. *Rol y evaluación de la diplomacia de cumbres. Construyendo el multilateralismo cooperativo,* in Aravena, Francisco Rojas (Comp.) Multilateralismo. Perspectivas latinoamericanas (Caracas: Nueva Sociedad, 2000).

Romero, meter. "U.S. Policy in the Western Hemisphere in the New Century." Fourth Annual Americas Conference, Miami, Florida, September 15, 2000, on www.state.gov/www/policy_remarks/2000/000915_romero_whpolicy.html.

Rossi, I. C. *SIVAM: A Case of Technological Dependence, 1990–1996.* Master Thesis (under my supervision)—Graduate Program of Sociology, College of Arts and Sciences, Campus of Araraquara, University of the State of São Paulo—UNESP, Brazil, September 2003.

Ruiz Marrero. "Carmelo: El Agua y el ALCA." December 2004.

USAID. Strategic Plan, 2000, on www.usaid.gov/pubs/.

———. Congressional Presentation FY 2000, Latin America and the Caribbean Presentation, on www.usaid.gov/pubs/cp2000/lac/.

———. FY 2000 Performance Overview, U.S. Agency for International Development, Washington, April 2001, Center for Development Information and Evaluation, on www.usaid.gov/pubs/.

USDS. (U.S. Department of State). Resources for American Values. Fact sheet released by the Bureau of Public Affairs. December 15, 1999 on www.state.gov/www/budget.

———. Report to Congress Pursuant to the International Anticorruption and Good Governance Act (Public Law 106–309), April 16, 2001, on www.state.gov/g/inl/corr/index.cfm?docid=2327.

———. Strategic Plan 2000, on www.state.gov/www/budget/stratplan_index.html.

———. Strategic Plan 2003, Fiscal Years 2004–2009, on http://www.usaid.gov/policy/budget/state_usaid_strat_plan.pdf.

———. What is the International Affairs Budget? January 21, 2001, on www.state.gov/m/fmp/index.cfm?docid=2342.

Valor Económico. *Exclusive Interview with Peruvian President Alejandro Toledo por Humberto Saccomand.* Valor Económico. Caderno Especial. São Paulo, April 11, 12, and 13, 2003, p. A-14.

Vanden, Harry E. and Prevost Gary. *Politics of Latin America: the Power Game* (New York and Oxford: Oxford University Press, 2002).

Vargas Llosa, M. "La Guerra del Fin del Mundo." Editorial *Seix Barral*, Barcelona, 1981.

VEJA. Interview: "Rogério de Cerqueira Leite. 'O SIVAM E Deles'. Physics From UNICAMP Says The Radar System in the Amazon Only Interests the US Government, and will be a Disaster for Brazil." *VEJA. Weekly Review*, São Paulo, December 27, 1995, pp. 7–9.

Index